Mary Nolan, Ziegfeld Girl
and Silent Movie Star

Mary Nolan, Ziegfeld Girl and Silent Movie Star

A Biography Including Her 1941 Memoir

LOUISE CARLEY LEWISSON *and*
MARY NOLAN

McFarland & Company, Inc., Publishers
Jefferson, North Carolina

LIBRARY OF CONGRESS CATALOGUING-IN-PUBLICATION DATA

Names: Lewisson, Louise Carley, 1957– author. | Nolan, Mary, 1905–1948. Confessions of a Follies girl.
Title: Mary Nolan, Ziegfeld girl and silent movie star : a biography including her 1941 memoir / Louise Carley Lewisson and Mary Nolan.
Description: Jefferson, North Carolina : McFarland & Company, Inc., Publishers, 2019. | Includes bibliographical references and index.
Identifiers: LCCN 2019035877 | ISBN 9781476677170 (paperback) ∞
ISBN 9781476636382 (ebook)
Subjects: LCSH: Nolan, Mary, 1905–1948. | Actors— United States—Biography.
Classification: LCC PN2287.N563 L49 2019 | DDC 791.4302/8092 [B]—dc23
LC record available at https://lccn.loc.gov/2019035877

BRITISH LIBRARY CATALOGUING DATA ARE AVAILABLE

ISBN (print) 978-1-4766-7717-0
ISBN (ebook) 978-1-4766-3638-2

Front cover: Mary Nolan in *West of Zanzibar*, 1928 (MGM/Photofest)

Printed in the United States of America

*McFarland & Company, Inc., Publishers
Box 611, Jefferson, North Carolina 28640
www.mcfarlandpub.com*

Table of Contents

Preface

In 1922, *New York Daily News* columnist Mark Hellinger wrote, "Only two people in America can bring every reporter in New York to the docks to see them off, one being the President of the United States, the other Imogene 'Bubbles' Wilson." Imogene "Bubbles" Wilson was in fact Mary Imogene Robertson, who began her career as a Ziegfeld Follies girl, and then had a tumultuous affair with comedian Frank Tinney that caused her to leave the country and start a film career in Germany. She appeared in 17 German films from 1925 to 1927 using the new name Imogene Robertson.

Upon returning to the U.S. in 1927, she attempted to break away from her scandal-ridden past and adopted yet another name, Mary Nolan. In 1928 she was signed to Universal Pictures and found some success in films, but by the 1930s her acting career began to decline due to her drug abuse and reputation for being temperamental.

She spent the remainder of her acting career appearing in low-budget films, mainly for independent studios. Mary made her final film appearance in 1932 and then went on the road appearing in various vaudeville acts, nightclubs and roadhouses. Her later years were plagued by ongoing financial turmoil and subsequent court cases, as well as by drug problems and frequent hospitalizations. She returned to Hollywood in 1939, spending her remaining years living in obscurity before dying of a barbiturate overdose in 1948.

Who was Mary Nolan, a.k.a. Imogene "Bubbles" Wilson? How did she go from being the youngest of a poor family in Kentucky, to the heights of fame and scandal, before dying as a drug addict, weighing a mere 90 pounds?

This is the story of her life, reconstructed from various sources, including from Mary herself. There have been many and varied accounts of certain aspects of her life, some fabricated by the various movie studios, and others that Mary probably invented herself to garner sympathy as well as attention, given her nature. As a child who did not receive much attention from her parents, lost her mother at a young age, and then was sent to a convent, she probably grew up feeling neglected. By having the spotlight on her, she may have been satisfying her inner need to be wanted and loved. This book attempts to corral all the facts, snippets from newspaper accounts and other published works, and finally from Mary herself, to try to create a fully formed picture of someone who had everything to gain, but everything to lose.

Also included in this book is the complete eight-part story that Mary wrote and sold to the newspapers in 1941. The overall goal of including this is to present Mary's writing as authentically as possible. In a few cases, her story contained factual errors, so it was necessary to add a few footnotes for purposes of clarification, and to give the reader a sense of Mary's thought processes as she embellished and revised her life story, in some cases perhaps to make the story more interesting, or to evoke in the reader a greater sense of sympathy toward her as a "victim." She also wrote an earlier life story which was published in 1931, also syndicated in the newspapers, yet another version of life up to that point. That account has not been included, but at certain points in this book, her 1931 versions of events will be referenced.

No matter the truth or imagined truth in Mary's mind, she was a victim, be it of her own naiveté, or battle with drug addiction, or her ongoing quest to find everlasting fame, true love and true happiness. None of which she ever found.

ONE

Beginnings

The town of Hickory, in Graves County, Kentucky, is in the western part of the state, 150 miles northwest of Nashville, 18 miles south of Paducah, and a three-hour drive southwest of St. Louis, Missouri. There is a handful of houses there today, a similar situation to what existed back in the late 1800s and early 1900s, when Mary's family lived there.

Mary Nolan was born Mary Imogene Robertson on December 18, 1902, in Hickory, then called Hickory Grove.[1] The town was initially established as a railway stop around 1856 along the tracks of the Illinois Central Gulf Railroad and named for the large hickory trees dotting the landscape. Mary was born in the year that Cuba gained its independence from the United States and Edward VII was crowned king of England. More relevant to her future career, it was also the year that the first movie theater, the Electric Theatre, opened in Los Angeles.

Tobacco was very much part of the economy in that area over the years, plus there was a nearby woolen mill which had been in operation prior to the Civil War. The area continued to expand with the growth of the men's clothing market, with several clothing companies being established in the county.

Mary was the fifth and last child born to Alfcanis Gabriel "Alf" Robertson and Viola Breckenridge Pittman.[2] Alf was born in October 1851 in Montgomery County, Tennessee, and Viola was born in January 1863. Alf was 51 when Mary was born, Viola 39. At the time of Mary's birth, the other Robertson children were Sallie Myrtle, then 19, Mabel May Farrie, nine, Canis Pearl, four, and Alton "Ray," who was one.

No record of Viola's death has been found, but she had passed away by 1910, as the 1910 census does not list her. This census now showed the family living on Fifth Street in Mayfield, Kentucky, with Alf working as a carpenter, Sallie Myrtle as a seamstress at a pants factory, and Mabel May Fairie as a telephone operator. Rounding out the household were the two youngest children, Canis and Ray. Mary was not living with the family at the time of the census, as Alf had placed her in the St. Joseph's Orphan Home in Louisville, Kentucky after Viola's death, even though she was not an orphan, just motherless.[3] Some sources also have her older brother Ray being placed there.[4] In later articles about Mary, she said that it was Sallie Myrtle who decided to put Mary in the orphanage.[5]

The Louisville cholera epidemic of 1832 had taken many lives and left many children orphans, and because of that, the St. Joseph Catholic Orphan Society was formed in 1849, with the first home built in 1850. The Ursuline Sisters of Louisville staffed the home from 1897 to 1972. According to Mary, while she was here, she was nicknamed "Bubbles."[6] This was probably because one of the chores she had to do every day, was wash dishes while standing on a wooden soda carton.[7] Other accounts say the nickname was given to her much later, after she had moved to New York, so the truth of the origin of her nickname is not definitively known.

Alf, 59, passed away of heart disease on January 22, 1911, when Mary was just nine years old. While still at the orphanage in 1912, Mary got word that Sallie Myrtle was dying, so she left to be with her sister, now married and known as Myrtle McDaniels. Myrtle died of tetanus on June 2, 1912. Mary then spent some time in Kentucky with her elderly grandmother Sarah "Sallie" Robertson, who had been a small-time actress at one point. Mary eventually returned to the orphanage, where she lived until she was 13.[8]

At some stage, Mary and Roy both moved to Worcester, Massachusetts, to live with Mabel, who was now an actress and married to Charles Rondeau, a small-time stage actor. Some accounts have Mabel meeting Charles when he was playing a one-week stand with a vaudeville troop. Charles had appeared in the 1912 and 1913 productions of the Edgar Selwyn play *The Country Boy* in New York, Philadelphia and Boston, with some sources also having Mabel appearing in the play. (No record has been found of her appearance in the play.) Jason Robards was also in the play with Charles, and he coincidentally later appeared with Mary in the 1932 film *Docks of San Francisco*.

Ray eventually got work as a bank messenger in Worcester, but by 1919, at age 17, Mary decided to move to New York. According to some sources, Ray gave Mary the railroad fare to get there.[9] Years later, several magazine articles reported that Mary found herself living on the streets at 14, but those stories came from Mary herself, who had made herself appear three years younger by always saying she was born in 1905. And it is also doubtful that she was living on the streets, so either this was fabricated by Mary to garner sympathy or was created later by the Hollywood publicity machine after Mary had become well-known. According to the 1920 census, Mabel, Charles, their daughter Maxine and son Charles Jr. were now living in Brooklyn, which means they may also have been in New York when Mary arrived around 1919, but this is not confirmed. Whatever the true circumstances, fate would now step in and alter the course of her life.

While living in New York, Mary met Arthur William Brown, a commercial artist originally from Canada, and she started working as an model for him. Brown is mostly known for his work as an illustrator for publications such as *The Saturday Evening Post*, *American Magazine* and *Redbook*. Mary went on to model for Norman Rockwell, Henry Clive, Charles Dana Gibson and Frederic Dorr Steel; Steel called her the "Angel Face" model. Graphic artist Gibson was best known for his creation of the Gibson Girl, an iconic representation of the beautiful and independent American woman at the turn of the 20th century.

Brown, or "Brownie" as his artist friends called him, was born on January 26, 1881, and died in 1968. He was a Canadian school dropout. While working on a steamer, he sketched in his spare time, and sold these sketches to various newspapers. Saving his earnings, he enrolled at the Art Students League and studied under Walter Appleton Clark, F.W. DuMond and F.R. Gruger. When a friend got a job from *The Saturday Evening Post* to cover a circus, Brown went along. The *Post* liked the article as well as Brown's circus drawings, and purchased the drawings; that was the beginning of a relationship between the publisher and artist that lasted for 40 years. He also contributed posters for the World War I effort and book art for various publishers.

In Mary's 1941 article series, she made certain creative embellishments to dramatize her start in modeling. It is not certain whether she really thought some of these events did happen to her, whether there are parts that are true, or if she made these embellishments to make the articles more enticing to the readers, as she was trying to eventually market these as a memoir of her life. The following account is from the various stories that were published about first meeting Brown.

Mary had just gotten off a tramcar in New York, and was standing there feeling lost, when a man asked her if she was okay. He had stopped to help her as he was drawn to her loveliness. She said she was lost and had no money, so the man offered to take her back to his house. According to Mary, she said yes and went with him back to his house, where she met Mrs. Brown, and ended up staying with them for a few days while Brown sketched her. The Browns then arranged for her to join and ultimately live at the Artists and Models Club, where she got modeling jobs from other artists.

At this time, not only were the models sketched, but they were also photographed, as by the 1920s the previously ubiquitous ink-drawn fashion sketches had given way to photographic representations of new designs, made possible by advances in commercial printing. Suddenly, a market emerged for photogenic young women whose elegant poses and gestures evoked the attitudes of the day while convincingly portraying the lifestyles and aspirations of the magazine or advertisers' target market. Models were recruited both from high society as well as the more risqué stage performers and Follies girls.[10]

Mary confided in Brown that her first love was dancing, and he encouraged her to go to Descha, a well-known dance instructor. Descha took her on. One day as Mary was leaving the Artists and Models Club to go to a dance lesson, she was asked to fill in as a model for James Montgomery Flagg, as his normal model was away overseas. Flagg, an artist and illustrator, is mostly remembered for his "Uncle Sam" poster created in 1917.

Mary posed for Flagg that day, and it turned into a regular job. Flagg asked her what she wanted to do, and when she again said she wanted to dance, he sent her with a letter of introduction to Arthur Hammerstein, who was just about to produce the musical *Daffy Dill*. Mary got a small part in the musical using her proper name of Imogene Robertson. She was in the ensemble as well as playing one of the two girls who opened the show wearing overalls and straw hats. In one sketch, she played the part of the main character, Lucy Brown's mother in a scene set in 1899.

Daffy Dill ran at the Apollo Theatre from August 22, 1922, until October 21, 1922, a total of 71 performances, and then went on the road for a month. Oscar Hammerstein,

Arthur Hammerstein's nephew, supplied the lyrics to the Herbert Stothart score. Arthur had teamed Oscar with writer Guy Bolton to write about a poor girl, Lucy Brown, who meets a rich boy, Kenneth Hobson, in a Cinderella-type story that had, as one critic put it, "just enough of a plot to not get in the way."[11] The show teetered dangerously on the brink of vaudeville, but its star, the popular blackface comedian Frank Tinney, kept it going for nine weeks.[12] Tinney played himself, performing his standard routines in each of the 12 scenes. At one time or another, he appeared as a Chinese magician, a coachman and a black porter, and every now and then he would stop and talk to the orchestra leader. (Tinney had previously partnered with the Hammersteins in the production *Tickle Me*.) In Mary's 1931 serialized biography, she wrote,

> I was a complete pest to the company. Time meant little to me. Often, I would be hours late to rehearsals. Then I'd sit in the wings, with the stage hands tumbling over me, reading a book. I don't know how many cues I muffed. But I was a well-meaning kid, so the directors didn't fire me. But I used to exasperate them, though![13]

As Buster Keaton revealed in his autobiography, Frank Tinney would become the first of Mary's "ill-starred admirers."[14] Mary had not yet turned 14 according to newspaper articles she later wrote about meeting Frank, but in reality, she was 20.[15]

Born in Philadelphia on March 29, 1878, Tinney was a comedian and actor who by the time of *Daffy Dill* had already achieved considerable success in vaudeville and on Broadway. He was 44 at the time, married to Edna Davenport, a former singer and dancer on Broadway, and they lived on a large Long Island estate with their four-year-old son Frank Jr. Frank was at the height of his career at this time and was earning around $4,000 a week, which would be the equivalent to around $100,000 a week today. His shtick was to tell corny jokes, involving others (bandleaders, audience members, etc.) in his jokes and sometimes bringing them onto the stage with him. He was also well known in theater circles as being a drunk and a womanizer, but it was his affair with Mary that was to be his undoing.

According to Mary's account of their meeting, she was just leaving the theater one night when Frank's car pulled up, and he offered her a ride home. That was the start of the on-again, off-again affair that would prove calamitous for all involved.

Two

On the Stage

Vaudeville shows of that period were typically made up of comedians, singers, plate-spinners, ventriloquists, dancers, musicians, acrobats, animal trainers and anyone who could keep an audience's interest for more than three minutes. Beginning in the 1880s and through to the 1920s, vaudeville was home to 25,000-plus performers and the most popular form of entertainment in America. From local small-town stages to New York's Palace Theater, vaudeville was an essential part of every community.

Mary's next theatrical turn was appearing in the ensemble of producer Oliver Morosco's musical *Lady Butterfly*, which ran from January 22, 1923, initially at the Globe Theatre, before moving to the Astor Theatre on March 19. It closed on May 12, 1923, after 128 performances. It was praised by the newspapers more for its dancing than the score or plot.

Lady Butterfly used the old device of a luggage mix-up for its thin plot. Albert Hopper, a clownish wastrel, discovers he has mistakenly acquired the suitcase and papers of Enid Crawford's fiancé, and he decides to pretend to *be* the fiancé, whom Enid has never seen. Most critics, passing over the book and the music, viewed the evening merely as a dancing show. It was staged by Ned Wayburn, who would go on to stage the *1923 Follies* in which Mary appeared.

Born on March 30, 1874, Wayburn spent much of his childhood in Chicago where he was introduced to theater and studied classical piano. When he was 21, he abandoned his family's tradition of manufacturing and began teaching at the Hart Conway School of Acting in Chicago. Wayburn subsequently spent many years in theater, staging shows for producers. In 1906, he began his own management group, the Headline Vaudeville Production Company. Through his own company he staged many feature acts, while collaborating with other producers such as Lew Fields. In 1915, he began working with Florenz Ziegfeld and became the main choreographer of the *Ziegfeld Follies*.

Wayburn's choreography was based on the five key techniques of musical comedy, tapping and stepping, acrobatic work, toe specialties and exhibition ballroom dancing. His choreography was influenced by the social dances of the time. He took dances such as the Tango, the Turkey Trot, the Grizzly Bear, the Black Bottom, the Charleston and recreated them for the stage by using strong exaggerations of movement. He created steps such as the Ziegfeld Walk and the Gilda Glide. Wayburn is credited with developing the talent of performers Fred Astaire, Barbara Stanwyck, Clifton Webb, Mae West, Groucho Marx, June Allyson and Fanny Brice, to name a few.

The *Follies* girls were also taught to walk a certain way so that they could descend the staircase on the stage in costumes that were as heavy as they were elaborate. To perfect the Ziegfeld Walk, dancers had to hold their chins high and jut their hips forward with a thrust from the opposite shoulder. The Ziegfeld Walk was the first of the *Follies'* many innovations. With the introduction of Wayburn in 1916, the girls also began to perform in kick lines and geometric formations, the same techniques that are still used today by the Rockettes, Vegas showgirls and even high school drill teams.

While appearing in *Lady Butterfly*, Mary entered a contest for the shapeliest feet on Broadway, and her picture appeared in various newspapers.[1] After *Lady Butterfly*, she appeared in the *Ziegfeld Follies of 1923*, which ran from October 20, 1923, through May 10, 1924, at the New Amsterdam Theatre, a total of 233 performances. A *Motion Picture* article about Ziegfeld Follies girls who had made the move to the big screen offered up this version of Mary's first meeting with Ziegfeld: The story goes that she waited outside his office for four days, unable to capture his attention. She was dressed in a simple woolen dress, her hair in braids down her back, no makeup, and Ziegfeld's secretary hoped that she would become discouraged and leave. But Mary came back every day. On the evening of the third day, the secretary told Ziegfeld that the only way Mary was going to leave was if he agreed to see her. She went into his office and he looked at her, and she was apparently immediately signed; Ziegfeld chastised his secretary, calling Mary, "one of the most exquisite beauties ever to come into this office."[2] Whether or not this is true, I do not know.

For 17 years it had been the custom to take each *Follies* show first to Atlantic City before taking it to Broadway, to do a dry run. The public rehearsals used to run from eight p.m. until sometimes past one a.m. in the morning, costing Ziegfeld between $40,000 and $50,000. He would use this as an opportunity to trim down the acts. This did not happen with the *1923 Follies* with Mary, as it has a "cold opening" on Broadway. It started at 8:50 p.m. and ran until 2:15 a.m. on Sunday morning, with seats going for $22. However, after a few performances, Ziegfeld cut many musical numbers based on initial audience reaction.[3]

The *Follies* were Broadway's most glamorous, spectacular production, being the most successful of all the musical variety shows that flourished during the first three decades of the twentieth century. Florenz Ziegfeld Jr., a daring and visionary showman, raised the revue to new levels of artistic creation. Born in 1867 in Chicago, the son of the founder of the Chicago Musical College, Ziegfeld began by importing bands and circus acts for the 1893 World's Fair. He launched his career as flamboyant showman with Sandow the Strong Man, who appeared on stage as naked as the law permitted then, performing feats such as lifting grand pianos and wrestling lions. After a couple of record-breaking cross-country tours with Sandow, Ziegfeld started to acquire a reputation as a logical successor to P.T. Barnum.

The breakthrough for Ziegfeld came on a 1896 trip to London, when he met the Polish-French soubrette Anna Held, famous for her hour-glass figure, saucy sexuality and well-publicised milk baths. Captivated by her looks and on-stage personality, Ziegfeld produced a series of Broadway musicals starring Held, and she and Ziegfeld eventually lived together for many years. At one time Held was under contract with the Folies Bergere, and she and Ziegfeld often saw the revue in Paris. It was Held who came up with the idea for the first *Ziegfeld Follies* in New York in 1907; it opened in the Jardin de Paris on the roof of the New York Theatre. *The Follies* produced lavish revues mingling the aesthetic of top Broadway shows and vaudeville variety, and Ziegfeld turned them into an annual tradition. The productions featured beautiful chorus girls, the Ziegfeld Girls, who sang and danced, adorned in either Erté or Lucile costumes.

Between 1915 and 1922, the elaborate productions reached their peak and became classics of the musical-comedy stage. The Follies were called a "national institution," the extravaganzas that every visitor to New York had to see.[4] What Ziegfeld really did was legitimize sexual objectification. He presented hundreds of beautifully draped females baring their long limbs to an audience that only a couple of decades before, had never even glimpsed a woman's ankle, let alone what Ziegfeld was now showing on the stage. He did so by scrubbing the girls clean, removing any hint of sordidness, any suggestion of the actual sexual act. His corporate credo was "Glorifying the American Girl."

The Ziegfeld Girls became recognized as the standard of female beauty. They became popular off stage as well, and several like Mary caused scandal and intrigue with their numerous high-profile romances with wealthy high-society men. Most of the girls dressed like flappers, wearing short skirts, getting rid of their corsets, wearing their hair short, wearing lots of makeup, and they also smoked and drank like their male peers. The Ziegfeld Girls included such well-known actresses as Marion Davies, Paulette Goddard and Barbara Stanwyck, who became the objects of popular adoration. The *1923 Follies* had Fanny Brice and Ann Pennington as its two main stars. This was Fanny's last year appearing in them.

Mary had entered the *Follies* when it was on the decline. As the teens and '20s passed, more and more producers had enviously tried to emulate Ziegfeld's success. Ziegfeld himself began producing some smaller scale shows called the *Frolics*. By 1922, the competition became much more intense, and as movies were now starting to come into their own, Ziegfeld found attendances dwindling and his incredible run coming to an end. By the time Mary was in the *Follies* in 1923, there were scores of competitive revues taking audiences away from the *Follies*: *The Negro Plantation Revue, Katinka, Earl Carroll's Vanities, The Greenwich Village Follies, The Passing Show, Artists and Models, Berlin's Music Box Revue* and the *Scandals*, to name just a few. Still, Ziegfeld managed to carry on for a few more years.

Some critics found the *1923 Follies* a "creaking gallery of exhausted concepts."[5] Theater critic Arthur Hornblower said it was "the most dreary, stupid, pointless, unbeautiful, unfunny show that Broadway has ever seen." The *1923 Follies* were the eighteenth rendition of the show, now unblushingly programmed as "The National Institution" and subtitled "Glorifying the American Girl." Like its predecessors, it did not single out any one performer as the overall star, but no doubt its biggest attraction was Fanny Brice. (Fanny was famously portrayed on stage by Barbra Streisand in the

1964 musical *Funny Girl.*) There was equally little doubt about it being a particularly weak addition in the series—short on good new songs and sketch material.

In November 1923, as "Imogene Robertson," Mary was voted the prettiest girl in the *Ziegfeld Follies* chorus.[6] As she recounted years later,

> That was probably the happiest period in my life. Because I didn't *think*, then. Life was just one great whoopee. It was fun, so help me Heaven, to be alive. If I had good luck, that was fine. If I had bad luck, I didn't have sense enough to realize it. When I fell in love—a state I was always in—it was another grand proof there was a Santa Claus. After my drab childhood in the convent, the world looked like a story by Hans Christian Andersen. I was dumb and dizzy—and happy.[7]

By 1925, the heyday of the *Follies* was well and truly over. There would be several more editions, but these shows lacked the luster of earlier productions. What ultimately caused the show's demise was Ziegfeld's own financial excesses, the growing competition from movies, and the desertion of many of the stars to Hollywood. Once the stock market crashed in 1929, the mood of the country changed to one of breadlines and unemployment. Ziegfeld's last production, *The Follies of 1931*, was staged during the peak of the Great Depression, and was clearly out of tune with the times. A year later, Ziegfeld, who had lost a fortune in the Wall Street crash, died in Hollywood in dire financial straits. A loyal friend to the end, Will Rogers paid for both his hospital and funeral expenses, oversaw the arrangement of the funeral, and helped console his family.

Ned Wayburn died on September 12, 1942. Fanny Brice died in 1951, age 59, of a cerebral hemorrhage.

THREE

The Frank Tinney Affair

Even though Frank Tinney was known to be a philanderer and heavy drinker and was married to a well-known actress, he and Mary began their affair after meeting in 1922. Who knows if Mary was looking for a father figure, someone to help boost her career, or genuinely fell in love with Frank. But regardless of the real reason, it was a caustic affair that had long-term ramifications on them, both personally and professionally. Later, Frank would say about neglecting to tell Mary he was married, "Sure I have a wife, a mortgage and an appendix, but why should I bring these things up and spoil a pleasant evening? I believe a man should keep his troubles to himself."[1]

As Marjorie Farnsworth wrote about Mary in her book *The Ziegfeld Follies*, "Almost from the day she was born, she lived with unhappiness in the form of loneliness, scandal, lawsuit, bankruptcy and above all hopeless love for Frank Tinney, the blackface comedian, a love that finally and inevitably was to wreck both their careers and, more important, their lives."[2]

This chapter in Mary's life would see her involved in the first of two life-changing tumultuous affairs and legal battles that would change the course of her life. In early May 1924, she gave a quote to the newspapers: "Tell girls to stay away from Broadway. Tell them there's only heartbreak there and shame—and bitter pain."[3]

Frank and Mary kept a relatively low profile after meeting. But in 1924 their affair became so volatile it spilled over into public fights and confrontations that made headlines across the country. The first major public disturbance was on Monday, May 26, 1924, when Mary "dramatically conceived a suicide," according to police: She took four sugar-coated pills which she said contained morphine.[4] The day before, she had also unsuccessfully attempted suicide, so she decided to throw a "suicide party" the following night, and had invited everyone over to Frank's apartment, at 157 West 72nd Street, where she was living. At the height of the party, Mary disappeared and came back a few minutes later, white and nervous, saying she had "done it." No one took her very seriously, and they even held a mock funeral for her still-breathing "remains." After everyone left, Carrie Sneed, her black maid, called the police and said that Mary had taken poison.

Policeman Alles of the West 68th Street Station, investigating the matter, found that Mary had taken harmless pills for indigestion. But on initially arriving and not yet knowing this, he had given her first aid by forcing her to swallow milk and eggs. The ambulance surgeon who subsequently arrived, Dr. Dibins of the Knickerbocker Hotel, examined Mary and confirmed that the pills were indeed harmless. To amplify the dramatic nature of this event, Mary had left a torn picture of Frank, along with a note supposedly written to her by Frank; she later admitted to police that she had written the note herself. The note read in part,

> Don't ever look for me, because you will never find me. I've gone far, far away, so far that God is the only living thing that can reach me. I know how terrible you are, but I love you in spite of yourself. I've tried to give you the things that money can't buy—love happiness and truth—because things that money can buy soon wear out, while love goes on and on through eternity.

A few days later, Mary appeared before New York City Magistrate Thomas McAndrews to file assault charges against Frank. She maintained that he had beaten her, causing bruises on her head and body, and had also "chastised" and injured Carrie, who accompanied Mary to court as a witness. Mary said the incident happened on the morning of May 28, when police were alerted as Mary ran from their apartment into the street wearing Frank's clothes and screaming at the top of her voice that Frank had beaten her. She said she had been naked at the time of the alleged incident and had grabbed the first items of clothing at hand and they just happened to belong to Frank. She was examined after the incident by Dr. Jerome Wagner (coincidentally, Florenz Ziegfeld's doctor) and he gave a statement saying, "The girl has all the appearances of having been struck by an automobile. It was a most brutal attack." Ziegfeld also made a statement: "I believe this little girl is an innocent victim. Her place in the 1924 edition of the *Follies* will be held open until she has recovered from the injuries she sustained. My policy is to stand behind all my girls when they are in trouble."[5]

Within a few hours, the story was all over the papers. Updates appeared daily in newspapers across the country as the public could not read enough about it. Frank was subsequently arrested by Baldwin Chief of Police Will Phillips at his home on Long Island on a charge of assault and was transported to Manhattan by detectives from the West 68th Street Station. The court case ended up being a circus. In stark contrast to how domestic violence would be treated if this happened today, it became a media joke.

Frank appeared in court on May 30 to face Mary's charges, but Mary was said to be too ill to attend and was reported to be in bed being cared for by two doctors. Her attorney, Edward V. Broderick, said she would appear in court on May 31. The packed courtroom contained a number of well-known theater people, but Frank just gazed over the crowd and seemed to look on the whole affair as a bit of a joke, telling the court that Mary's antics were all just a publicity stunt to the extent that his wife Edna had even thrown him out of their car on Broadway after she read reports of Mary's "suicide party." He then denied all the charges against him. Broderick stood up, denounced Frank, and asked the court to fix a high bail. Hearing that, Frank's expression turned glum.

"This man has left a trail of maimed women behind him," Broderick said. "His latest victim is too ill to appear today, and I would like a postponement." Broderick told the court that Frank had booked a passage to Europe for the coming Saturday, and that he also had information that Frank had mistreated other women in the past.

When Frank was questioned by the court, he told them that he didn't think Mary would appear against him, and that she was not as badly injured or as ill as she pretended to be. "She will not appear," he said. "Nobody ever appeared against me—and nobody ever will." He went on to say, "I don't feel like the Diamond Brothers or like Hoffman, and I have no intention of going to Europe over this affair."[6]

The laughter died and the smile faded from Frank's face when, after hearing both sides, Magistrate McAndrews upheld the charge of Frank feloniously attacking Mary, and Frank was held on $2,500 bail.[7] Wearing a tan suit, with a swagger overcoat flopped over his arm, holding his straw hat in his hand (Frank was what Broadway called "a nifty dresser"), he was stunned when the bail was set. Edna, who had threatened to divorce him in 1921 but changed her mind, went out of the court into the lobby frantically looking for someone to help with securing the bail. One of the bondsman agreed to fund it, and after that Frank and Edna left in a taxi to head home. The next day, Edna told the newspapers:

> What can a poor girl do when a man lies to her? Frank told her he was not getting along with his wife and she believed him. I saw Miss Wilson with my husband several years ago and warned her to stay away from him. I have not devised any punishment for him. I think he is getting punished enough. She is just a foolish little girl that has believed everything Frank told her. She has my sympathy and I am very sorry for her.

When the case readjourned in late May, Mary appeared and, while being interviewed by a reporter, confirmed her claim that Frank had beaten her and Carrie. She stated that she had just entered their apartment, accompanied by the reporter to whom she was relating her life story, when the attack took place. Frank was already in the apartment when Mary and the reporter came in, and Mary said he was wearing her blue silk kimono plus a pair of earrings belonging to Carrie.

Mary told the court that Frank refused to believe the visitor was a reporter. After the reporter left, Frank kicked her in the instep. Mary said she cried, "Frank, don't kick me," and he said, "Come here, honey," and when she did, he hit her on the side of the head with his fist. She said she fell to the floor and then Frank sat on her and beat her between the shoulders until she was bleeding from her mouth and nose. When talking about this incident, the court asked Mary why Frank beat her up, and she replied. "Judge, he considers that one of his star indoor sports." Mary then told the court that Frank had told her that Edna was going to California to file for divorce, after which time he would marry her. "I love him like many other little fools," she said.

Will Page, who was then Florenz Ziegfeld's publicity man, wrote about Mary during this time:

> She was the talk of New York, the toast of hundreds of admirers, and had the world of cavaliers at her feet. Then came the crash. She was beaten up by an actor—let no one ever tell you this was a press agent story. I know, because in my official capacity I was sent to visit her and found her with two nurses, a badly bruised, hysterical, pitiful young woman. The colored maid was still cowering upon a couch in the corner, wailing and crying because she, too, had been beaten.[8]

The next phase of this saga came about on May 31, and again it was in front of a packed courtroom. Everyone who was anyone showed up. Mary, still nursing her injuries, was carried into the court on a stool (and later left the same way). A huge crowd had also shown up outside the courtroom, to try to catch a glimpse of the main players, as it was the talk of Broadway. To add to the melodrama, Carrie was also carried into the court on a stool. It was noted that she limped a little on the off foot when she got off it and took a seat.

Mary appeared in court this day wearing a brown outfit, covered by a coat with a gray fur collar. Her hair at this stage was a light brown, and she was assisted down the aisle by both Carrie and her attorney, the former holding a small jar of smelling salts in case Mary needed them.[9] She did not acknowledge Edna, who was waiting outside the courtroom. As Mary entered the courtroom, Edna, who was amongst the earliest spectators to arrive, was then joined by Frank. According to reports, Frank looked tired and even yawned. He said he needed a glass of water, but when he went to get one, he was called upon to come into the courtroom. When he did, he passed by Mary without even acknowledging her.

Frank gave his age as 38, denied the charges, and then left the courtroom, again passing Mary without acknowledging her, although some witnesses said it looked as if he made a tentative move to step towards her to have a conversation. Frank went off in search of a glass of water, so when his name was again called out by the court clerk, he was not there. The clerk explained to the court that Frank was getting water, and Magistrate Goodman asked, "What does he think this is, a social party? He had better be back in a minute, or I'll forfeit his bail."

Frank re-entered the courtroom and stood to await the judgment. He was served with a summons in favor of Mary's charges for $100,000 in damages, and then subpoenas were obtained for 27 witnesses, both for and against the claim. Mary's lawyer Edward V. Broderick got 15 and Frank's lawyer Monroe Goldstein got the remaining 12. They each did this in a separate session, so neither knew what the other lawyer had done. The magistrate exclaimed, "What are you lawyers doing—subpoenaing the whole of the theatrical profession?"[10] Mary's charge of felonious assault was put off until a hearing scheduled for June 7.

The court case was covered in every major paper, and there were many editorials published, either for or against Mary. One article quoted William J. Fielding, a well-known psychoanalyst who said that in his opinion, the whole episode was a result of emotional temperaments running riot:

> It is found among stage folk, whose very work is one of emotions. With it comes a temporary mental aberration, in which high-strung persons often are subject. Even though beaten, the subject keeps on loving. But when the beating is accompanied by so much shock, as that is indicated in Miss Wilson's statement, revulsion sets in—and love turns to hate. I doubt very much if the girl will ever again be able to love her funny man—whose humor may just be a forced tendency to overcome a serious brooding that might have been dominant.[11]

The June 7 hearing was held in front of Magistrate Levine at the New York West Side Court, with the court denying Frank's motion to dismiss the charge of assault. The case was adjourned until June 11 after Mary, Carrie and Mary's doctor, Herbert Adler of the Hotel Alamac, had given testimony. Frank's counsel had tried to claim that the case was just a publicity scheme by Mary, but his motion was denied.

But things were not going Mary's way, as during the proceedings, Dr. Adler had told the court that after examining Mary, he felt that the pains in her abdomen might have been caused by something other than Frank's foot. He also admitted that Mary had complained of an ache in the affected area before her fight with Frank in her apartment.[12] After this testimony, Mary decided to dispense with Dr. Adler and she told the court she would select a new doctor before June 11, obviously to ensure she could get a testimony that more fully supported her charges.

The case got more interesting when, back in court on June 11, Frank's valet Bobby Gray was called on to testify in support of Frank. He stated that Mary had threatened to stab Frank to death with a kitchen knife during a quarrel they had, *before* the incident in Mary's apartment where Mary said Frank had beaten her. Gray called Mary a regular wildcat.[13] This incident, he said, took place on the night of May 19, when there was a furious battle between Mary and Frank at a New York Railway Station when Frank refused to accompany her back to their apartment.

"She slammed Frank with a suitcase, tore his suit open, ripped off his necktie, and hit him on the nose so hard it bled," Gray said. Arthur O'Brien, a friend of Frank's, confirmed Gray's story. The incident happened after O'Brien, Mary and Frank had left the Music Box Theatre, where Frank was appearing. Frank wanted to go to the railway station, saying he was heading home, but Mary said he shouldn't go, and the fight ensued.

Gray also spoke of an occasion when he took Mary to Frank's Long Island home and Edna refused to let them in. it was then that Mary produced a knife and threatened to stab Frank. Gray said Edna had just turned up her nose and told Mary that she had better go back to town and start hunting for a husband of her own, as that was the only way she was ever going to get anywhere in this world. He said that Mary then left Frank's house and returned to New York.

Frank appeared next and kept the courtroom in an uproar all that afternoon as he spoke about his difficulties with Mary (or, as he kept on referring to her, "Bubbles"). He recited a litany of things that Mary had supposedly done including smashing his apartment door, brought in her trunks so he was compelled to move out, hit him with a heavy handbag, hit him with her fists, left deep fingernail marks on his face and neck, and kicked the windows out of a taxi to demonstrate her anger when he told her he was going home to his wife. Frank said Mary also tore the clothes off his back, kicked his shins until they were black and blue, and then threatened to slash both Frank and Edna with a potato knife.[14]

Frank mentioned all these purported attacks to back up his story that Mary had threatened his life on more than one occasion. To prove this, he pulled up his pants leg to show the court his bruised shins. On the day in question in Mary's suit, Frank said he had gone to see Mary to tell her off for staging a "fake suicide party," and to let her know that he did not want that type of publicity. Regarding the assault that Mary alleged took place after the reporter left, Frank testified that he only used what force was necessary to keep Mary from using an ice pick on him.

Frank's version of the event was that he was in their apartment waiting for Mary to come home and had accepted a Scotch and ginger ale from Carrie that made him so ill he had to go to bed, wearing Mary's kimono. When Mary walked in with the reporter, he came out of the bedroom, and for a laugh had put on a pair of her earrings. After the reporter left, Frank said he had tried to find his clothes, so he could go home, but Mary had locked them in a closet. When he tried to get them out, the alleged assault occurred.

Despite the physical evidence presented, a grand jury refused to indict Frank, apparently agreeing with his lawyer's assessment that the incident was nothing more than a publicity stunt by Mary. Two days prior to the hearing, Frank had written to the grand jury foreman, asking for permission to appear and relate his side of the affair. They agreed, and both he and Mary attended the hearing and both spent 15 minutes in front of the jury. Appearing with Frank were his attorneys, Monroe Goldstein and Julius Kendler, as well as Catherine Lovely: The nurse who attended Mary was now appearing as a witness for Frank. Mary had her maid Carrie and Dr. Adler with her, and also brought detective Simon Tierney (who did not testify).

After they had all presented their evidence, the jury deliberated and decided there was not enough evidence to bring any charges. All the charges were dismissed. Frank, informed of the grand jury's decision, said,

> It is just what they should have done. Do you realize the number of American homes these glorified girls have broken up? It was nothing but a publicity stunt. This is the first time I have ever made good without getting a laugh. When a woman beats a man, that's no news. But when a man beats a woman that's news. I know just how Fatty Arbuckle felt now.[15] I realize now why they call actors and actresses hams. She's cured, she is.[16] A week ago, I was best man for another tragedian like myself.[17] Today I appear before the grand jury. Everything will be "jake," if I can find a happy medium in between.[18]

The reality was that this was not Frank's first incident with a showgirl. In 1920, when he was starring in *Sometime* at Chicago's Studebaker Theatre, one of the company's most beautiful chorus girls was titian-haired Mary McDonald. Frank threw a party for the cast at the Marigold Gardens, and for some reason McDonald failed to show up. This apparently annoyed Frank, so he left the party and went to the Lorraine Hotel where she was staying. A situation occurred that resulted in McDonald being taken to a hospital. She told doctors she had been beaten, but would not say who did it. Her body was covered with bruises and a handful of her hair was missing. She also had an eight-inch wound that necessitated stitches, resulting in a permanent scar.[19] Edna went to the hospital to see her, and then finally Frank showed up as well. After Frank left Chicago, it was reported that Edna had stayed on, not only paying all of McDonald's hospital bills, but giving her $3,600 in return for signing away all claims against Frank.

After McDonald left the hospital, she went to Philadelphia where she rejoined the cast of the show. She did end up giving a brief interview, and while not mentioning Frank by name, she did say, "I hope that a few of these fellows keep on with their roughhouse tactics till they get what they deserve." Coincidentally, McDonald appeared in the *Ziegfeld Follies of 1922,* a year before Mary was in them.

Mary's lawyer in her case against Frank, Edward Broderick, went go on to represent Wayne Thomas Lonergan, convicted in one of the most sensational trials of the 1940s. Lonergan was charged with killing his wife Patricia, heiress to a New York beer fortune, and was eventually sentenced to 35 years to life after his conviction on second degree murder charges. Because of the case's tangled drama, which included elements of love, hate, jealousy, the scandalous behavior of the young "cafe society" set of New York and a $7 million fortune, the Lonergan trial of 1944 attracted international attention. Lonergan was paroled in 1967 and died in Canada in 1986, at age 67. Broderick died in 1960 at 67. Frank's lawyer Monroe Goldstein was also a well-known theatrical lawyer; Milton Berle and Edward G. Robinson were among his clients.

In early August 1924, Frank booked a trip to England on the *Columbus*; in England, he was scheduled to play some music hall engagements. On August 4, two days before he was set to leave, he and Mary reconciled and were seen together outside a Broadway theater. Frank smashed the camera of photographer Nicholas Petersen, who attempted to take a picture of the couple as they were leaving a Broadway restaurant. Petersen filed a claim against Frank on August 5, but these charges were eventually dropped in the West Side Court by Magistrate Edgar S. Frothingham. Since Mary and Frank reconciled immediately after the court case, it is obvious that they both were putting on some type of charade during the trial for some reason, but it was possibly more on Mary's side: If she had won the court case, Frank would have to had to pay her whatever the court decided was the final settlement.

To avoid another incident like the one with Petersen, as well as to avoid reporters, Frank decided to board the *Columbus* the day before his scheduled departure. However, while waiting to board, he was served with papers informing him that Edna was filing for a legal separation, charging that Frank had deserted her.

In a *Brooklyn Daily Eagle* article, Edna was quoted as saying, "I've had all I can stand. I've tried to be a good fellow. I've tried to play on the level with Frank and be a regular pal. But you can only use a postage stamp once, and I guess that about describes me."[20] Edna declared that she would not sue for divorce and did not really want a divorce, and that a separation would suffice for the present. She added that she already had the separation papers drawn up, and that she would file them as soon as she had an opportunity to come into the city and meet with her attorney, Harry H. Osbrin. Edna continued:

> I could say a whole lot of things, but what good would it do? I don't want anybody to think that I'm ready to join the rest of the mob that wants to jump all over Frank. Frank has a whole lot of good qualities but he, apparently, hasn't sowed all his wild oats and perhaps never will. There never will come a time when I won't be a good friend of Frank's and help him all I can. There is no ill feeling, but I've just had about all I can go.

Edna then announced she was going to go back to the stage.

At eight the following morning, Mary showed up to bid Frank farewell but the two stayed in Frank's cabin to avoid reporters, with Mary having to eventually be physically escorted off the ship after she kept ignoring the departure whistle. She wept as she watched the *Columbus* depart and told reporters that she was still in love with him:

"[He's] the only thing in my life. I know it. You know it. So why should I beat around the bush?" It was also reported that Frank gave $5,000 to a friend to give to Mary just before he sailed.[21]

Mary's tearful goodbye to Frank was covered by the media, which prompted Florenz Ziegfeld to fire Mary later that day. Ziegfeld said that he had fired her because she had promised to break off her relationship with Frank, and she hadn't. He added, "She broke her promise and I discharged her because of the notoriety and to prevent a possible disruption of the morale of my cast. I have given Miss Wilson the benefit of the doubt up to now. But this ends it. She is no longer with the company."

After Frank sailed, Mary went up to Saratoga Springs, New York, where Frank's friend turned the money over to her. "Give this to 'Bubbles,'" Frank had told him. "Things are likely to get hard for her now she has lost her job. Give her the entire amount now, or pay it to her in installments, as she needs it," were his parting directions to his friend. The check was made out to Frank's friend, who endorsed it and turned it over to Mary. Mary was not seen attending any races there but was sometimes seen out at night in the company of bookmaker Joe Zuker.

On August 20, Mary gave an interview to Mark Sellinger, the reporter she was with in the case she brought against Frank.[22] The article is reproduced below in its entirety:

Imogene, Drooping Flower, in Upper West Side Flat
Awaits Call of Her Frank

"I Can't Go to England Yet, for It Would Hurt Him Professionally," She Wails—
If Her Comedian Grows Tired of Her, She Has a Prescription "And the Drugstores Will Always Be Open."

The beautiful Imogene Wilson, former "Queen of the Follies," has not gone to England with Frank Tinney, her beloved comedian. And she has no intention of going, she says, until Tinney cables that he needs her. It was a different Imogene whom a reporter located today in a select hotel on the upper west side.

"Only Thing in My Life"
No longer is she the brilliant show girl, who was known as "Broadway's most beauteous fragile blond." Nor is she the girl who told a Judge and a Grand Jury Frank Tinney had beaten her insensible. She is now but Imogene Wilson the woman. She spoke slowly and quietly. There was a droop to her head, as if she was tired. She was asked if she was happy.

"Happy? And why shouldn't I be? I have something that nobody else in this world has stronger than I. I have love," she cried. "Frank Tinney is the only thing in my life. You know it. Everybody knows it. So why should I beat around the bush?"

Here she was interrupted. But doesn't Tinney seem a poor lot on whom to lavish your devotion. Don't you know—

"Stop." She cried.

"Every Man is Rotten"
The mantle of languor dropped from her. She sat rigid. Her eyes flashed. She bit her lower lip so hard a trickle of blood appeared.

"Don't preach to me about Frank Tinney," she screamed. "Every man in this world is rotten—and Frank is no worse than anyone else. Maybe Frank does drink. Is he the only man who does? Perhaps Frank was not true to his wife all the time. Is he the only married man who has had another affair?

"But no, just because I am Imogene Wilson and he is Frank Tinney, people point at us and whisper. Whisper? I should have said broadcast."

Her voice fell low again. She clutched at the reporter's arm, clenched it tightly. A woman's soul was being laid bare.

"Wherever I go I can feel accusing eyes on me."

Glories in Her Love

"I have lived with Frank Tinney. I am not ashamed to admit it. More than that, I glory in it. But Frank is the only one and, with God's help, he will always be the only one. I am only twenty-one, but I have lived twice that many years in the last six months. What have I gained? The knowledge that I belong to Frank Tinney, and that I will belong to him until the end of time.

"But how can you love a man who has beaten you so brutally?" she was asked.

"Don't ask me how I can," was her tired reply. "I only know that I do. And even if Frank has beaten me, is there any shame attached to that? He has not hurt me half as much as you and all the other papers have. He has bruised my body, but the newspapers have broken my heart."

Longs to Go Away

"Oh, I want to go someplace far away from all this. I wouldn't care if I never saw Broadway, or people, or lights again. If Frank would only take me away." She gazed dreamily out of the window. Three children passed with a maid. Imogene turned suddenly.

"I could marry a millionaire tomorrow if I wanted to. You can believe me when I tell you it would be very simple, and if I did not want marriage, I could have all of them calling on me at the same time. But that's where I differ from other girls. Whereas others think that wealth, no matter what the man, is the only thing to be desired. I learned of love and dream of children. That's right. Everybody laughs, you might as well, too. Sounds funny from a chorus girl, doesn't it? Especially from a girl of my type." She drew the last words out with a cynical intonation. Her voice grew bitter. Her mood changed rapidly.

"And I don't blame you for laughing. Maybe I ought to laugh myself. Have I been wise, or have I been the most foolish of women? The world thinks it knows, but only Imogene Wilson really knows."

Lied for Love

"I have lied for Frank Tinney. I lied to you, to Ziegfeld, to everybody. But I couldn't lie to myself. And so, I am waiting. I can't go to England yet, because it would hurt Frank professionally. That's the reason, and I'm not ashamed to tell you or anybody else." The former Missouri convent girl's closing words were barely audible, so softly were they spoken.

"Maybe Frank will grow tired of me some day. Maybe I will grow old and ugly and not worthwhile. But I have a prescription and that may be ugly, but it never grows old. And the drugstores will always be open."

In early August, after the media circus around Mary's court case had subsided, she traveled to Boston to embark on a tour of dancing engagements in New England. By August 25, she was back in the newspapers. Apparently annoyed by reports that Massachusetts women would attempt to prevent her from going on with a dancing act, Mary told the newspapers she would dance anyway: "I'm going to dance a ballroom dance with my partner at Merriman Pavilion, Lawrence, tonight, and I am sure that no one is going to stop me there or anywhere else in Massachusetts." She also appeared as a judge in a ballroom dancing competition on August 26, at Whalon Park in Lunenburg, Massachusetts.[23]

In September, Mary announced she was going to England to join Frank, and on September 20, she set sail for Plymouth aboard the *Columbus*, where she said she would then go on to France, as she was scheduled to appear in a Paris vaudeville show.[24]

Although newspapers reported that she was accompanied by her sister Mabel, brother-in-law Charles and their son Charles Jr., the ship's passenger list has no record of them being aboard, so they may have just come to the dock to see her off.[25] Before the ship sailed, Mary gave an interview to half a dozen reporters. "I certainly am not going to dodge Frank if we happen to meet in Europe." she said. She told the reporters she was going abroad to fulfill the Paris vaudeville engagement, which she had arranged well before Frank left for England, and would be there for four months.

"I am very unhappy, and I want to go away. I may stay away forever." she said. "I don't care to talk of Mr. Tinney—or love. Love is too sacred a thing to discuss, especially with newspapermen." She told them she had not heard from Frank since he had gone to Europe, but she admitted to sending him a congratulatory message when he began his London engagement. She went on to say that she was going to lead a quiet life. Coincidentally, Frank's former valet Bobby Gray was also a passenger on the ship, so Mary and Frank had obviously been in touch despite her denials.

When Mary arrived in Plymouth, Mary told the waiting press, "I am not Miss Wilson. I am Miss Robertson. I don't know Miss Wilson. Please don't bother me." Wearing all black, except for a touch of red in the trimming of her gown, her now blonde hair peeking out from underneath a black cloche hat, she was escorted from the ship by Gray. While she was getting her passport inspected and telling them her occupation was a "dramatic artist," a message arrived from Frank via his London manager.

Frank's music hall engagement at the Empire Theatre had just been extended by eight weeks, so he had sent his manager to guard Mary against newspaper reporters and photographers, as he was in bed with indigestion. Mary told Immigration officials she was going to be staying at the Ritz, which is also where Bobby Gray was staying. Her fellow passengers said that Mary was seasick for the first five days at sea and kept to her stateroom the rest of the voyage, only appearing in the dining room for dinner twice. After going through Immigration, Mary caught the train to London and hid herself in her compartment for the whole journey.[26]

Mary had told the newspapers she was going to Paris, when she arrived in London she told the International New Service that she was on her way to *Italy*. On September 29, she gave an interview from the Ritz Carlton Hotel:

I am only a girl of 20.[27] Why all this fuss about me? Naturally, when I stopped over in London I looked up Frank Tinney just as I would anyone else in the profession if I knew them. What's wrong with that? I haven't really got a story to tell. I'm simply going to Italy to make pictures. It's my first visit to London and I like it immensely, but I cannot stay long. I'm leaving probably Wednesday or Thursday for Italy. I'm not telling the newspapers whom I'm working for or under what name I have contracted. Once before, the newspapers concocted wild stories and I lost it. Never again.

Frank didn't know I was coming. Why should he? Why all this interest in us? The English public doesn't care what Frank does, as long as he makes them laugh. They don't care if he has six wives or eight other women. Neither do the Americans. It's all the newspapers' fault. They've made an old woman of me, when I'm only a girl of 20. I'm fed up on it. I'm determined to make good in the movies. I won't have my chance spoiled by newspaper gossip. Most reporters remind me of schoolboys. They should be spanked.[28]

Although articles and newspaper reports say Mary went to Paris and appeared in shows there, no record can be found of this. It *is* known that she stayed in London where she reunited with Frank. At this stage, Frank had once again started to drink and he physically abused her: On October 8, Mary, wearing a patch over her eye, was seen moving out of the hotel into a 25 Germain Street flat that had previously been occupied by Frank.[29]

While she was in London, it was reported that Frank and Mary had many public fights, including a rather loud one at a dinner party in a fashionable Jermyn Street hotel. Fifteen people had been asked to a dinner party to celebrate Frank, who had had a triumph with his show there. According to newspaper reports, Frank was called upon to make a toast and rose, a glass of champagne in his unsteady hand. He bowed to the assembled group, but then pointed to Mary and shouted, "There she is! She's nothing but a modern Cleopatra, who delights to dig pitfalls for men!" Mary, clutching her satin wrap with as much pride as she could, looked at Frank with hurt and indignation, and then left. This caused the other diners to feel so uncomfortable that they promptly left as well. This incident cemented Mary's resolve to walk out of Frank's life for good, and in early 1925 she finally ended their relationship.

In 1941, Mary described her affair with Frank that she said began when she was just 14 as a "nonsensical mixture of fights and laughs, and half and half."

FOUR

Germany

By early 1925, Mary had received an offer to make movies in Germany, so she made her way to Berlin and worked there for the next two years under the name Imogene Robertson. German newspapers used to refer to her as "Sprudeln," which they had translated from her nickname "Bubbles." Several sources say that well-known gambler Arnold Rothstein paid for her to go to Europe, but this is largely unsubstantiated. In one of Mary's numerous articles that she or publicists wrote, she said she was in London sitting in Piccadilly when a man came up to her and told her how beautiful she was, and asked if she would come to Germany to make movies. Whether that happened or not, we will never know, but there would have been no language barrier, since these were silent films.

Filmmaking was a new experience for Mary. Even so, her acting skills garnered excellent reviews after her first German film, *Verborgene Gluten,* was released in 1925. In an interview many years later, Mary said of her time in Germany,

> My first picture was a shock to my sanity. The most difficult lesson to learn is naturalness. Every self-conscious thought seems to register more quickly than a smirk does away from the camera. I never saw anyone look or act so stilted. I recalled each strained effort to hold this or that pose, and realized that rehearsal should perfect technique, that once in a scene, emotional expression is more natural. So, my work does for me subconsciously, what I tried to teach myself to do intentionally.[1]

In 1924, the British distributor W&F Film Service Ltd. signed a production agreement with the German production company Emelka, under which the first film was to be *Verborgene Gluten.* Emelka had its own theaters and was its own distributor. At that time in the United States, only a handful of companies produced movies; in Germany there were as many as 80 small companies producing films. Emelka, founded in 1919, was the second largest of these, and in the 1920s it produced nearly five percent of all German films.

Mary made four more movies in 1925: *Die unberührte Frau, Wenn die Liebe nicht war! Die Feuertänzerin* and *Mrs. Worrington's Perfume. Die Feuertänzerin* received excellent reviews, prompting Germany's largest film company, UFA, to offer her a $1,500-a-week contract. Mary told a newspaper in 1927, "In America, I was just one of a flock of pretty girls, but in Germany I had to stand on my talents. They require a great deal of an actress over there."[2]

The saga surrounding Frank had not gone away: Frank's lawyer George A. Hopkins traveled to London in February 1925 to get testimony from him, as Frank was going to appeal the separation order that Edna had served on him before he sailed to London the year before. But by April, Edna had changed this to a divorce suit, naming Mary as a co-respondent. The process that Edna had to follow was to discontinue the separation suit and then file a separate motion for the divorce, and she was granted permission to do this on April 11 in King's County Supreme Court.

Part of Edna's suit was her claim that she had obtained evidence that on March 15, 1925, Mary and Frank had registered as man and wife at the Royal Turk's Head Hotel in Newcastle-on-Tyne, and she was going to call on hotel employees and detectives to be witnesses. Edna had obtained this piece of damning information as her lawyer Harry H. Oshrin had secretly gone to London on March 7 and found Frank and Mary at the hotel, where they had registered as "Frank Tinney and wife."

By March 1925, Frank was appearing in the London show *Sometime*.[3] On March 21, he told newspapers that after the divorce was final, he was going to marry Mary. He said,

> I'm very happy that my wife decided to adopt that plan. It makes everything so much simpler. It's too bad Mrs. Tinney's lawyer had to spring a surprise to get his evidence. Had I known he was coming, I would have had Imogene remain in England to he could take motion pictures of us. Bubbles will become Mrs. Frank Tinney as soon as the present Mrs. Tinney gets her divorce.[4]

On his return to the U.S. in April, Oshrin told newspapers that the trip to London had been necessary due to Frank's inability to stop seeing Mary, even though he had promised Edna he would, as well as failing to send her any money. According to Oshrin:

> I sailed from New York on March 6, arrived on March 13, and at once took the route of Tinney's company. I found that a "Mr. and Mrs. Frank Tinney" had registered at the Royal Turk's Head Hotel, Newcastle-on-Tyne, on March 15. When I finally met Tinney, he was very good-natured about the matter, and he admitted that Imogene Wilson had come over from Berlin to spend a few days with him in England. She is now in Vienna, making motion pictures. Tinney told me he intended to marry her if his wife would divorce him, and he will probably fight the amount of alimony, but he will not fight the divorce.
>
> Mrs. Tinney is practically penniless. The house in which she lives is in the joint names of herself and her husband, so she cannot sell it. She has disposed of her motorcar and is trying to sell her furniture. She says there's nothing for Tinney to come home to now—she has sold the cocktail shaker.[5]

According to Frank, one morning about dawn, a knock at his hotel door woke him up and the hotel manager, two maids, two waiters and Oshrin walked in and asked if he was Frank Tinney. When he replied he was, they said it was merely a formality to secure his identification. With him in the room was Johnny Fields, an American actor also playing with Frank in *Sometime*, and as they been out drinking the night before, Johnny had crashed in his room.

Edna's divorce petition was asking for $500 a week in alimony and $10,000 to cover lawyer's fees, and she had petitioned for sole custody of their son Frank, Jr. Frank later said he would not contest the actual divorce but was going to fight the amount of alimony Edna was asking. Newspapers reported that Frank had left Edna with no money, plus a pile of unpaid bills. To perhaps gain sympathy or to point out the dysfunctional relationship that Mary had with Frank, Edna told the newspapers that Frank had supposedly asked Mary if she wanted him to buy her a car. She agreed and together they went shopping for one in New York, until they finally agreed on a roadster. Frank had it outfitted with balloon tires, a cigarette lighter and several other costly extras. The day they came to pick it up, he wrote out a check for it, but then promptly arranged for it to have Edna's initials engraved on it, and then sent to her. The car was not to be Mary's after all.

When Edna arrived back in New York that night, Frank surprised her by picking her up in the car—but also telling her that they may get a visit from Mary at their house, because Mary thought the car had been purchased for her, not Edna.

Mary was so upset about this incident that after her performance that night, at around two in the morning, she had Frank's valet Bobby drive her to Frank's Long Island house. According to Edna, she was woken by the sound of Mary and Bobby arguing. Frank was pretending to be asleep, so Edna called the police. Mary was now hiding in the bushes either waiting for the police to arrive or hoping Frank would come out, so Edna invited Mary into the house to wait there. Mary went inside and told Edna that she had come there to get the car she felt was rightfully hers, and to tell Edna she was in love with Frank and that she wanted to be with him. Edna said the conversation went as follows:

> EDNA: What do you wish at this ridiculous hour—in my home?
> MARY: I—I—I—I want Frank!
> EDNA: You do? Why?
> MARY (sobbing): Because—I—I—I love him.
> EDNA: Oh, you mean my husband?
> MARY: Yes, I love him. And *you*—you don't understand him.
> EDNA: Well, perhaps you're right. After 14 years of married life, a comic is up to all sorts of tricks. Are you one of 'em?
> MARY: I won't talk only except in front of Frank. And I—

According to Edna, Mary never got to finish her sentence as at that time a policeman arrived. Mary still insisted on seeing Frank, but Edna could not persuade him to come downstairs and see Mary. Police escorted Mary out of the house. She then got into an argument with him, but it ended when the police called a taxi. Mary got in it and returned to New York.

By May 1925, Frank said he was broke. He occupied a small single room in an obscure hotel in London, living on crackers and cheese. This was probably somewhat true as he had had very little work since November 1924, and *Sometime* had proven to be a financial failure. He was owed $4,500 in back salary and he told reporters that he himself had paid for the *Sometime* cast to go from Cardiff back to London.[6] Frank returned briefly to New York in June for some initial court proceedings related to his divorce, and appeared before Supreme Court Justice Benedict in Brooklyn, to see Edna initially awarded $200 a week in alimony and $5,000 in legal fees pending trial of her suit for divorce.[7] Frank appealed the amounts, which meant the divorce would not be final until his appeal had been heard.

By July 1925, Mary had finally left Frank. Meanwhile, Edna was telling the newspapers that she was willing to take him back. She said that when Frank went to England, he promised to send her $400 a week, but he never sent her any money even though she had written to him more than 20 times.[8]

Because of Mary's notoriety, there were numerous newspaper articles written around her frolics in Europe. Some of them were possibly written by Mary herself or by her publicity machine. While she was in Europe, Mary was supposedly seen with Henri Letellier, proprietor of *Le Paris Journal*, often called the "best-mannered man in Europe"; she had met him in Rome. He was often associated with the Moulin Rouge and was the recently elected mayor of Deauville. Henri asked Mary to join him on his yacht, which was moored at Naples, for a week with various other guests. Mary also made the acquaintance of King Alfonso of Spain, who allegedly gave her an expensive brooch. She had met Alfonso in Madrid, when she was invited to the palace with about 20 other people.

From there, the story went, she finally went to Germany to fulfill a contract she had with Ben Blumenthal, who had supposedly offered her a role in *Samson and Delilah*. While she was on the train there, she met the "sausage guy" or "Herr G." He asked Mary to honor him by coming back to his villa where he was having a party. According to Paul Prys of the *Vaterland*, Mary decided to blow off the Germany trip and followed Herr G. When she did not show up in Germany, the film company dispatched various people to find her. At the same time, Frank was supposedly telegraphing around Europe, also trying to track her down. The search for Mary was the headlines in many papers on the Continent.

In September 1925, Edna was quoted in a newspaper saying,

> A year ago, when Miss Wilson was issuing these rather undignified statements to the paper, she very thoroughly emphasized her devotion to the gentleman who happened to be my husband. She said something to the effect that wedding rings really didn't count for much when a heart's ardor was pitted against the poor little old-fashioned golden circlet. And that her love for Mr. Tinney was such that poor circumscribed wedding ceremonies were as nothing by comparison. So, Miss Wilson explained, and undoubtedly my husband was considerably flattered. Any man would be, to know that he has raised such riot in a heart so young and tender.
>
> I am sure when Miss Wilson crossed to the other side and turned her really fine eyes toward my husband, he must have felt again that his drawing power off the stage was enormous, in fact, quite as great as it was on. And—also—I am sure Mr. Tinney felt that the heart, affection, loyalty of Miss Wilson was all his, to accept, or trample upon, forever. But lately, I hear, something happened which seriously shocked Mr. Tinney. Miss Wilson crossed the English Channel and went to Munich, Germany. Hardly had she arrived in Munich than a sausage manufacturer, as red as his own bologna and as plump as his own frankfurters, came paying Miss Wilson his court.

Edna went on to say that she had heard that Mary had gotten engaged to this sausage man, and so Frank then traveled to Munich, and having found Mary, handed her a gift, saying it was a beautiful necklace. But according to Edna, Frank was up to his old tricks, and when Mary opened the present, she found a necklace made of sausages. Mary did not see the joke and told him to leave and never come back. Edna added, "My husband then went back to England, and as he went, my sympathies went with him. I am fond of my husband, as always, no matter what has happened or may happen." She went on to allege that Frank then took up with Aileen Stanley, an English actress, but there is no record that this ever happened.[9]

In September, Frank was sued by his lawyer, George A. Hopkins, who was trying to collect $7,250 in unpaid legal fees. Hopkins asserted that Frank had only paid him $2,750, against a debt of $9,000, for legal services that Hopkins had provided from August 1924 through September 1925, including Frank's defense in the suit brought by Edna.[10] At the same time, Mary told reporters that she would never set foot on Broadway again "unless they spread a red velvet carpet on it for me."[11]

By October, Edna had returned to the stage as "Mrs. Frank Tinney" and her divorce proceedings had started again in the Mineola Long Island Court. On October 16, a deposition, obtained by Oshrin on his March trip to England, was read in court. It was from an Elizabeth McIntyre, a waitress at the Royal Turk's Head Hotel in Newcastle-on-Tyne when Frank and Mary stayed there. She said she had served Mary breakfast in bed and had heard Frank call her "Bubbles." Other depositions were heard from hotel employees Blanche Horsman, Samuel Marshall and Thomas Turner. A note of issue was filed suggesting that November 2 was going to be the date for the actual trial, but the divorce case was eventually heard on November 5.

Edna and Frank's divorce was heard before Supreme Court Justice Riegelman in Mineola. Hopkins, still representing Frank, opposed Edna's application for $750 a week alimony because, he told the court, Frank was now drinking heavily and had not worked for the past three months. He also told the court Frank had formerly made $2,500 a week appearing in London music halls and nightclubs but was no longer making that kind of money, so he could not possibly afford to pay that amount of alimony. To show how chaotic this whole affair was, just before the case was heard, Frank's agent Percy Reiss sent two telegrams to Edna on November 4, asking Edna to think about doing a double act with Frank on the stage in London. She never took up the offer.

Frank returned to the U.S. on November 23, 1925, on the *Antonia*, while the divorce proceedings were still going on, and was seen out and about shopping with Edna and their son. Edna had apparently agreed to try again with Frank, although she was not stopping the divorce proceedings. The divorce was finally granted on November 28 and Edna was awarded custody of Frank Jr. and an initial settlement amount of $200 a week in alimony. She told the press that she thought there might be a slight possibility that she and Frank would marry again within a year. That never happened and their attempts to salvage their relationship were over by March 1926.

Frank's career and marriage were ruined after his affair with Mary and his subsequent divorce. In July 1926, his house and furnishings at "Foxhurst," Frank and Edna's 35-acre estate in Baldwin, Long Island, was sold as part of their divorce settlement for $11,000 against a judgment of $10,000.

After Frank and Mary split in July 1925, he continued to work on stage. On his return to the U.S., he found that many of his friends had deserted him and that his popularity with the theatergoing public had waned. While performing on the stage in Detroit in October 1926, he collapsed and was hospitalized suffering from a pleural infection and from the two broken ribs sustained in the fall. It was also reported that he had major psychological issues, with doctors holding grave fears he would recover from the latter. He left the hospital in mid–December but was back in January 1927 after a relapse. He never fully recovered, and by 1930 he was in Philadelphia living with his father, his career virtually over. Frank died at age 62 on November 28, 1940, of a pulmonary condition after a long stay at the Veterans Hospital in Northport, Long Island.

According to Charles Chaplin biographer David Robinson,

> The idea for Chaplin's film *Limelight* was suggested by Chaplin's memory of Frank, whom he had seen on stage when he first came to New York at the height of Frank's popularity. Some years later Chaplin saw Frank again and recognized with shock that "the comic Muse had left him." This gave him the idea for a film which would examine the phenomenon of a man who had lost both his spirit and his assurance.[12]

Mary made 12 more films in Germany: *Fünf-Uhr-Tee in der Ackerstraße, Unser täglich Brot, Die Welt will belogen sein, Wien, wie es weint und lacht, Die Königin des Weltbades, The Armored Vault, Adventures of a Ten Mark Note, Eleven Who Were Loyal, Das süße Mädel, The Girl of Paris, Erinnerungen einer Nonne and Halloh–Caesar!* Regarding her performance in *Uneasy Money, Variety* said, "The picture's chief merit is the remarkably good acting of Mary Nolan. Not that she's any cinema Bernhardt, but she does extremely well for the simple purposes of this tale."[13]

At the end of 1926, Mary finally relented to the offers coming in from Hollywood and took the one offered by Joseph M. Schenck, head of United Artists, and made plans to return home. Some reports say that Schenck was supposedly browsing through a European movie magazine when he saw a picture of Mary, and then cabled his Berlin representative saying, "Understand Imogene Robertson is an American. See if she will consider a Hollywood contract." Other accounts say that it was while viewing one of Mary's German movies that Schenck became enamored of her and had searched her out to take her under his wing.[14]

But the version that seems to be the most factual is that John M. Considine, the head of Feature Productions (a United Artists subsidiary) and Schenck's right-hand man, saw Mary on the screen and immediately signed her. As was the custom with a foreign actress, he arranged transportation from Germany as well as a standard contract for $400 a week. At that time, it was reported that he did not know that Imogene Robertson was Imogene "Bubbles" Wilson.

In a February 1927 interview with the *Los Angeles Times*, Considine came clean: "This story is not exactly true. I knew Miss Wilson, of course, and I brought her here for tests. If they are satisfactory, we will use her in pictures. If not, I can release her at any time."[15]

Regardless of how Universal came to offer her a contract, this was a big career boost for Mary. Joseph M. Schenck (1878–1961) started in the entertainment business with his younger brother Nicholas, operating concession stands at New York's Fort George Amusement Park. In 1909, the brothers purchased Palisades Amusement Park and afterward became participants in the fledgling motion picture industry in partnership with Marcus Loew, operating a chain of movie theaters. In 1916, through his involvement in the film business, Schenck met and married Norma Talmadge. Schenck supervised, controlled and nurtured her career in alliance with her mother, but they divorced in 1934. After parting ways with his brother, Joseph moved to the West Coast, and within a few years, he was made the second president of United Artists. UA had been formed by D.W. Griffith, Charlie Chaplin, Mary Pickford and Douglas Fairbanks with the intention of controlling their own interests, rather than depending upon the commercial studios to decide their fate.

In 1933, Schenck partnered with Darryl F. Zanuck to create Twentieth Century Pictures, which merged with Fox Film Corporation in 1935. As chairman of the newly formed 20th Century–Fox, he was one of the most powerful and influential people in the film business. Caught in a payoff scheme to buy peace with the militant unions, he was convicted of income tax evasion and spent four months in prison before being granted a presidential pardon. Following his release, he returned to Fox, where he later became infatuated with the then-unknown Marilyn Monroe and played a key role in launching her career. One of the founders of the Academy of Motion Picture Arts and Sciences, he retired in 1957 and shortly afterwards suffered a stroke from which he never fully recovered.

Mary's reputation in Germany may also have fueled her desire to return to the U.S. She had gained a reputation for being a prima donna, faking fainting spells and breaking contracts. There were also rumors that she fled Germany as she was facing court cases over unpaid bills.

Whatever the real reason, by the end of 1926 Mary had set her sights on the next stage of her career back in the U.S., to once again be caught up in a vicious public brawl, this time with a much more highly influential and powerful man than Frank Tinney.

FIVE

Hollywood and Eddie Mannix

A large crowd of press and paparazzi were anxiously waiting on the docks in New York, anticipating Mary's arrival back in the U.S. on January 31, 1927. Earlier in January, newspapers had reported that she was fleeing Germany as she owed $25,000.[1] Other reports said that she had fled Germany not because of debts, but to escape a married man who had beaten her, as well as fleeing the jealous rage of his wife. That report was from Mary's purported legal representative in Germany, Dr. Erich Frey, who also said that her debts in Germany were less than $2,000, or less than two weeks' salary, not $25,000 as had been previously reported.

Frey went on to say that Mary was fleeing from more than just one man. He characterized one of them as being a "caveman" who had slapped Mary's face repeatedly in the presence of witnesses and said that it was because of this man that Mary did not have any money, as he had made her turn all her earnings over to him. He said that he had eventually managed to get this man deported from Germany. Frey also said that Mary was involved with yet another married man, and that this man's wife had threatened to shoot Mary, so Frey said she took refuge in a fashionable sanitarium at Grunewald, but the man ultimately tracked her down there. At the same time, the first man returned to Germany and ended up also trailing Mary to Munich. Fred reported, "In her distress at finding this out, Imogene changed her ticket for Berlin where she had wanted to settle everything, into a ticket for America and left immediately."[2]

He reported that Mary had failed to appear in court in Germany on ten different occasions but that the judge refused to order her arrest, so Frey opined that the charges against her would eventually be dropped. There were other reports in various newspapers backing up Frey's story that Mary had fled Germany due to man troubles and jealous wives and girlfriends, as well as financial difficulties.[3]

With all this hype about her homecoming appearing in the media, Mary finally landed in New York, disembarking from the *Majestic* accompanied by German actor Nils Anton Asther, with whom she had starred in *Das süße Mädel* (*The Sweet Girl*) in Germany. She gleefully sashayed down the gangplank to greet the crowd who had been there for hours waiting to catch a glimpse of her. Nils later wrote, "There was much talk in the papers when I arrived in America, because Mary was on the same boat as me. They said I was brought here by her. We had played in a film together in Berlin, but I did not know that she was on the same boat as me until after we had set sail."[4]

Why Mary officially became "Mary Nolan" is not known. Some reports say it was

Schenck who, wanting to disassociate Mary from her past life and scandals, insisted she change her name to Mary Nolan before arriving in New York. Other stories say the name-changer was director Herbert Brenon, who had just announced that he had cast her in her first movie back in the U.S., *Sorrell and Son*.

As Mary's return was widely covered by the press who were still interested in the scandalous "Bubbles" Wilson, it prompted backlash. Several women's groups protested her coming back to make films in the U.S., while Will H. Hays, president of the Motion Picture Producers and Distributors of America, expressed doubts about her embarking on a Hollywood career.

After arriving in New York, Mary stayed only a few days before making her way to Hollywood, where she checked into the Hollywood Plaza Hotel, then popular with actors and actresses. After a few weeks, on February 18, Mary announced to the press that she was now formally under contract.[5]

Legal troubles were still plaguing her. In February 1927, she filed a $100,000 suit against press agent Will A. Page, author of the just released book *Behind the Curtains of the Broadway Beauty Trust*, saying it included false claims about her in the chapter "A Little Bit of Fluff."[6] Playwright George Bernard Shaw also sued Page as, without Shaw's permission, the book included numerous letters Shaw had written.

Here is what Page wrote about Mary in his book:

The winds of Fate play funny tricks, they catch a speck of dust and throw it into the eyes of rich and poor alike; they grasp a scrap of paper and toss it into a whirlwind as ruthlessly as a cyclone or a tornado sweeps everything before it; and so it is not strange that they seized upon a little puff ball from the corn fields of Kentucky and wafted it four thousand miles to the edge of the lagoon under the trees of Armenonville, the garden restaurant of Paris.

She came to us from the land of fair women and brave men; from a State hallowed with the chivalry of two hundred years. Blown upon the winds of Fate she came, an orphan raised in a convent, knowing little of life except that all men told her she was beautiful.

Of course, she came to the *Follies*; the most widely advertised beauty market of the world, for here alone could she get full market value for her marvelous form and features. Henry Clive saw her first, as an artist's model. He brought her to Ziegfeld; and overnight she blossomed forth as the fairest of all flowers in that wonderful garden of girls.[7]

Artists went mad about her; magazine editors begged for her photographs; costumers and modistes flooded the country with her pictures, displaying their wares; dramatic editors who loved to print beautiful pictures, used up more than three hundred photographs of her in less than six months; Cheney Johnston had to put on a night shift of men in his studios to turn out enough photos of this wonderful girl, and Ziegfeld declared her the most beautiful girl he had ever glorified.[8]

As press representative of the *Follies*, at that time, it became my duty to act as her official chaperone, I consulted with her on various plans of publicity that would make her famous and a great star. She loved publicity; adored it; was never fed up with too much free space in the papers. Her scrapbook, kept by my office boy, soon ran into a second volume. Cranks began to besiege her; strange men waited at the stage door; flowers and presents from admirers came like a deluge; the stage door man at the *Follies* became rich in a few weeks from tips for delivering mash notes; in other words, she was distinctly IT; she was the talk of the town, the toast of a dozen admirers, the world of cavaliers at her feet.[9]

Then came the crash; beaten up by an actor. A famous comedian, jealous of the attentions of other men, smashed her one on the nose and a couple more on the side of her head for good measure.... A sympathetic doctor had given the show girl first aid; her head was swathed with bandages, and one of the nurses told me there was a gash an inch long in her scalp.

The whole affair is over now; it was tried in the courts and the comedian was given a Scotch verdict of "not proven." WHY? Because when the grand jury heard the fair young damsel's story, she had relented; he was HER MAN; he had a right to beat her, and it was nobody's business if he did.

And so, the winds of Fate blew the little bit of fluff from Broadway and across the seas. But not until the affair had ruined the comedian's drawing power for theatergoers; not until the puff-ball herself had come in for some unpleasant notoriety and had been fired from the *Follies* for being "too notorious"—rather a doubtful compliment if you analyze it carefully.

"I don't fancy I shall ever return to America," said the "Puff Ball" softly, as she sipped the champagne…. "I have learned many serious lessons since those days when I was a mere foolish girl. I fancied that because I had won fame and publicity, it would bring me fortune at once…. If I had never met the comedian, if I had never become infatuated with him, my career would have been vastly different."

Darkness came; the lights of the Bois flickered through the trees. The Puff Ball shivered slightly. I paid the check—think of it, champagne at $3.00 per—and we sped back to town in a taxi. Around the Arch de Triomphe, down the beautiful and brilliantly lighted Avenue de Champs Elysee, and then into a side avenue not far from the Etoile district. It was nine o'clock; I left the Puff Ball at the door of her apartment house. "I always retire early! I never go out late to parties; I have been in Paris for three months and I have never seen Montmartre; I am working hard studying French, also Italian, and I have my lessons early tomorrow. And so—good night."

A pretty bit of Fluff; I feel sure that someday winds of Fate will blow the Puff Ball back across the seas. Knowing her as I do, I have found by experience that one should always "copper the bet,"[10] on whatever she says. But here's good luck to you, Puff Ball, whichever way the winds may blow you henceforth.[11]

Page's book never actually names Mary as being the "Puff Ball," but in the middle of the chapter of the book is a picture of Mary. Mary's suit against Page was eventually dismissed. Just 49 years old, Will Page died of heart disease in 1928.

Mary waited several months before finally being told that director Herbert Brenon was ready to start shooting *Sorrell and Son.* July 1927 saw Mary travel to Chicago, and then onto New York before sailing on the *Majestic* on July 18 for London and Cambridge, where she was going to shoot some exterior scenes for the movie with the cast and crew. Brenon was an Irish film director during the era of silent movies, right through to the 1930s. Some of his more noteworthy films were the first movie adaptations of *Peter Pan* in 1924, *Beau Geste* in 1926 and *Sorrell and Son,* for which he was nominated for the Academy Award for Best Director in the first Academy Awards. As the Famous Players-Lasky Company was uninterested in the story, Brenon had chosen to produce it independently.

Based on the 1925 best-selling novel by Warwick Deeping, *Sorrell and Son* starred H.B. Warner in a father-love melodrama about paternal devotion in the face of personal and social adversity. Set in England in the aftermath of World War I, the film tells the story of Stephen Sorrell, played by Warner, a returning war veteran who suffers all sorts of humiliations in order to support his young son, following the desertion of his self-centered wife. Nils Asther plays his grown son Kit, and Mary plays Molly Roland, Kit's love interest. Brenon filmed many of the location scenes in England, including sequences on a moving open-top London bus and a punt on the River Thames with Nils and Mary.[12] Overall, it cost Brenon $75,000 to take the cast to London, as it took 13 days before they could even set up their cameras due to rain and fog.[13]

After filming finished, Mary returned to the States on the *Mauretania* on August

6, arriving back in New York on August 12. Her address on the passenger list was noted as 503 N. Beachwood Drive, Hollywood, a modest bungalow near the Wilshire Country Club.

In the summer of 1927, while still under contract to United Artists, Mary began her second abusive relationship with a married man: She started seeing MGM studio executive Eddie Mannix. Mannix had a gravelly voice, the face of a bulldog, and bearing to match. The legend about Mannix, spread largely by Mannix himself, was that he had worked in construction as a bricklayer, with supposed gangster acquaintances, at the Palisades Amusement Park, until he landed a job as a bodyguard for Nicholas Schenck. Born in 1891 in Fort Lee, New Jersey, Mannix entered the movie business in 1916, managing Joseph Schenck's New York studio. Sent to California by Nick Schenck in November 1924 as a comptroller, and to supposedly keep an eye on Louis B. Mayer, who was reporting to Schenck, Mannix soon became a valuable force in handling grievances and departmental rifts and was named MGM's Comptroller and General Manager. He worked in tandem with MGM's dapper head of publicity Howard Strickling, a former journalist who controlled how the press reported on MGM's stars and films.

Strickling made sure that scandals didn't make the papers, which often meant giving reporters alternate stories to print, and giving them made-up stories about other stars as misdirection. Meanwhile, Mannix's job was to make sure the scandals went away. So, while Strickling distracted the media, it was Mannix who arranged to get unruly stars out of the drunk tank, who paid off the victims of their car accidents and fistfights, or in Mary's case, arranged abortions. When he couldn't scare a star straight himself, Mannix would call in an old friend from New Jersey—i.e., a gangster—to deliver the message for him. He would read every telegram sent or received through the studio, including personal messages sent by the stars. This was one way he could stay on top of any trouble brewing, so that he could plan how to respond to a scandal before it happened, or even prevent it from happening. He and Strickling were known as fixers. Back then, each of the big five studios had fixers whose job it was to keep scandal and bad publicity at bay.

Mannix was married to Bernice Froomis at the time of his affair with Mary, but this did not stop him from being a notorious womanizer. He had met and married Bernice in New Jersey, and although they had been married since 1916, this had not stopped his wandering eye. Because Bernice was a strict Catholic, divorce was out of the question. But with Mary, the situation was different. Instead of his normal one-hour or one-night stand with someone anonymous, he broke his own rule and got involved with Mary on a more permanent basis because, according to friends, he was a sucker for a dancer. Mannix had a fondness for gambling and drinking, and his bad temper was exacerbated when he indulged in the latter. Mary was soon to bear the brunt of this.[14] Hollywood knew all about the true nature of Mary and Eddie's relationship, which would continue for several years.

In August 1927, Mannix persuaded Mary to leave United Artists and sign with Universal for six months. Her first film there was to be *Good Morning, Judge* with Reginald Denny, directed by William A. Seiter.

Sorrell and Son was released on December 2, 1927. Brenon always regarded it as his favorite film, but after its release his career went into decline, in part due to his criticism of the introduction of sound (he called it a fad). *Moving Picture World* said of Mary's performance, "Mary Nolan fails to impress. Her performance is entirely negligible, even her vaunted beauty failing to register."[15]

Brenon had a different story to tell about Mary, in part perhaps to help promote his picture: He told *Moving Picture World*,

> I would stake my reputation as a judge of screen talent on Mary Nolan's future. She has everything. She has poise, reserve, delicate beauty, wistfulness, personality, vitality, physical charm and a perfect screen face. I predict that in a year, Miss Nolan will be one of the screen's best leading ladies. She is already very popular in picture circles. Every other woman in the *Sorrell and Son* company likes her immensely—an unusual situation with a beautiful woman involved.[16]

Mary's last movie under contract with United Artists was to be *Topsy and Eva*, starring the Duncan sisters Rosetta and Vivian. Ultimately her bit part was cut out. *Topsy and Eva* was a silent movie based on the Duncan sisters' stage hit and was partially directed by D.W. Griffith. Nils Asther, also in the cast, married Vivian Duncan in August 1930. Nils was in fact gay, so theirs was what was known as a "lavender marriage," where one or both partners were gay. They had one child and divorced in 1932. Between 1935 and 1940, Asther sought work in England after an alleged breach of contract led to his blacklisting; he made six films there. He returned to Hollywood in 1940, and although he made another 19 films up until 1949, his career was never the same; he appeared mostly in small supporting roles. In the early 1950s, Nils tried to restart his career in television, but managed only to secure roles in a few episodes of some minor TV series. In 1958, he returned to Sweden, almost destitute. There he managed to get an engagement with a local theater and had four film roles before he finally gave up on acting in 1963 and devoted his time to painting. Nils died in 1981.

Six

A Movie Star

At the end of January 1928, Mary's six-month contract with Universal was due to expire, but they extended it for another year to January 1929. It was also announced that she had been cast in director Edward Sloman's *The Foreign Legion* with Norman Kerry.

Good Morning, Judge, released on April 29, 1928, had a simple plot: A wealthy young man is "rescued" by a wealthy young woman after he has been arrested for inciting a riot. According to *Variety*, "Mary Nolan, the former Imogene Robertson, should get applause for her work. It is not only sincere and convincing but registers her as pos-

"GOOD MORNING JUDGE" A UNIVERSAL PRODUCTION

Lobby card from *Good Morning Judge*.

sessing all of the camera and lighting appreciation of an old timer."[1] *The New York Times* said her work was "all right."[2]

Director Robert F. Hill's *Silks and Saddles,* her second Universal, was based on Gerald Beaumont's story *Thoroughbreds.* Filming started in late 1927 and it had wrapped up by early January 1928. It premiered in New York on November 27, 1928, with its final release date being January 20, 1929. Jockey Johnny Spencer (Richard Walling), an employee of the rich Mrs. Calhoun (Claire McDowell), is fired as the jockey for her racehorse Lucky. Johnny manages to be rehired when the new jockey proves unable to handle Lady. After winning a race, he regains the confidence of Mrs. Calhoun and wins the love of her daughter Lucy (Marian Nixon). Mary played Sybil, an adventuress.

Released on June 28, 1928, Mary's next Universal was *Foreign Legion,* directed by Edward Sloman and starring Nor-man Kerry. Mary played Sylvia Omney, fiancée of Capt. Arnaud (Crauford Kent). The movie contained many of the elements that had caused an uproar when the similar movie *Beau Geste* was released in 1926. The French thought both movies featured insulting slights on their methods of colonial administration, but *Foreign Legion* was "just an imitation of a proven money spinner."[3] Universal had to make cuts to the movie and change the villain from French to Russian to receive approval from the French. *Variety* said of Mary's performance, "Mary Nolan plays a selfish gold-digging blonde and does it very well. She is the type of impersonal, characterless beauty and within a narrow range of characterization should prosper on the screen. Here she was distinctly as asset."[4] *The New York Times* said, "The director has endeavored to place her in the part of conscienceless person and Mary Nolan is not suited to the role."[5]

At some stage during Mary's life, she was exposed to and

Lobby card from *The Foreign Legion*.

became addicted to drugs. Pain killers. Amphetamines. Uppers. Downers. It could have been during her time in the *Follies* when cocaine was widely used. It could then have been exacerbated during her time with Frank Tinney to ease the pain of the physical battles she had with him. By all accounts she was already a heavy drug user before she started her relationship with Eddie Mannix, which only increased her dependency on them.

Cocaine was a popular medical drug in Europe for decades before it became popular in America. In 1886 when Coca-Cola was introduced, it contained syrup derived from coca leaves. That same year, the Surgeon-General of the United States Army endorsed the medical use of cocaine. Over the next few decades, various unregulated medicinal "tonics" were sold in the U.S. containing cocaine, and hundreds of Hollywood silent movies depicted scenes of cocaine use. By 1902, there were an estimated 200,000 cocaine addicts in the U.S. Cocaine was finally outlawed in 1914 and declined in usage over the decades until it regained popularity in the 1970s as a glamorized recreational drug.

By the mid–1920s, drugs had become widespread in Hollywood. Cocaine was the drug of choice among the fashionable and wealthy. Flappers wore little spoons around their necks to scoop the so-called "joy powder." One well-known addict, silent movie star Barbara La Marr, kept her cocaine in a gold box on her grand piano. Twenty years old, she died of drug abuse in 1926. Film stars Wallace Reid and Alma Rubens also died due to drug addiction. Pushers hung around movie studios, supplying actors with drugs. Heroin was also commonly used at that time. The Harrison Narcotics Tax Act, passed in 1914 to control its sale and distribution, allowed it to be prescribed and sold for medical purposes. But by 1924, it was illegal.

So whatever drug Mary was using or when she started to use them is unknown, but what is known is that she was having trouble hiding its effects as early as 1926.

In June 1928, Mannix managed to get Mary loaned to MGM for their film *West of Zanzibar*, directed by Tod Browning and starring Lon Chaney and Lionel Barrymore. Mary was cast as Chaney's young daughter Maizie, who becomes a prostitute. Released on November 24, 1928, it was an instant hit, with Mary receiving favorable reviews for her work. One critic pointed out, "There is a tragedy in Miss Nolan's eyes that seems more heartbreaking than the histrionics of two dozen more experienced actresses."[6]

West of Zanzibar was based on the Broadway play *Kongo*, written by Chester De Vonde and Kilbourn Gordon. Lon Chaney gave his ninth movie performance for Browning as Dead-Legs Flint, a ruthless monster who engineers a horrifying revenge upon the man who stole his wife. *West of Zanzibar* was remade as *Kongo* in 1932, with Walter Huston in the Chaney role that Huston had originally played on Broadway. The art director on *West of Zanzibar* as well as Mary's next film *Desert Nights* was Cedric Gibbons, who famously designed the Oscar statue, and won it himself 11 times out of his 37 nominations. He supervised over 1500 movies for MGM.

In late 1928, Mannix got Mary another role at MGM, this time as John Gilbert's leading lady in what was initially called *Thirst*, a romantic drama, ultimately re-named *Desert Nights*.[7] Filming started in November and wrapped by mid–December.

Mary's brother Ray Robertson was in trouble in early January 1929. On January 15, he was taken before Municipal Judge Gibbs for arraignment on two forgery charges. He had in fact been sought by police since May 1928. He was ordered held under a $1,000 bail to await a preliminary hearing which was set for January 15, and his bail was furnished. Ray, then living at 436 South Catalina Street in Los Angeles, was accused by Deputy District Attorney Holland of forging two checks, one for $50 and one for $49.75, signing the name Don Saunders, trustee, to each. Saunders, a real estate agent who resided at 625 South Western Avenue, was named as a witness, along with Mrs. M.E. Firman, who lived at 803 California Street. One of the checks was made out to her and the other to the Regina Corporation.[8]

Also in January, several newspapers and movie magazines were including Mary's name on lists of movie stars who were then "considered to have made the greatest strides in popular regard and ability during 1928."[9] Carl Laemmle announced that Universal had taken up the annual option on Mary's contract, and that her next movie would be *Come Across*. Mary did not appear in that film; the role went to Lina Basquette. When *Silks and Saddles* was released in January, Mary's performance was not called out by any of the reviewers, but they did mention her on-screen beauty.

In *Desert Nights*, released on March 9, 1929, John Gilbert starred as a diamond mining executive kidnapped by jewel thieves, with Mary as one of the thieves. The kidnapping turns into a death march through the desert with California standing in for the Kalahari Desert. Director William Nigh and fabled cinematographer James Wong Howe allowed the stars to look realistically sweaty, disheveled and filthy, with Gilbert's beard growing heavier day by day. *Desert Nights* had cost a modest $209,000 but brought in a profit of $292,000 at a time when silent movies were attracting smaller and smaller crowds.[10] It was one of the last silent films made by MGM, which had been reluctant to make the switch to talkies and was still producing silent movies over a year after every other studio had made the change to sound.

Another financial success for MGM, the film served to boost Mary's career as she received good reviews for her performance. *Motion Picture News* said, "Mary Nolan is not only beautiful, she shows ability that cannot be kept under cover very long."[11] According to *Variety*, "Miss Nolan does better work than usual in this picture. A good teammate for Gilbert."[12] This was John Gilbert's last silent film; later that year he made his sound debut in *His Glorious Night*. His voice was said to have sounded high-pitched and odd in that film, but in fact that was not the case—although his performance was marred by bad dialogue and nervous delivery, and audiences reportedly laughed at him at inappropriate moments. A popular rumor at the time was that the reason his voice sounded high and reedy was that MGM studio head Louis B. Mayer had a grudge against him and told the film technicians to speed up the soundtrack. This myth spread because the movie was rarely screened after its initial release. However, the film itself shows Gilbert's voice was completely normal and it was not tampered with.

Shortly after *Desert Nights* was released, Mannix abruptly ended his affair with Mary, expecting her to go away quietly.[13] She didn't. Enraged by being dumped, Mary threatened to confront him at his home in front of his wife Bernice. Mannix then beat her so badly, she was taken unconscious to the hospital. It was not the first time he had injured a woman, as he had once broken Bernice's back during an argument. After this latest incident, Mary was constantly in and out of hospital and required 15 abdominal surgeries to repair the damage he had inflicted on her. During this time, she was prescribed morphine for the pain, which she said was the start of her ultimate addiction to drugs, but in reality she had been hooked on drugs for many years prior to this.

In March it was announced that Mary would play the role of Dolores Dupre opposite Eddie Leonard in her next film *Melody Lane*, which was to be a sound movie. *Variety* reported on April 9 that production had been halted due to Mary coming down with "influenza." Mary was admitted into a hospital on April 23, supposedly still suffering from the infection. By then, however, Universal had decided to replace her in the movie with Josephine Dunn. Mary was back in hospital again in May after an operation that followed on from her "influenza."

Universal announced plans to star Mary in four sound pictures to be released in the next season: *Mademoiselle Cayenne*, *Flaming Daughters*, *The Come-on Girl* and *Winnie O'Wynne*, the latter an adaptation of a story by Otto Henry. None of those movies ever eventuated.

On May 24, 1929, it was reported that Mary had to have a second operation because of a car accident. No further details have been uncovered, so this could have been a story put out by the studio to cover up the real reason for the operation, which was related to her drug usage. To boost her image (perhaps considering the recent Mannix saga), Mary gave an interview to *Picture-Play Magazine's* Margaret Reid at the Hollywood Athletic Club; it appeared in the May 1929 edition under the heading of "A Girl Who Had No Childhood." Like previous articles, this was a mixture of truths, half-truths and more than one embellishment on her early life.

To keep it light and airy, Mary covered many topics: beauty, men, even her stage name. In one section she said, "And my hair is really red. If it wouldn't be thought a little eccentric, I could wash off all this mascara, and show you that my eyelashes are red too. I've been a blond ever since I was 14, and it's been a terrible expense and annoyance. It hardly seems right to have spent so much time and money on a head with nothing in it."

About her name, Mary said, "I should be either a schoolteacher or a bride, with that name. But I like it. It suits one part of me—the nicer part. Mary is an awfully nice person—sane and sensible and easy to get along with. Imogene, on the other hand, is a great care. She is flighty and reckless, and I don't encourage her at all. She is a black sheep. It is for Mary that I entertain great hope."

In June, Mary attended the Shriners Convention at Universal City along with movie stars Hoot Gibson and Laura La Plante. Eight thousand people attended a rodeo that was put on by Carl Laemmle. Laemmle was a pioneer of American films and one of the founders of Universal Studios, and he produced or worked on over 400 movies. The writer Harold Robbins, a former Universal employee, based the main character in his novel *The Dream Merchants* on Laemmle. On June 15, it was reported that Mary was home from the hospital again, after having a second major operation that was a result of a car accident that she and Mabel had been in.[14] In reality, this story was covering up the real reason Mary was in hospital, which was to try to end her ongoing struggle with drug addiction.

The Universal publicity machine once again spun stories to the fan magazines when in July 1929 Mary received some good press in *Universal Weekly*:

> Miss Nolan has more than her share of "It," which coupled with a fragile and blonde beauty, spells box-office. Mary Nolan's charm is not the typical movie "vamp" sort; it is infinitely more finished and subtle. Fans will remember her remarkable performance in *The Foreign Legion* as a blending of unconscious magnetism and deliberate yet well-bred seduction. She wears clothes divinely (a factor not to be overlooked from an audience angle) and has built-up fan appeal that is growing in leaps and bounds.

Mary's next movie was *Charming Sinners,* based on the work of Somerset Maugham and directed by Robert Milton. Her second talkie, it was released in August 1929. The film was something new for the cinema, as it was not about action, but it was about words, expertly delivered by a well-seasoned cast, including Clive Brook, Montagu Love and William Powell, all of them stage veterans since the 1910s. Critics were impressed by the film and its players, but complained about the sound quality.

It was shot in the early hours of the morning, typical of early sound features, and it was also co-directed by Dorothy Arzner. Mary, the only non-stage veteran, held her own as the pampered schemer with whom Brook is smitten. Reviews said that she was always thinking and plotting and had turned her distasteful character into something peculiarly fascinating, and she also proved that silent stars didn't need to fear the influx of stage veterans to movies with the advent of sound films.

Charming Sinners was a pre–Code film, referencing the brief era in the American film industry between the introduction of sound in 1929 and the enforcement of the Motion Picture Production Code censorship guidelines, popularly known as the Hays Code, in mid–1934. The Hays Code was named after Will H. Hays, who in 1927 had voiced his concern over Mary coming back to America to start her film career.

Although the Code was adopted in 1930, oversight was poor and it was not rigorously enforced until July 1, 1934, with the establishment of the Production Code Administration. Before that date, movie content was restricted more by local laws, negotiations between the Studio Relations Committee and the major studios, and by popular opinion, more so than strict adherence to the Hays Code, which was often ignored by filmmakers. As a result, many films of this era included sexual innuendo, profanity, illegal drug use, promiscuity, prostitution, infidelity, intense violence and homosexuality.

Reviews of *Charming Sinners* were quite flattering about Mary's performance, with *The New Movie Magazine* saying, "Mary revealed great ability, unfolding none of the flaws so common in chorus and show girls."[15] *The Film Mercury* said, "It seems to me that Miss Mary Nolan's portrayal of the shallow flirtatious wife who caused all the trouble ... was so shrewdly and subtly humorous, that it was not only the best thing in the film, but also suggested that this handsome young blonde is one of the best histrionic bets of the current screen."[16]

In a September 1929 interview by Harry T. Brundidge, Mary said:

Mary Nolan, Ziegfeld Girl and Silent Movie Star

Women do not like me, they hate me and snub me, and yet I would love women friends. What woman, who had the experience that I had as a child, and all the suffering of the terrible aftermath could love a man? I know that I attract men. I have known it ever since I was a little girl. But I despise that about me which attracts them. I own neither a diamond ring nor an automobile, and I live in one hotel room.[17]

The rest of the interview is reproduced here in its entirety. Like most of Mary's interviews and stories about her, the details always keep changing to the extent either you start to think that Mary herself had started to believe her own fabrications, or she just wanted to make each interview more interesting. Either way, buried in all of them are snippets of truth.

"What kind of story is this to be?" she asked Brundadge. "Shall I begin by telling you that kissing John Gilbert is like kissing a relative, or that to me Lon Chaney and Emil Jannings have more sex appeal than any other men in Hollywood? Or shall I tell you that I'd rather kiss Lon in a picture than any screen Romeo? Would you be interested in knowing that I hate nervous men? Or what kind of a story do you want?"

"I would like a story that is 100 percent true," replied Brundidge.

"No one has ever written a word of truth about me—would you write the truth if I told it?" she asked. He replied that he would.

On December 18, 1905,[18] a baby girl was born in Louisville, Kentucky, and there was mystery in connection with the event. Those who know about the circumstances won't tell, but anyhow, the baby was called Mary Imogene Robinson.[19] I was that baby and my first recollections of life date back to a convent in Louisville. Never have I known a real home.[20] As a child I worked washing stockings and handkerchiefs in the convent and as I grew older did more washing and served as a waitress. It seemed I was atoning for the sins of others. I had little chance to attend classes and learned little save my prayers. Even now I am going to school three days a week, trying to learn the things that are taught in the grammar and high schools.[21]

When I was 13 years old I was allowed to go to the funeral of a relative and as I heard the clods of dirt fall on the casket, I made up my mind I would never return to the convent. I ran away to Worcester, Massachusetts, but I was not wanted there.[22]

Then I managed to get some money to buy a ticket to New York. When I got there, the first thing I did was to board a streetcar and ride for hours trying to decide what to do and where to go for lodging. The conductor said I would have to get off, after he began to notice that I had been on the car for a very long period. I stood on a street corner crying, and soon a little man, wearing glasses, asked me what the matter was, and I told him. The man was Arthur William Brown, an illustrator, who took me home to his wife. I lied about my age and said I was seventeen. Mrs. Brown introduced me to a Miss Foster at the Artist's Models Club in New York, and I began posing and got a room at the club, where I lived for many years. I changed my name to Imogene Wilson and became a famous model.

Frank Leyendecker, the portrait painter, painted me, and Louis Betts did me as "A Little Bit of Sunshine" and as "The Sun Flower," two prize-winning pictures. I posed for painters, illustrators and photographers, and got a dollar an hour, working nine hours a day. James Montgomery Flagg was the first to pay me $5 for a three-hour sitting. In the meantime, I was going to dancing school at night because I wanted to be a chorus girl. Someone told me I was too pretty to be a model and introduced me to Oscar Hammerstein and a few nights later I was in the chorus of *Daffodils*. That was in 1919.

Let those who have condemned me, and those who will condemn me in the future, remember that I was an innocent child who knew nothing of life. Before I knew what life was all about, I was seeing it from an angle from which few people ever see it and it dazzled me. I had never seen a big show until I walked out on the stage in *Daffodils*. Men with whom I had contracted as a model, treated me with respect because they were the biggest men in the arts, and because they knew my age. There was a man in the *Daffodils* show, however, who followed me with his eyes so steadily, that I was afraid of him.

One night it was raining and as I started for the Eighth Ave. "L" to go back to the Artists and Models Club where I still resided, this man's secretary offered to drive me home. I got in the car, a little red Buick. The man who had followed me with his eyes was in that car and he did not drive me home. A few days later I went to a relative and told what had happened to me but received no sympathy. Then I went back to the man.[23]

Five years passed, during which I played in *Lady Butterfly* and Ziegfeld's *Follies*. The little dance that I did with balloons won me the name of "Bubbles" and I became the most famous of all the *Follies* girls.[24]

I was determined to reclaim myself and make good professionally and I got a chance in German pictures. As you know, I became a star. I hated the United States and its people. I certainly had been mistreated in my native land. Just a poor kid out of a convent. I had been jerked by fate into the ranks of a chorus when still too green to know what lay ahead of me. Those who should have helped me turned thumbs down.

I made pictures throughout Europe—Germany, France, Italy, England, Switzerland, Holland and other countries,[25] I then had a breakdown and lay in a hospital in Berlin with a heart attack.[26] The doctors said I had poisoned myself with my bitter thoughts and hatreds of those persons in life who had wronged me. I was given up to die, and as I lay there, God came to me and took me in his arms and said: "Little girl, I am sorry for the way the world has treated you, but you shall yet find happiness and use the talents I have given you, and use them well." It WAS God! I got well, and life opened up a new vista to me.

Despite the fact that you will find plenty of people here in Hollywood willing to rake up the past and point a finger of scorn at me, let me tell you this—I know the true principle of life, and it is God. Nothing else matters.

October 1929 saw the stock market crash which touched off the Great Depression, the worst economic recession in U.S. history. The nation had only weathered a recession as recently as ten years before, when the end of World War I had sent the economy into a temporary dive before the Roaring Twenties of peacetime consumerism set in. However, no previous recession had been so severe, so long-lasting, or so widespread as the one that began in 1929. By December of that year, almost one-fourth of working adults in major cities were unemployed, while some schools closed due to lack of funding from local tax bases.

Most film studios were hit as hard as the public, since people with no money to spare were hesitant to pay to go to the movies, and studio heads who had thought to make a bundle in the stock market were instead saddled with huge losses. In 1929, as an example, Universal's operating budget was only $12 million, an amount intended to finance 20 films, as well as to pay all salaries. Even with limitations in place on expensive productions, the studio would post a loss of $1.2 million in 1932.

Mary's medical issues continued when she went back to the Good Samaritan Hospital in November 1929, for re-examination of a leg injury that was purported to have been received in her car accident. The accident had resulted in a fracture of her right thigh, which despite treatment was still causing her almost constant pain. She had been on set the day before at Universal, but her doctor had advised her to return to the hospital for further examination and possibly a minor operation.[27]

Mary's next film, *Shanghai Lady* with James Murray, was about an American prostitute in China. Released on November 17, 1929, it was based on the play *Drifting*, written by John Colton and Daisy H. Andrews. It followed the daughter of a Methodist deacon who determines to defy all conventions, leaves home, travels to Shanghai and becomes a prostitute. She then meets an American soldier who was unjustly dishonorably discharged from the army. Falling in love with him, she confesses to her checkered past, and the two decide to continue their lives together. The original play was on Broadway in 1922, with a young Humphrey Bogart making his Broadway debut in it. It was also made into a 1923 silent movie starring Wallace Beery and Anna May Wong. Mary's version was shot on location at Noah Beery's Paradise Trout Club, located 88 miles outside of Los Angeles. It was her first movie since her supposed automobile accident, and a nurse accompanied her on location.

Mary in a publicity still for *Shanghai Lady*.

With this remake, the plot was substantially changed, placing the emphasis on action scenes such as a train being attacked by bandits. This was the first talking movie that director John S. Robertson had done. Mary got mixed reviews for her performance as the sluttish blonde. Some said that she needed more versatility, that she sometimes overacted and could have been more subdued.[28]

Other reviews of Mary's *Shanghai Lady* performance were positive, with the January 1930 edition of *Photoplay* stating, "Mary gives a sincere characterization, and because her voice is a bit harsh, she is perfect for the part."[29] *The Exhibitors Herald* said that Mary "walks away with the picture, although she does over-play considerably."[30] Director Robertson said that Mary had been a conscientious worker while making the movie. "She tries very hard, and there is a sincerity about her portrayal of this girl that is really fine."[31]

In December, *The New Movie Magazine* named Mary one of the best new star bets in a list that included Claudette Colbert, Loretta Young and Walter Huston.[32]

SEVEN

On Her Way

On January 14, 1930, Mary was a featured singer on the Paul Whiteman radio show *Old Gold Hour*. She sang the hit song of *Shanghai Lady*, "I Wonder If It's Really Love."

On February 16, Mary's next picture, *Undertow*, directed by Harry A. Pollard, was released. It boasted a promising lead in John Mack Brown, who had made a name for himself as Joan Crawford's love interest in 1928's *Our Dancing Daughters*. Featuring John as a blind lighthouse keeper and Mary as his isolated, discontented wife, the plot depicted the development of their relationship from courtship to hardship to the reappearance of Mary's former love. The film ends with the reconciliation of John and Mary, as well as the restoration of John's sight.

The film did not impress the critics, with *New York Times* critic Mordaunt Hall griping, "[T]he dialogue is so faulty and ill written, the scenery so pasteboard-like and the photography for the most part so indifferent, that any attempt to make of this simple tale the bit of O'Neill-like realism that it might easily be would necessitate a revision of everything." Most reviews felt that Mary did not handle the drama well and was completely submerged by it.[1] But *Variety* said, "Just three good performances, and Mary Nolan tops."[2]

There are many conflicting reports about Mary's fight and subsequent exile from the set of the film *What Men Want* in March 1930. Ernst Laemmle was a German screenwriter as well as a film director and the nephew of Carl Laemmle. Some trade papers said that he and Mary fought because she was the only cast member who hadn't received a close-up shot, while others reported that Mary was forced to withdraw because of illness. *Talking Screen* said that Mary was upset over a couple of close-up shots that she did not like, and she objected to Laemmle using them. Other reports said she was upset as she was left out of some close-up shots. Whatever the real reason, Laemmle looked up a clause in her contract to the effect that they were at liberty to lay her off without pay for a period of up to 12 weeks each year, and he put this into effect immediately after the incident.[3] It was also rumored that Eddie Mannix had suggested to Universal that they fire Mary.[4]

On March 14, *The Oakland Tribune* reported that Mary said she was going to leave the movies altogether. It stated that Mary said that director Laemmle had treated her unfairly and had refused to let her to return to work after showing up to the movie set on March 13, and she found out that Pauline Starke had been assigned to replace her. She said she was going to file a suit to break her contract and would also ask for damages.

But no matter the true story, Mary's career and reputation took another hit. This would be one of the last movies Pauline Starke made, as her career stalled after the advent of sound. She had been a well-known silent-era actress with more than 60 films to her credit.

At this stage, Mary had two years remaining of her initial five-year contract with Universal. Carl Laemmle called her charges "ridiculous" and added, "She is simply suffering with an attack of temperament, as we have only shot ten scenes in five days." Mary's response was to say that she considered her contract had been broken because of their refusal to allow her back to work and said she would never set foot on the lot again, even if she had to sacrifice her career to do so. She then announced she was leaving Hollywood immediately.[5]

Mary headed to a cottage at Lake Arrowhead where she used to go regularly. Lake Arrowhead was a popular destination for movie stars because of its proximity to Los Angeles. The nearby San Bernardino Mountains were often used as a backdrop during the silent movie days because of its bright sunlight, excellent weather and unspoiled wilderness. In the 1930s and 1940s, over 60 films were made at Lake Arrowhead.

By the end of March, Mary had instructed her lawyer, W.I. Gilbert to break her contract with Universal, and demanded damages because they had broken an agreement to increase her weekly salary by $500 a week, which Carl Laemmle called "ridiculous."[6]

By now there were several negative stories appearing in various publications about Mary and her fight with Laemmle, the *Exhibitor's Herald* summarizing most of the views when it said, "Mary Nolan has upset the apple cart again. It's the talk here that she disappointed a lot of friends who sincerely wished she had outgrown her Imogene Wilson days. Her current offense is a row with a Universal official."[7]

But by April, Mary and Universal had mended their relationship as *Picture Play Magazine* reported that Mary had signed a new five-year contract with Universal for a reported salary of $1,000 a week. A May 1930 article by Louella Parsons noted that Mary had gone back to Universal after agreeing to be a "good girl."[8] To show their renewed support of her, Universal announced in late May that it had cast her in *Outside the Law*, directed by Tod Browning and starring Edward G. Robinson. She was to play gun moll Connie Madden to Robinson's gangster Cobra Collins.

Mary's next film to be released was *Young Desire*, which was initially called *Romance Wanted*. William Janney falls for a carnival performer (Mary) and tries to help her plot a better course in life. He wants marriage but she hesitates, feeling her reputation will alienate him from his parents (George Irving and Claire McDowell) and jeopardize his future. She solves the dilemma by jumping to her death.

Interviewed years later, Janney said,

> Mary Nolan took dope and practically everything else. She was supposed to have had all these venereal diseases and it scared me to death. She would rub herself all over me, and I didn't like it when she played with my toes, sticking her fingers all between them. Then we'd do these love scenes in which she would stick her tongue down my throat. After the director yelled cut, I would go to the dressing room and gargle with Listerine, because I was afraid she would give me something.[9]

Once again reviews of Mary's performance were mixed. *Motion Picture News* said that she was "miscast,"[10] but *Photoplay* said that Mary "gives an excellent performance."[11]

The June 1930 *Photoplay* had this to say about Mary's fight with Carl Laemmle:

> The Nolan girl has torn Universal limb from limb. She has passed fighting talk to everyone from Carl Laemmle down to the boy who waters the elephants. She has demanded, raged, stormed and caused more trouble than a hundred ordinary actresses. Hollywood had faith in her and nursed her along, but an open break came during the making of *What Men Want....* Mary Nolan has been hounded to here and back. She's had a tough life, and the Frank Tinney trouble, when she was Imogene Robertson, would have completely licked a weaker girl.
>
> Mary, however, stood up under the rough handling, and everyone's been giving her a hand for her success at Universal. Then, with bad advice from a gentlemen friend and her own spirit of fight, the Universal trouble has come. It is now reported that things have been patched up, and that she will go back to work. Mary Nolan has been making a big mistake with these bitter scenes. She's not enough of an actress to get away with that sort of thing. She is still showing promise, and that's all. If she's smart, she'll settle down and work hard, and get in the big money. There's danger in all this temperament business. Studios won't stand for it nowadays. A little more, and Nolan will be out, before she is really in.[12]

Mary's abstinence from controversy never lasted very long. In July 1930, newspapers were reporting that federal narcotics agents had been unable to serve Mary a warrant for her arrest on charges of possessing narcotics, as she had checked herself into a hospital. The warrants were to search her hotel and beach club rooms, as well as her Universal dressing rooms, for drugs. The warrants were issued as two nurses, Caroline Clark and Claire Anderson, gave sworn affidavits claiming that they had seen Mary using large quantities of narcotics illegally every two or three hours daily since June 20. The nurses told U.S. Commissioner David Head that Mary also suffered an intestinal ailment curable by operation. They said that Mary's arms were "full of punctures from hypodermic needles." The hospital refused to discuss the situation, apart from saying that Mary was

Mary on the cover of *Motion Picture Magazine* June 1930.

"very nervous, and an operation may be performed."[13] Los Angeles D.A. Samuel McNabb launched an investigation.

But by August, Vincent H. De Spain, a federal narcotics inspector, said he was satisfied after examining Mary that she was not a narcotics addict and he would return three search warrants for various charges to Commissioner Head, with the suggestion that the case be dropped. He said he had looked carefully at Mary's arms and "I failed to find a single needle mark. I am firmly convinced Miss Nolan is not an addict. I will not search her residence places. I will return the warrants and that will be the end of the case." He wrote across the warrants, "Film actress is not a narcotic addict." Being a drug addict does not mean you use a needle. Mary could well have still been addicted to pain relieving pills or she could have been snorting cocaine. But it is a mystery why the nurses gave sworn affidavits about the needle marks.

Mary had told De Spain that she was the victim of a plot to extort money from her. "The charge is too ridiculous for words," she said. She said the affidavits were part of a ploy to blackmail her under threat of ruining her reputation. She told him she had been called repeatedly by phone and threatened that she would be branded an addict unless she paid $600.[14] She had offered to have an intensive examination by a woman operative, but De Spain told her it was unnecessary.

It turned out that the real reason Mary was in hospital, or at least the one that was finally reported, was that she had gotten a severe case of sunburn caused when she fell asleep on a boat at Lake Arrowhead. "I, a drug addict?" she said. "I never heard of such a thing. Such a report is utterly without foundation—it is ridiculous.... I am stunned. I can scarcely believe anyone could say such things about me."[15] By September, Mary had been completely exonerated.[16]

Outside the Law was released on September 18, 1930, with Mary getting top billing. The movie's premise was about a crook and his girlfriend who double-cross a local crime boss when they attempt to pull off a high-stakes bank heist in his territory at Christmas. A remake of Browning's 1921 silent film of the same name, this was Browning's second talkie and his first in a three-picture deal with Universal. The story, by Browning and Garrett Fort, would be filmed for a third time, also at Universal, in 1946 under the title *Inside Job*.

Inside Facts of Stage and Screen said that Mary "was given an ideal opportunity to show her stuff and she handled the part admirably. It had everything in it from the hard-boiled chorus girl in a joint, to the emotional mother-love of a love-starved woman. She was beautiful and magnetic, and at times her acting was powerful."[17] Other publications were not as kind, with *Motion Picture News* saying, "Miss Nolan's work is spotty. At times she is very good, and other times she over-acts greatly."[18] Other review quotes: "Mary Nolan is the worst" and "Mary Nolan gives the poorest performance of her career, but no fault of her own."

In November 1930, Mary was again in trouble when she was charged with forgetting to pay for $640 worth of clothes when she was in Munich, Germany. The action was filed by Simon Lewald, who had been assigned the claim by Adolph Rothschild of Munich.[19] Also in late 1930, she also got caught up in the affairs of the silent actress

Lila Lee. Lila was fighting for custody of her son with James Kirkwood Sr. and had for a time moved four doors down to move in with Mary.[20] Lila's marriage ultimately ended in August 1931 on the grounds of her desertion and she lost custody of James Kirkwood, Jr., who went on to become a highly regarded playwright and screenwriter (his works include *A Chorus Line*). Lee died at age 72 in 1973.

Mary ended 1930 with some positive publicity with *Picture Play Magazine* saying,

Mary Nolan grows more and more interesting as her pictures grow less and less important. This is unfortunate, for it makes even more difficult the uphill climb before her, until she reaches the position she deserves, if ever. With such beauty as hers, talent might be taken for granted. But such is not the case. Miss Nolan's command of emotions is certain and sure, and she is more sympathetic than the situations. All this is evident in *Outside the Law*, a tolerably interesting crook opus in which the characters—even Miss Nolan—are just a bit too hard-boiled and strive rather too hard, to talk out of the corner of their mouths to be real.[21]

EIGHT

Legal Troubles Abound

In January 1931, Mary threatened to file a lawsuit against Universal, but the studio decided to buy out her remaining contract, and the lawsuit was dropped. Mannix then tried to get Mary a role in an MGM movie, but when Irving Thalberg tried to cast her in *Trader Horn*, she was so addicted to drugs she couldn't work. She lost the *Trader Horn* role to Edwina Booth, less than a week before the cast and crew left for Africa to start filming.[1] Mary may have dodged a bullet on this occasion as the film set was plagued with multiple accidents. Many crew members including the director, W.S. Van Dyke, contracted malaria, an African crewman fell into a river and was eaten by a crocodile, and then another one was killed by a charging rhino. Edwina became infected either with malaria or schistosomiasis during filming, and it took six years for her to fully recover from this and the other conditions she endured. She retired from acting soon after and then sued MGM. The case was settled out of court for $35,000 (around $650,000 in today's money).

In February, Mary was charged with petty theft after Lambert Hillyer, a film director from whom Mary had rented a house at 612 Foothill Road in Beverly Hills, accused her of stealing a $200 rug from the house. She was exonerated in the Los Angeles Justice Court by Justice of the Peace, H.E. "Josh" Billings when Mary said that she had sent the rug to the cleaners when she vacated the house and had completely forgotten about it. She then gave the name of the cleaners and Hillyer said he was satisfied. There was another report that the rug later turned up at the home of a doctor who claimed Mary had given it to him in exchange for payment for medical care.

On the same day she was exonerated of that charge, Mary faced two new charges from her former cook Joseph Bayse and her former maid, Alma McNair, for failure to pay $165. 24 for services they say were rendered during the previous two months. Bayse said he was owed $136.67 and McNair $28.57. Mary settled out of court with both plaintiffs.[2]

In March, Mary signed with producer Edgar Allen for a vaudeville tour in Philadelphia.[3] And on March 11, *Variety* reported that she was in New York to play a week at the Palace for RKO and would then go into Mae West's new show *Diamond Lil's Daughter*. The report went on to say Mary was going to get a cut of the takings, with Jerry Mayer having negotiated her contract.[4] In reality the show never happened, and Mae West stopped the play from going on. Jerry Mayer was in fact Louis B. Mayer's brother, born Gershon Meir. He started working at MGM in 1918 and left in 1930 to form a talent agency. His brother refused to hire anyone connected with Jerry's agency, so Jerry gave in, returned to MGM in 1938 and acted as general manager until he died in 1947.

Mary started the *Forward March* vaudeville tour on March 13 at Philadelphia's Mastbaum Theatre, alongside Teddy Joyce, Healy & Cross, Norman & Rio, Eddie Bruce and Anne Zeke & Judy. Wearing a pink and gold gown, Mary walked gracefully down to the footlights and, after saying hello to the audience, said she was sorry but she was not going to be able to do anything, as she had not had adequate rehearsal time.[5]

On March 26, Max Grah, the acting German consul, filed a complaint against Mary in Los Angeles to collect the judgment returned five years earlier in a Berlin court. The complaint said that in Berlin on April 1926, Mary contracted to work as an actress for Glashaus Films, but failed to fulfill her agreement; on May 19, 1926, she was ordered to pay 2712 marks damages to the company. It is assumed that Mary settled this out of court.[6]

At this time, Mary was still seeing Mannix, but she had picked up an ardent admirer in Wallace Macrery. Mary later wrote that Mannix found out about Wallace and his infatuation with Mary and, seizing on an opportunity to completely remove Mary from his life, he ordered them to marry. Because of her fear of Mannix, and what he could do to her career, they both agreed to go through with the marriage. Mary and Wallace then left Hollywood, secretly arranged by Mannix, and at 7:30 p.m. on the evening of March 29, 1931, Mary married "stockbroker" Wallace Talbot Macrery Jr. at the Christ Episcopal Church, Seventy-third and Ridge Boulevard in Brooklyn, New York. Only seven relatives attended the ceremony. Mary wore a white satin gown, matching slippers, an ermine wrap and a shoulder corsage of orchids and lily of the valley.

Wallace Macrery Jr. was born on July 25, 1908, in New York. His father operated a private detective agency in Brooklyn, the Macrery Detective Bureau on Nightshore Road. Wallace was the nephew of New York Magistrate Andrew Macrery, who was beaten to death in 1929. Wallace's father took on both civil and criminal cases and supplied guards to both banks and railroads. At the time of their wedding, Wallace lived at 166 Seventy-First Street. The Rev. Dr. J.H. Fitzgerald performed the ceremony, and the witnesses were Wallace's brother John James and his sister Lily. Mary was 29, but said she was 25 and living at the Park Central Hotel. Wallace was just 23. One week before they married, many newspapers reported that Wallace had lost $3 million on bad investments, but this was purely publicity as Wallace had never been a stockbroker, nor did he have any type of fortune.

There were numerous stories about how Mary and Wallace actually met, all supplied by Mannix and the film studios. One story said that they had supposedly been engaged for a year and a half, but they had only obtained the marriage license at the Municipal Building the day before the wedding. Some other reports said that Mary had known Wallace since she was a child.[7] There was even one report that said Mary was having dinner with Walter Winchell and Harry Richman in a New York nightclub when Wallace said they should be married instantly. They supposedly called up Mary's business manager at three a.m. and told him about it.[8]

Before the wedding ceremony, Mary and Wallace spent the afternoon chatting with journalists. Newspaper reports said that Mary was going to go back to Hollywood in six weeks to start filming *The Racketeer of New York* at Metropolitan Studio, but this movie never eventuated.[9]

The day after their wedding, April 1, the *L.A. Times* published an article saying that Mary was being sued by Universal for $11,887.[10] The complaint, filed by the law firm of Loeb, Walker & Loeb, claimed that she had borrowed $20,698 over the past four years, but had only repaid $8,811. This case was also settled out of court and, given Mary and Wallace's precarious financial situation, it is highly probable this was settled by Mannix, to avoid further bad publicity. At the same time, *Variety* reported that Mary was now rehearsing a five-person sketch by Harry Delf, that was being produced by Edgar Allen.[11] Whether Mary tried out for the part in this production, *Any Family*, is not known, but she never appeared in any of the various productions that were staged.

In a *Motion Picture* article, "Do You Look Like a Movie Star" (April 1931), Mary's beauty was once again called out: "The oval face of Mary Nolan is a study of fine delicate quality, it is the face of an impractical person, a dreamer of dreams, one hesitant to face the realities of life. Mary Nolan may have been raised in an orphanage, but there is aristocratic blood in her."

The following month, Mary was to appear in the Broadway play *Strong Stuff*, depicting youth and its propensities for alcohol and drugs. It was cancelled because of issues with the script.

Mary's next film was *Enemies of the Law*, directed by Lawrence C. Windom and starring Johnnie Walker. It finished filming in May 1931. On June 6, more legal trouble surfaced when it was announced that Mary was now suing the producer of *Enemies of the Law* Sherman S. Krellberg, for $900 in back salary and charging a breach of contract. It was subsequently announced that he was countersuing her for $25,000. "She is as gifted a woman as there is in pictures today," quoted Krellberg's attorney, A.S. Krellberg. "But, temperament—my word!"[12]

Mary was in the middle of filming *Enemies of the Law* in Fort Lee, New Jersey, when it was halted by Mary's supposed temperament. "I'm merely trying to collect my salary," Mary said. "For ten days I have worked. When I asked for my money, they told me I was through." The case was eventually dropped.

By June, Mary and Wallace were living on the 27th floor of the St. Moritz Hotel in New York. On June 18, a Los Angeles sheriff, armed with a warrant, accused Mary of passing a bad check. Sheriff Walter Shay of San Bernardino said that Mary needed to return to Santa Barbara to face the charges.[13] No further mention of this case exists so once again either the case was dropped, or it was settled out of court.

Enemies of the Law was eventually released on July 21, with mixed reviews. One review said, "Mary Nolan looks good as usual, but her acting simply isn't. The fault seems to lie in the direction and poor cast."[14] Another one said, "Mary Nolan does fine work as the stool pigeon."[15]

This picture represented one of the few talkie appearances by former Broadway matinee idol Lou Tellegen, and was in fact the last film he made. Tellegen was a Dutch-born silent film actor, director and screenwriter. He had appeared in numerous films before his face was damaged in a fire on Christmas Day in 1929, when he fell asleep smoking. He had extensive plastic surgery in 1931. In 1934, he locked himself in his bathroom and fatally stabbed himself with a pair of sewing scissors multiple times.

In this movie, Mary was cast as cop Florence Vinton, who goes undercover to get the goods on rival gangsters Eddie Swan (Tellegen) and Larry Marsh (Johnnie Walker). One of the few gangster pictures of the era to feature a female protagonist, *Enemies of the Law* was also one of the few of its kind produced in New York.

By July, on a charge of failing to pay her mounting debts and facing ongoing legal battles, Mary announced she was bankrupt. Papers reported that she had been collecting $250,000 a year in salary, but her lawyer David J. Landau said that he was going to file a voluntary petition in bankruptcy for her. Landau explained that Mary wanted to clear her financial plate so that her debts would not trouble Wallace, as her debts were incurred before she married him. Mary said she was embarrassed, after she had moved into the St. Moritz Hotel with Wallace, to have process servers stalking her wherever she went.

Mary's bankruptcy petition was filed on August 1, 1931, with debts totaling $92,796.03, and her assets only $2,998. Among the creditors were Dr. E.C. Fischbough of the Good Samaritan Hospital, and Doctors C.T. Sturgeon and Harold Van Meter of Hollywood, for a total of $6,000. Mary gave her address as the St. Moritz Hotel and listed the hotel as a creditor for $750. Other creditors were Universal Pictures Corporation for $13,067, the Glashaus Film Company on a judgment for $50,000, and General Motors Acceptance Corporation for $3,497.

On August 14, newspapers reported that Mary's representative Henry Fink had signed a contract with RKO-Pathe for Mary to star in the forthcoming film *The Big Shot*, to be directed by Ralph F. Murphy and starring Eddie Quillan and Maureen O'Sullivan, the latter borrowed from Fox for this production.

By August 1931, Mary and Wallace were back in Los Angeles, but on August 20, Mary was arrested on a charge of not paying wages to some former employees. The wages were $355 to eight employees, including a cook, a maid, a chauffeur, $46 owed to nurse Phoebe Knudsen, and $50 to violinist Louis Elst. Mary pleaded not guilty before H.E. Billings, whom she had appeared before in court back in February. She was released under a $300 bond for a trial set for September 11.[16] Her lawyer Keith Carlin said that Mary would clear everything up when she got paid. Mary ended up sending through the monies owed and prorated the cash so as to satisfy the claims of five of the eight claimants.[17] Elst said at the time, "I played in her home to soothe her nerves. I played for five hours at $10 an hour. I want my money." Billings ended up reducing Elst's claim to just $37.

Wallace had his own legal issues that year: On August 21, Hannah Menihan filed a complaint against him. A manicurist at the St. Moritz Hotel, she said that she had been summoned to Wallace's room, but told police Wallace had a different type of service in mind when she arrived. "He should have called the gymnasium, and then some Lonely-Hearts Association." she told police. She said that as soon as she entered his room, Wallace began to make violent love to her, and when she resisted, he began hitting her and eventually knocked her to the floor. Her complaint cited that Wallace beat her and attempted to criminally assault her. Detective Gray, investigating the claim, was informed that Wallace had since joined Mary in Hollywood, so he would be seeking an indictment so that Wallace could be extradited back to New York. Menihan said she delayed making the complaint because she had been ill at her home since the incident.[18] Another court case, another complaint settled out of court.

In early October 1931, Mary started shooting *X Marks the Spot*, for Tiffany Pictures, directed by Erie C. Kenton and starring Lew Cody and Wallace Ford. Released on November 29, the film got good reviews for its plot featuring libelous journalists, omniscient newspapermen and publicity-mad showgirls. Mary's role was much smaller than her previous films as she plays a showgirl murdered early in the film.

Mary decided to write her life story up to that point and sold a seven-part serialized version to the newspapers: "Mary Nolan: my tragedies and triumphs." In 1941 she would write a new version, vastly different from this 1931 version.

The next curious event that happened was that Mary and Wallace decided to open a Beverly Hills dress shop, supposedly capitalizing on Mary's fame. Although it was suggested that it was funded by Wallace, it could well have been funded by Mannix, to further isolate Mary from him. (With their constant money struggles, as Wallace and Mary would have been hard-pressed to find the funds to open a new business.) The shop opened in September or October 1931.

Soon a barrage of wage and debt claims were being filed against Mary and Wallace. It was obvious that they were trading on Mary's fame, but also managing to get deeper and deeper into debt, so when payments were not forthcoming, the claimants had no choice but to take them to court. On October 14, Mary's agent Henry Fink filed a civil suit saying that Mary had borrowed $1,821 within the last two years but had failed to repay him.[19]

On October 22, Mary entered a denial plea in the bankruptcy court against the allegation that she had attempted to conceal assets through her relatives, saying that only the name on the Mary Nolan shop belonged to her. She had been summoned before Referee N.I. Mulville to explain why she had failed to pay two judgments totaling $1,385. Accompanied by Wallace, Mary said the two judgments obtained against her in January 1931 had been included in her petition for bankruptcy, which was pending in the New York courts. The hearing was therefore postponed until November 20, to allow Mary to go back to New York to testify in that bankruptcy hearing, which was slated for November 3. One of the claims was the one that was lodged in November 1930 for $685 for clothing she purchased in Germany four years ago and the other was for $100 owed to a drug company.[20]

Dr. Charles F. Nelson filed a suit against Mary, claiming she failed to pay him $142 for services rendered.[21] Nelson was a well-known doctor in Hollywood, at one time the head of the Beverly Hills and Hollywood Hospitals. He treated many of the actors and singers of the day, including Mary Astor, Tom Mix and Lilyan Tashman.

On November 12, Wallace surrendered in the Los Angeles Municipal Court when he learned that a warrant had been issued charging him and Mary with failure to pay wages. He pleaded not guilty and said that Mary would surrender on November 16. Mrs. Sonia Sovere, a clothes designer, claimed that Mary and Wallace owed her $50 for work that she had done in Mary's clothes shop.[22] Mary then appeared in the Los Angeles Municipal Court on November 14 and pleaded not guilty to Sovere's charge, and she was told that she would face a jury trial on December 8.

As Mary was leaving the court, she was again arrested on a fugitive warrant from Beverly Hills, charging her with failure to appear in court relating to yet another wage claim. She was taken to the Beverly Hills court and she paid $100 in settlement against two of the claims; a third claim, which she disputed, was set for trial on November 23.[23] This payment was for six claims against Mary for failure to pay $209 in wages, the largest claim being for $61 to a tailor. Another claim was filed by a seamstress and a third claim, for $18, from a model, Diana Humphrey.[24]

On November 24, Lindley Carpet Associates Ltd. filed a suit against Mary and Wallace for $572, alleging they bought a rug on the installment plan but had failed to pay for it.[25]

On December 7, Mary and Wallace again failed to appear in court and a second bench warrant was issued for Mary's arrest, on a charge of failing to appear in answer to a summons in a $59 wage claim filed by Phoebe Knudsen. Mary also left an agent for the California State Labor Commission waiting in court; he was there to see what the outcome was going to be with the additional 14 wage claims against Mary, these totaling $900. These charges also stemmed from Mary's dress shop.[26]

On December 9, it was reported that Mary had been given a long-term contract by M.H. Hoffman, and that her next movie role was to be in *Vanity Fair*.[27] Hoffman was the founder of Liberty Pictures, and a former general manager at Universal. He was later the president of Tiffany Pictures and Allied Pictures. Mary did not appear in the movie, which was made with Conway Tearle and Myrna Loy. On December 11, 13 new warrants against Mary were issued after more people came forward asking for Mary to be arrested for not paying $500 in wages. This was settled out of court.

When her shop closed, Mary told the press the closure was just temporary. She said that she had designed the clothes herself and had sold all the original models. "They went so fast," she said, "that I had to shut up the shop—so as to design some more."[28]

The Big Shot was released on December 31, 1931. Reviews for the movie and cast were good, but there was no special praise for Mary's performance.

NINE

More Legal Battles

On January 6, 1932, Mary appeared in court on a charge of not paying wages to some former employees of her Mary Nolan Gown Shop. She was released on her own recognizance and the case was to be continued on February 4. Mary said she was now working as an actress and earning money, so she would soon be able to pay the back wages.

On January 8, Municipal Judge Robert W. Kennedy entered a judgment of $47.50 against Mary and Wallace in favor of a sign company, representing the cost of erecting a sign on their dress shop. Mary was still facing a count of 14 complaints of evading state law, which was to be heard again in March.[1] But on February 4, Mary did not show up in court and produced a doctor's certificate saying she was ill, postponing the case until March 2. The case was settled out of court when Mary found the funds to pay the outstanding wages.

Mary's next movie was *The Docks of San Francisco,* directed by George B. Seitz and starring Jason Robards. It was released on February 1, 1932, and got mixed reviews. All one review had to say about Mary's performance was that she was "blonde and rather attractive."[2] But *Variety* said, "Mary Nolan, a Universal star until a couple of years ago, doesn't have the most desirable support, but as the scarlet gal, picking up a living as a holdup moll for a small-time mobster, plus other things, turns in a nice account of herself."[3]

Mary next appeared with Lew Cody, William Collier Jr. and Clara Kimball Young in *File 113,* directed by Chester M. Franklin, released on February 19, 1932. *Film Daily* called it an "[e]ngrossing detective story aided by an able cast and containing plenty of goodness."[4] Mary was seen only twice, very briefly. By the end of February, newspapers were saying that Mary was in debt to the tune of $42,000 and had no assets.

Mary and Wallace were back in the papers on March 13 when she faced a possible jail sentence for violating the State of California labor laws. Sentences were to be passed on March 14 by Municipal Judge Clement Nye. The maximum penalty on each of the eight counts was six months in jail and a $500 fine. Chief witness for the eight complainants, all former employees in Mary and Wallace's Nolan Gown Shop, was Salvatore de Santaella, a musician. He was called to show that Mary really did have money, although she had failed to pay her shop employees.

He testified ruefully that a smile from Mary cost him $1,200, the amount of his wage claim. Santaella said he was riding along Hollywood Boulevard in his limousine, when he noticed a beautiful blonde in a taxi. He said she smiled and he smiled back. He then asked her to ride with him and he told the court that Mary said yes, so long as he would pay for her taxi fare, and she did ride with him after he paid her $6 taxi fare. They then went back to his apartment and during the conversation, he wrote Mary a check for $45, and later wrote more and more checks. He told the court, "Why did I do it? I don't know. I was a big sucker."

Mary was in court for this testimony, wearing a stunning green ensemble, and denied his charges. "I do recall meeting De Santaella and going to his apartment, but that was purely a professional call. I recall he wanted to be my husband's partner—I believe he was in business with my husband." she said. Mary added that the gown shop, even though it used her name, was operated solely by Wallace, and he testified that this was true.[5] One can only surmise why De Santaella paid Mary $45 after she went back to his apartment, but given the state of her financial affairs, she was obviously desperate for money.

This saga continued on March 12 when Mary and Wallace paid $1,300 in the wage claims against them and they were each sentenced to 30 days in jail. Judge Nye initially sentenced Mary to 750 days and Wallace to 840 days but suspended all but 30 days for each of them and set bail at $200 each. In suspending a major portion of the sentences, Judge Nye said he took into consideration payment of the $1,300 against the claims, but he said that to free them after they had "flagrantly violated the law" would not be in the interests of justice. Mary and Wallace filed a notice of appeal after being denied a new trial, saying six sections of the state laws were unconstitutional.

On March 15, Mary gave an interview to the *Los Angeles Times* from the office of her attorney Arthur S. Guerin, asking Hollywood for "just a fighting chance to make good." She continued:

> I'm going to reach the goal I set for myself at childhood—if they will just give me a chance. Nothing can stop me—this I know, for I feel that I am destined to prove to the world I am an artist. But there have been so many barriers, so much to thwart me since I came to Hollywood. Why, they didn't even meet my train when I arrived here—and it's been like that since. People who on the set have been nice to me, seem to shun me in public.
> They don't know the real Mary Nolan out there. The homes of film folk have not been open to me since I arrived. Why this must be, I don't know. They haven't given me a chance to show them the real Mary Nolan. And who is there among them all who can point a finger at me? Not one of them can. Their own private lives are not being aired, while unpleasant incidents in my own have been given the spotlight of publicity. What if this spotlight were turned on everyone else?
> I humbly ask Hollywood for just a chance to realize my ambition, and for an opportunity to show them the real Mary Nolan. Star after star has passed me out there, rising on the wings of personal influence. But I don't want that type of success. I want to make it for myself if they'll let me. I'm not sorry because I've been dragged through the muck and mire of this court incident and the other unhappy circumstances that were widely publicized. It will just give me that much more insight into life in the raw and will make me a better actress, I believe. One must live to really know and feel. Even though I face a jail term simply because I loaned my name to a gown shop, I bear no one ill-will for it all, and I have faith in it, justice. I feel that I shall never go to jail, that the courts are just and will give me justice. But Hollywood must do the same. I must have my chance.[6]

Mary went on to say that she made her appeal after being told that her contract for eight pictures with Worthy Pictures Inc., on which she had been slated to start work on the day before, had been canceled due to her conviction on the wage law charges. Worthy Pictures was a company based in Medford, Massachusetts.

Her attorney Guerin said the producers explained to Mary that the contract was canceled because its morality clause had been violated when Mary was convicted. But he said that the contract had no such clause and that if the Academy of Motion Picture Arts and Sciences failed to influence the producers and re-consider the cancellation, that he would be forced to file suit against the studio to force them to abide by the terms in the contract or make proper reimbursement. Mary asked:

> Why must people be so vindictive? I could probably have several persons prosecuted on bad-check charges if I wanted to. I hold checks for my work that are worthless, but I'm going to be patient and give the people who issued them a chance to make good, even though I need money now. But it seems as though nothing will satisfy the world but my incarceration in a jail because of my conviction. And all I had to do with the non-payment of wages charges, was loan my name to my husband's gown shop, letting him call it the Mary Nolan Shop.

She tearfully concluded the interview by saying, "I'll make good in spite of it all—unless the appeal should fail, and I should have to go to jail, in that event, there just wouldn't be any more Mary Nolan, real or otherwise, for I think jail terms are dishonorable and I'm not doing anything dishonorable."

Mary and Wallace's wage case was heard in the Los Angeles Appellate Court on April 1. Pleading her case, Guerin said, "If Miss Nolan is required to pay debts contracted by her husband, every married woman in California could be criminally prosecuted if her husband engaged in a community business enterprise and failed to pay his debts."[7]

Mary's movie career was continuing, but her parts were getting smaller. In February she shot her next movie, *Midnight Patrol,* directed by Christy Cabanne, and starring Regis Toomey, Betty Bronson and Edwina Booth, the actress who took over Mary's *Trader Horn* role. Released on April 10, 1932, the movie got very good reviews with *Variety* saying, "If independent producers could consistently release features like *Midnight Patrol,* exhibitors would have no concern.... It is an action picture, exceptionally well cast with names that are known, and too strong a bet to be sacrificed on a double-feature program."[8] The *Motion Picture Herald* said that Mary "gives an excellent portrayal as the tool of the scheming lawyer."[9]

On April 12, another warrant for the arrest of Mary and Wallace was issued, charging failure to respond to an outstanding summons concerning their assets. This warrant was issued for a case where there had been two judgments against Mary and Wallace, one for $783 for a dress, the other for furniture valued at $1,700. Included in the furniture was a chaise lounge in silk with a special velvet tower valued at $300, a silk canopy for the bedroom valued at $100 and a statue of French bronze and enamel valued at $275.

In court on April 15, Mary and Wallace said their assets were only 15 cents and they said they had basically been living on the charity of their friends. With the court case still ongoing, it was reported that Mary was now returning to the stage: She had signed with Joe Tenner to appear in several productions at the Duffy Theater in Portland, Oregon. It was thought that her first appearance would be in a production of *Rain*. But this never materialized.

Joe Tenner was another shady character that circled Mary's world. He was having legal troubles of his own in 1932 when he was arrested in Portland and accused of transporting a Seattle woman across a state line for immoral purposes. He was sentenced to four years at the McNeil Island Federal Penitentiary but was released early on parole. In February 1935, he was arrested on a charge of parole violation and went back to McNeil to complete his sentence. In 1941 he was in San Francisco managing the popular Stairway to the Stars nightclub when he was again jailed by order of the State of Washington parole authorities. Tenner also served time in San Quentin on a sodomy charge and in 1949 was implicated in the ambush shooting of gangster Mickey Cohen.

On April 16, Mary's next film was released, the short *Beautiful and Dumb*. It was directed by Emmett J. Flynn and starred Lew Cody and Dot Farley. Cody, who had once been married to silent star Mabel Normand, died not long after, at age 50, of heart disease. Dot Farley was in 280 films between 1910 and 1950. She was most notably associated with Mack Sennett in his silent films.

In May, Mary was in Omaha, Nebraska, doing a week of personal appearances at the Moon Theater, but she appeared for only for two days due to illness. This was just another example of her deteriorating health. Also, her drug dependency was becoming more evident in her constant "illnesses."[10]

On May 4, the Appellate Department of the Supreme Court upheld their conviction as well as the 30-day jail sentence imposed from a prior conviction, so on May 5, Mary and Wallace said they would make an application for probation, or an appeal against that sentence to the California Supreme Court.

A minor legal issue surfaced on May 7, when J.B. McDonnell, owner of a local motor car company, complained that Mary owed him $43.50 after evading a taxi fare. On May 20, the $200 bonds that had been posted for Mary and Wallace on March 12, were forfeited, and they now faced arrest on a bench warrant. Judge Nye forfeited the bonds after a Deputy City Prosecutor pointed out that Mary and Wallace's appeal had been denied, and the time for them to appear and surrender had expired. August Nardoni, who posted the bonds, told the court he would leave that day by plane to return Mary from New York, where he said he had located her.

By July 1932, Mary realized that she needed to divorce Wallace, especially as they had been formally separated for some months. She told newspapermen on July 17,

Yes, I am going to get a divorce from Wallace. He is the nicest man I know, and I am terribly fond of him, but we are a drawback to each other. We have been separated for several months, and as soon as I can straighten my business affairs I will go to Reno. It's just another lot of trouble. We were married in New York a week after he had lost his whole fortune—$3,500,000—in one afternoon on the Stock Exchange. Like children, we thought money didn't matter and married anyway. We went to Hollywood, but Hollywood did not want me married. Everything I do is wrong, even when it is the right thing it seems. Everything went wrong for me out there. Wallace had just $9,000 left and he invested that in a dress shop using my name. All the world knows that was a failure, and he lost his last stake. In addition, I was dragged into court for failure to pay his employees, even though I had never been in the store but once.

In August, Mary was back on stage appearing at Brooklyn's Fox Theatre in a single sketch in a vaudeville act called *Singapore Sal. Variety* reviewed her performance:

> Mary gives a colorful imitation of Sadie Thompson. Apparently, she finds it difficult to hold up in a sustained effort instead of the 20–60-second scenes of a talking picture, and she never suggests the underlying tragedy in what is supposed to be a dramatic sketch of racial pull. Most of the time she has the stage to herself for long speeches delivered in a colorless voice. Sometimes she sits down and sometimes she stands up. Three or four times she walks around, but the actress is singularly static.[11]

In September, Mary appeared in a show with Opie Cates and Al Shayne at the Club Mayfair on Long Island. Cates, then a prominent band leader, went on to direct the music for a radio comedy known as *Granby's Green Acres*, the basis 15 years later for the TV series *Green Acres*. He was also host of the long-running radio show *Lum and Abner*. Andy Griffith's TV son was named Opie as an homage to Cates, as both its star Andy Griffith and its producer-director Sheldon Leonard were big fans. *Variety* announced on September 20 that Mary, Jack Squires and Fred Hildebrand had just finished touring but reports of Jack and Fred's tours in the local newspapers made no mention of Mary appearing.

On October 4, Mary was appearing at the Albany Place with the husband-and-wife team of Edith Evans & Ray Mayer as well as Russ & Edwards in the second half of a vaudeville act.[12]

By late October, Mary had scored the title role in the play *Lilly Turner*, staged by the Bainbridge Dramatic Stock Company at the Schubert Theatre in Minneapolis. The reviews were poor, and it ultimately grossed less than $3,000.[13] *The Minneapolis Star Tribune* said that the role of Lilly

> contrives to put [Mary's] physical qualities on display, but which allows of no considerable exercise of the acting powers. It must be said that she manages quite well, with what she has been given. There is a frankness and an honesty in her performance, yet there is present a superficiality. At times on Sunday it seemed that Miss Nolan was seeking the camera and not finding it, developed a stage consciousness. Her portrayal of the part however, has appeal.[14]

Afterwards, Mary returned to New York. On December 19, 1932, she was arrested for being a fugitive from justice after endorsing a check for $304.48 drawn on the Citizen's Trust & Savings Bank of New York, Seventy-Third Street Branch. Since no such bank existed, she was taken into custody at Loew's Orpheum Eighty-Sixth Street Theatre where she was appearing in a vaudeville sketch.

Arresting officers from Minneapolis accused Mary of "larceny by aid of a bank check" as she had issued a worthless check to the Radisson Hotel there. After spending several hours behind bars, she was released once a $1,500 bail bond was issued. She described herself at the time as being 26 years old (she was actually 30), married and living at the Hotel Salisbury at 123 West 57th Street.

Mary said she had gone to Minneapolis to appear in *Lilly Turner*, but it had flopped. She had been told the theater was large enough to bring in $13,000 a week, of which she was promised ten percent. She said,

This action of the Minneapolis authorities is an outrage. I went to that city in October to fill a theatrical engagement but broke the contract because the facts about the capacity of the house where
I was appearing had been misrepresented. I told the hotel manager, Carl Olson, I was without
funds in any New York banks, and offered to give them a note. They insisted I sign a check, my
understanding being I'd make it good after coming to New York. I was astounded when the detective walked into the theater with a warrant this afternoon.

A court hearing was set for the end of December, but a telegram was produced in a
Harlem court that day, saying Mary was no longer wanted on that charge, and she was
free.

Mary then appeared in the short film *Broadway Gossip No. 3*, released on December
27. Directed by Raymond Kane on a budget of $8,000, it was the third in the *Broadway
Gossip* series starring Leo Donnelly in the role of a Broadway columnist. In this short,
he interviews former star Lillian Walker, now struggling to make a living on a small
farm, and Mary, who makes a confession of sort. (Walker was a prolific actress during
the silent era, making more than 170 movies between 1909 and 1934. She did one last
film in 1934, before retiring from acting.) The third and last interviewee was Madame
Sylvia, a former movie studio beautician.

By January 1933, Mary was in Poughkeepsie, New York, making live appearances
at the State Theatre, typically as part of the showing of a movie. The local newspaper
mentioned that she would forever remember playing in that city as when she had been
performing there in the past, she had been forced to use a barber shop as a dressing
room (the theater didn't have one); she had to walk there to get changed into her costume.[15]

Back in New York, Mary was a guest at a reception given for Jack Osterman at the
Club Richman, celebrating his Broadway comeback. Also present were Jack Benny,
Fanny Brice and her husband Billy Rose.[16] Osterman was a vaudeville headliner and
Broadway star, whose career peaked around the mid–1920s. He was a comedian and
singer in the Al Jolson-Eddie Cantor mode and was also a songwriter. His comeback
was short-lived, however, as his last Broadway show in 1935 only lasted a couple of
weeks. His career had declined so badly that by 1937 he took out a full-page ad to
remind everyone how significant his career had been. He died of pneumonia in 1939
at age 37.

In March 1933, *The Akron Beacon* reported that Mary had taken an overdose of
drugs at the Lido Apartments on 65th and Columbus, but this was never corroborated.
Mary was now traveling around the northeast appearing in small vaudeville shows. In
April and May, she was in Middletown, New York, appearing in a vaudeville show at
the State Theatre.[17] In mid–May, she was on the stage in Massachusetts at the Bowdoin
Theater.

In July, Mary was back in Massachusetts where she appeared for two days in a
vaudeville show with four other acts, including one-time movie star Agnes Ayres. The
program consisted of vaudeville acts, two feature movies and a prize contest, with the
admission price being ten cents. Like Mary, Ayres was forced to take whatever piecemeal
work she could get, but in her case, she lost her fortune (including real estate holdings)

in the crash of 1929. Mary and Agnes were also with the same company in Hartford, Connecticut, appearing for two days at the Cameo Theatre.[18]

Both former stars were reported to only be getting $75 for the two days' work, which compared starkly to the $2,500 they used to earn a week in their heyday. Agnes managed to return to acting in 1936, but she was unable to secure any starring roles, so she retired from acting for good in 1937. Becoming despondent, she was eventually committed to an asylum, and lost custody of her daughter in 1939. She died at age 42 from a cerebral hemorrhage on Christmas Day 1940, after being ill for several weeks.

In August, Mary was back in court, this time in a case involving a cosmetics line labeled "Mary Nolan"; she claimed they were using her name without her permission. When Jerry Nolan set up Mary Nolan Cosmetics Inc. several years previously, he had started to advertise his products with a Mary Nolan signature, but he said he never intended to capitalize on Mary's fame as an actress, as he named it after his wife Mary. Mary applied for an injunction in the New York Supreme Court which would prevent the further use of her name in conjunction with the cosmetics business. She claimed that not only had they used her name, but they had also used her photographs, and a signature very similar to her own in its advertisements. Jerry Nolan said he could not stop stores using photographs of Mary when they chose to advertise his products, and he could not help it if his wife's signature was very similar to Mary's. After some deliberation, Justice Hofstadter agreed with Mary, and the advertisements were halted.[19]

Film Daily reported in August that Mary was back in New York after a Long Island "vacation" and was looking for a vaudeville act to appear in. It was also reported that Arthur G. Solomon, a well-known New York lawyer, was handling her affairs.[20] Long Island probably referred to Mary being at Brunswick House, a private institution for those with mental illnesses and drug dependencies, and where she would end up again years later, as by then her addiction had become dangerous.

On September 11, Mary told Massachusetts newspapers that she had been divorced from Wallace for around eight months and also told them that she and Wallace had divorced in Connecticut. "I am free of any romance at present, free of any thought of marriage. My husband divorced me eight months ago. I have only one objective now—to win back what I have lost professionally." At the time, it was reported that she was appearing on stage at the Lynn Theatre in Massachusetts, but no record of her performing there at the time has been found. It well may have been in a small uncredited part.

In November 1933, newspapers reported that Mary was in critical condition at the New York Medical Arts Hospital, after having her fourteenth operation for an abdominal ailment. Dr. Harry Gilbert, who performed the operation, said it would be at least four days before she was out of danger. Mary had been taken to the hospital after collapsing in her St. Moritz Hotel room.[21] Given Mary's financial state at this time, one has to question how she was paying for a room, given she was only bringing in paltry sums of money at the places where she could get work, plus she had to support her drug habit. In December, *Variety* reported that Mary was in talks with Universal about making a movie based on her career, including her various legal issues and drug problems. Again, this was probably a story that Mary made up to keep her name in the entertainment headlines.[22]

But by the beginning of 1934, Mary has started to drop out of sight both in a legal sense and in an entertainment sense. Advertisements appeared in *The Film Daily* in February, saying that Mary was now under the personal supervision of Harry R. Chards and Max Golforb, who could be reached care of WMCA Bldg., Room 707, 1697 Broadway.[23] Chards and Golfarb were low-ranking entertainment agents placing acts in bars and nightclubs across New York. Mary seemed to have booked no new engagements until August, or at least none that were worthy of any advertising, when *The Film Daily* reported that she was now appearing at the Hotel Beau Rivage in Brooklyn. No other mention of this engagement has been found.[24]

In October 1934, Mary opened at the Green Gables Club in Hazelton, Pennsylvania. However, on November 5, it was reported that the police were now hunting for her, as theatrical booking agent Frank Keffman said he was missing $2,000. Keffman, of Newark, New Jersey, said he had gone for a drive with Mary early on November 4, after Mary had finished her act at the Green Gables Club; they then returned to the Green Gables, had one drink together. According to Keffman, he didn't remember anything until he woke up the next day at 7:30 a.m. Police reported that Mary had called for a taxi at five a.m. to take her down to New York. Driver Harold Smith reported that Mary asked to be dropped off on the New York side of the Holland Tunnel, where she got into another taxi. The police reported that she had not collected her salary, and her hotel bill had also not been paid. She had also left her trunk in her room. Police said Mary had fled in an evening gown.[25]

Mary went back to Hazelton on November 5, where she was arrested and booked as Mary Nolan, 23 years old, of 3 West 92nd Street.[26] She was kept overnight before police confirmed that the charges filed by Keffman were dropped. This happened when attorney Henry Zeltner, acting for Mary, notified Hazelton Sgt. Frank Dolan that it was all a misunderstanding and notified them to cancel the charge.

Mary was quoted as saying that Keffman wanted to act as her personal agent, and that he had brought along a document for her to sign, but that she said she needed time to think about it and had gone back to New York to decide if she wanted to take him up on his offer. She said she had received $50 from the manager of the club, Alfred Gottesman, for the expenses of the trip. If this was a publicity stunt, it didn't work: Her arrest was overshadowed by a major event that happened only five miles away. On November 5 at Kelayres, Pennsylvania, five people were killed at a Democratic rally and convention. This made front-page news at the time, across the country.

Mary's last advertised appearances that year were in November, when she appeared at Tiny's Chateau on the Philadelphia Turnpike, near Reading. She was featured with the regular floor show and appeared for one week only. In December, she started performing at the Roosevelt Gardens on Roosevelt Avenue in Jackson Heights, Queens.

TEN

The Final Curtain

The Roosevelt Gardens was one of the many cabaret venues that sprang up after Prohibition was repealed in December 1933. There were red-checked gingham table-cloths and patrons could get a meal for 75 cents. The girls who appeared in the floor show had to use the office for a dressing room; it was located at the front of the place, so after each act, the girls had to run past the patrons, often dressed in scanty outfits. The place was noisy as it sat beneath an elevated IRT Flushing Line.

Mary arranged to give an interview to journalist Joseph Mitchell there on the night of January 5, 1935. She came on around two a.m. and started her act, which was a combination of doing scenes from her various movies as well as singing. That night she sang "Out in the Cold Again." She gave an interview to Mitchell after her show had finished:

> I am trying to make a comeback. I don't like nightclubs, but I have to live. I'm not a singer, but I have to make a living. You know what I have been doing? I've been studying English. I am going back to Hollywood and I want to be physically and mentally in perfect health when I go. And, also, I want my English to be perfect. I am only 28. I'm not old. I can make a comeback.[1]
>
> All I want in this world is to act in moving pictures. And I want people to let me alone and not get me in trouble. Also, I have been studying science. I mean Christian Science. No matter what goes wrong, when I read the words of Mary Baker Eddy, I am peaceful. It is the most beautiful thing in my life. I used to be a Catholic, but I changed. Catholics make very good Scientists. Also, I am going to write a book and call it *Great People, as I Have Known Them*. God, I want to go back to Hollywood. I don't want to work in these nightclubs.

Mary went on to tell Mitchell that after this engagement had finished, she was being considered for the lead in the play *The Trial of Helen Dean* by Mark Linder.[2] She finished by saying, "If it is a success, I am going to rest for a while and get in shape. Then I am going back to Hollywood and try to make a comeback. I wish I never had to see a night-club again. My God."[3]

Up until this point, Mary's legal skirmishes, apart from her saga with Frank Tinney, had been relatively minor, and were predominantly around her failure to pay her debts. This changed when on July 9, 1935, Mary made headlines when she filed a lawsuit against Eddie Mannix for $500,000 in damages (the equivalent of five million dollars today). She charged him with assaulting her physically; with using his influence to prevent her from obtaining work; and also for "personal and professional damages." The suit was disclosed when Supreme Court Justice Peter Schmuck signed a warrant of attachment against any property Mannix may have in New York. The whole affair became very public, with many newspapers and magazines recounting in detail the numerous occasions that Mary said Mannix had beaten her. Why Mary chose this particular time to file this suit could be linked to the fact that by this stage she was very nearly destitute, and perhaps saw this as a way of getting some money, as well as once again appear in the headlines.

In her four separate causes of action, she said she had met Mannix in 1927 at the Cocoanut Grove in Hollywood and from the fall of 1927 until 1930 they had lived together as man and wife in his suite at the Ambassador Hotel in Los Angeles. She claimed they later moved to a private home, because Mannix thought it was too conspicuous to continue living together at the hotel.[4]

In the first claim, Mary said that one night in 1931, Mannix woke her up in bed at the Ambassador and "violently and criminally attacked her." She said that attack caused her to be rushed to the Good Samaritan Hospital for an emergency operation. One attack happened in the hospital itself, when Mannix came visit her, and according to her claim, "again brutally and criminally attacked the plaintiff, inflicting great pain, and causing the bandages to be torn and ripped from the plaintiff's wound." She asserted that Mannix struck her in the face and assaulted her and ripped and tore the bandages from the operation from which she was recuperating. Because of these attacks, Mary said she was forced to undergo as many as 20 more surgeries.

In the second cause of action, Mary said another attack occurred while she was recuperating at Frank Orsatti's Lido Club in Santa Monica Beach on February 19, 1931, where Mannix threatening to kill her if she did not leave the West Coast. In the third action, which happened in November 1933 in New York City, Mary said Mannix came to her East 44th Street apartment and struck her. In the last claim, Mary alleged that in the spring of 1931, while appearing at Philadelphia's Mastbaum Theater and receiving $2,750 for a week's engagement, her second week was canceled because of Mannix's influence. For that claim alone, she was asking for $250,000 in lost wages.[5]

Mary's claims stated that prior to the first incident, the pair had "lived happily together as man and wife, both parties showering valuable and expensive gifts upon each other, and in every way, in mutual love."[6]

According to Mannix's biographer E.J. Fleming, Mannix was incensed that Mary exposed their affair in front of his wife. The affair included three abortions according to Mannix's friends, abortions that he had supposedly paid for. At the time of Mary's claims, she had been appearing on movie sets with bruises and black eyes, as he allegedly beat her regularly. It was also said that he had beaten his wife so badly that he had broken her back.

Mannix denied Mary's claims, and Howard Strickling (MGM's head of publicity) and his PR staff leaked unflattering stories about Mary's sexual past. According to Fleming, it was Mannix, not Carl Laemmle, who had gotten Mary fired from Universal in 1930. Then, knowing that Mary had become hooked on the morphine that had been prescribed for the constant pain that she had been suffering from his multiple bearings, Mannix had a detective intimate that she would be arrested for drug possession. With an MGM car waiting at the curb outside her house, the detective told Mary she could stay and fight Mannix and face drug charges or leave Los Angeles and the matter would be dropped. Days after, Mary left Los Angeles for New York City, which is when she married Wallace.

In July, Mary was appearing at the 20th Century Tavern in Philadelphia, and in August at the Silver Slipper in Atlantic City.[7] After that engagement, she went to a week's engagement at Joe's Casino at the Black Cat in Atlantic City, where she was to appear in two shows each night.[8]

While she was still in Atlantic City, Magistrate E.J. Dugan refused to issue a warrant at the request of Philadelphia authorities, who charged that Mary had bought two dresses from a shop there, for which she had refused to pay. When Mary was notified of the charge, she asked the police to search her room, which they did, but they failed to find either one of the dresses. Mary's second encounter was when she was charged with failure to pay a $42 flower bill. When Magistrate Archie Toffler issued a warrant for her arrest, she paid the bill and the case was dropped.[9]

On October 9, Mannix appeared in the New York Supreme Court, telling them that he had never been served with a summons in Mary's $500,000 suit. However, Mary's legal counsel had filed an affidavit saying that the process servers handed Mannix the summons on the night of the Joe Louis-Max Baer fight, September 4, 1935.[10] The case continued, and on December 12, New York Supreme Court Justice Aaron J. Levy denied a subsequent motion by Mannix to dismiss the suit claiming the summons was never served. Mary's attorney countered their claim with additional information saying that after months of effort, Mannix was finally served at the Sherry-Netherlands Hotel in New York on the night of the fight. This ruling meant that Mannix now had no way to avoid Mary's suit, and he needed to do so within 20 days or a judgment would be granted by default.[11]

Mary went to London in early December to appear in a Piccadilly Theater show starting on December 21. According to her, she had been bankrolled by a "kindly gentleman." But she withdrew from the production after only one afternoon performance, claiming she had lost her voice, and was paid $625 for the effort.[12] She was replaced by Gillie Potter. Mary blamed her loss of voice on the London fog and cold: "I have not really been well since I have been here. When I began to sing, the notes would not come," she was quoted as saying.[13]

In January 1936, Mannix's lawyer, Nathan Burkan, obtained a court order to compel Mary's lawyers, Herbert Tenzer and Henry Zeltner, to show cause why she should not accept an "unverified" answer to her $500,000 suit against Mannix. The motion was set to be argued in court on January 29 before New York Supreme Court Justice Charles B. McLaughlin. The "unverified" answer was a statement by Mannix that he had previously paid Mary $3,000 to settle any claim against any and all further litigation. Mary claimed the signature on the $3,000 receipt was gotten under duress from representatives of Mannix while she was recuperating at the Medical Arts Hospital in New York. Mary said she thought the money was just to cover her medical expenses.[14]

Burkan, a well-known celebrity lawyer, had argued cases involving Charlie Chaplin, Lillian Gish and Colleen Moore. In his most famous case, he represented Gloria Morgan

Vanderbilt in her unsuccessful battle for custody of her young daughter. He was also Jean Harlow's business manager.

By the end of January, Mary was appearing in a special matinee session as Karen Andre in Ayn Rand's play *Night of January 16* at the Ambassador in Brooklyn, with the proceeds going to the Actors Fund.[15]

The case against Mannix was continuing and on March 30, Mannix's co-counsel James A. Murray filed an application for an order to force Mary to reply to his defense that she had released Mannix "from all claims of every nature" on payment of $3,000 to her. Murray said his client would produce a copy of the check to support his claim, and that this clearly destroyed Mary's cause of action in her suit.[16]

Mary was continuing to make appearances in small clubs and revues in New York. In March, Mary, now 34, was a cast member in a revue at another obscure cabaret club on Queens Terrace in Woodside, Long Island. In May, she made a personal appearance at Oriole Terrace in Detroit, as the added attraction to the Jack Pomeroy musical production *Rhythm Fantasies*.[17]

In July, she appeared at the Vendome in New York, and by August, she was in Pittsburgh appearing at the Plaza Villa.[18] But her career took yet another nose dive when in September, she was reduced to performing in a business that was a cafeteria during the day and a nightclub at night on West 46th Street, a half block from Broadway. The cafeteria had hit on a plan of helping the business by installing an entertainer and a band, that entertainer being Mary.

Mary's suit with Mannix was finally settled out of court in October with the terms of the settlement never published.[19] It is doubtful that Mary walked away with a lot of money, as by December she was living at a cheap rooming house for actresses on West 48th Street.[20] She was spotted briefly in Philadelphia in February 1937 and seen in a New York nightclub that February as well.

Mary had been born with red hair but had dyed it blonde when she went to New York; she was now back to be a redhead, due to the cost of keeping it blonde. In May, she was back in jail in New York City for failing to pay a four-year-old dress bill to the Wilma Gowns Inc. for $405.87. The claim said that Mary took the clothing and disappeared, never attempting to pay any part of the bill. At the time of her arrest, she was staying in a dollar-a-day room just west of Times Square, barely eking out a living. She was arrested by City Marshall Abraham Adisky on a court order. At the time of her arrest, she was in her room with Al Reinis, described as her booking agent.[21]

Mary had been recently appearing at small roadhouses and nightclubs. When Adisky showed up to arrest her, she pleaded with him not to as she said she was seriously ill, and "had forgotten about the bill." Her plea was ignored, and he told her she had to pay up or go to jail. Unable to pay, she was taken to the prison ward of Bellevue Hospital. After she spent four hours there, her attorneys promised to pay, and she was transferred to St. Vincent's Hospital.[22] Bellevue Hospital's prison ward was opened in the early 1930s to treat prisoners and inmates with psychiatric issues. It contained a courtroom to process the various cases, where Bellevue's psychiatric staff would assess a suspect's competence to stand trial.

Al Reinis told reporters that Mary was unable to pay the bill as she already owed her landlady $100 in back rent. Either he or Mary's lawyers ended up paying the bill or came to an agreement with Wilma Gowns and persuaded the authorities to release her.[23] Upon being discharged, Mary told reporters that she had been sent to Bellevue because the shock of her arrest caused her "severe nervous strain" which required hospitalization.

On May 26, Mary's attorney Henry Yarm pointed out to New York Municipal Judge William Matthews that a woman in New York State could only be jailed for debt when "willful injury" was involved, so Justice Matthews signed a vacating order which prevented Mary from being sent to jail again for that charge.[24] After her release from St. Vincent's Hospital, Mary returned to performing in nightclubs. In June 1937, the Actors Fund of America sent her by ambulance to the Brunswick Home in Amityville, Long Island, for psychiatric treatment. Attendants said she was "a very sick girl."[25]

Brunswick Home was a private institution that had been set up to care for the treatment of epileptics, paralytics, so-called "feeble-minded" and aged people, and many actors and actresses lived out their last days there. It had been supported by the Actors Fund of America since 1917. The Actors Fund of America was founded in 1882 largely through the efforts of Harrison Grey Fiske, the owner of a theater trade publication, the *New York Dramatic Mirror*. In the founding year, the *New York Herald* generously donated $10,000 to the Fund. The primary mission of the Actors Fund was to care for members of the theatrical community when they fell ill and to bury the dead.

In the late nineteenth century when the Actors Fund began, actors and actresses often ran away from home to join the theater, and had cut ties with their families. Consequently, if they did not find either fame and fortune, and died early or even during a tour, often there was no one to claim the body or make funeral arrangements. Thus, the Actors Fund, from its very beginnings, looked on burial and funeral arrangements as a central and necessary component of its work. It also had a long-standing arrangement with the Brunswick Home, and funded many stays for actors who were having mental and/or financial issues.

In the early years of the Actors Fund, benefit performances were held annually, generally taking the form of vaudeville-style multi-performer revues, to rise funds. In 1927, a significant breakthrough in fundraising was achieved when the Actors Fund and the Actors' Equity Association reached an agreement whereby theater companies would put on special performances of productions, sometimes a ninth show during any given week. All proceeds were to benefit the Fund.

In Mary's case, Robert Campbell, the secretary of the Fund, said that Mary was too proud to ask for aid, so when some of the girls in the Ziegfeld Girls' Club found out that Mary was very sick and living in a cheap rundown room, they did what "they were supposed to do—we helped her." It was noted that a physician was attending to Mary daily, but a complete recovery was doubtful.

Only a few days before being sent to Brunswick Home, Mary had given an interview to journalist Marguerite M. Marshall:

There have been three men in my life whom I loved. And every one of the three has abused me and brought me ill fortune. I can tell any girl that to have a romance with a man who already has a wife is one of the most foolish and hopeless performances in the world. She is asking for trouble and she usually gets it. When Mr. X drove me out of Hollywood and—I am confident—barred my return, I went to England hoping in London to win new fame in pictures. Not a chance! I did obtain an opportunity to do a vaudeville singing act at the Piccadilly Theater in 1936. All alone before the audience in the center of a brilliantly lighted stage, my voice went. I could not utter another note.[26]

When Marguerite asked what the trouble was, Mary said, "London fog, for one thing." When Maxine asked about her past issues with a dope habit, Mary said,

It was one of those things for which, in the beginning, nobody was to blame, or, rather, one person was emphatically to blame—Mr. X, who sent me to the hospital for 21 major operations. Because of the intense pain I suffered on the operating table, my doctors were compelled to keep me much under the influence of opiates. It is my heartfelt belief, shared by Al Reinis, my manager, and Dr. Frank Fink, my physician, that those times will never return. The shock of my recent arrest and brief imprisonment for an old debt put me under a severe nervous strain. But I am sure that in the near future, I shall be a strong healthy woman. I still believe that it is in Hollywood that I belong.[27]

Mary was released after a few days, and in August she was back appearing in nightclubs. She then filed a claim that she was maliciously libeled and her reputation damaged to the extent of $25,000, through a *New York Amsterdam News* article which had appeared the previous May referred to her as the former wife of Dr. Eugene Nelson, a black Hollywood doctor, by saying, "Imogene and her Negro husband, Dr. Nelson caused a sensation in Hollywood seven years ago when it became known that that dashing doctor was colored." Mary filed a lawsuit in the New York Supreme Court against Powell-Savory Corporation, the owners of the publication, but ultimately lost the case.[28]

Dr. Nelson's real wife was Helen Lee Worthing, who, like Mary, was also a Ziegfeld star in the 1920s. In a cruel twist of fate, Helen died in Los Angeles the same year as Mary in August 1948, and like Mary she was also all alone at the time. Helen's career had faded after she was arrested for forging a narcotics prescription. After attempting to take her life, she was confined to a state hospital. After being released, in her later years she was repeatedly arrested on drug charges, at one stage spending five months in jail on a drug conviction.

In August, Mary's ex-husband Wallace pleaded guilty to a charge that he forced the rear window of a restaurant at 250 West 47th Street and stole $50 worth of liquor and cigarettes. He was sentenced to up to three years in prison by General Sessions Judge Owen Bohan. After his marriage to Mary, Wallace had found employment as an usher in Hollywood. In his probation report, his probation officer had noted him as a "gigolo type."[29] Twice more married about he divorced Mary, Wallace died in Los Angeles in October 1984.

By October, Mary was back in Bellevue Hospital, supposedly suffering from alcoholism, morphine poisoning and barbituric acid poisoning. There were even reports that she had taken an overdose of sedatives. Reinis was once again there to take her to hospital. He wanted her released, but the doctors persuaded him to let her stay.[30]

In November 1937, Eddie Mannix's relationship with his wife Bernice came to an end. She had been living quietly in Palm Springs, but that month she finally decided to divorce him. But just before she filed for divorce, she died in a mysterious car accident. It appeared the car she was in was run off the road, but no charges were filed.

In September 1938, there were newspaper reports that Mary was back in Hollywood, hoping to restart her career. The *Ohio Circleville Herald* said that she had been in a sanitarium for her health. "I am a competent actress, and there should be a place for me here," she said. "I want to go back to work." With Mary's health regained according to her published story in 1941, she left Bellevue in October 1938 and caught the train to Los Angeles, to live with her sister Mabel and her niece Maxine, at 4848 Oakwood Ave, where she took the name Mary Wilson. Mabel had been living in Los Angeles since 1930 and Maxine was now working as a dancer at the studios. With her looks fading, unable to get work, and suffering from a chronic gallbladder condition, Mary started receiving treatment at Cedars of Lebanon Hospital.

Before the year was over, Mary had increased her use of heroin to ease her pain. No longer living with Mabel, she now resided alone at 1504 South Mansfield Avenue in Los Angeles County in a tiny furnished apartment. Mary, who had been accustomed to the finest things in life, was now surrounded by mundane furnishings, except for a grand piano formally owned by Rudolph Valentino. Shopkeepers in the area were accustomed to seeing her when she would go into their stores with an item of value she wanted to sell.[31]

In 1941, she sold the second version of her biography to *The American Weekly*, which serialized it under the title "Confessions of a Follies Girl." It is reproduced in its entirety at the back of this book. Nothing was really heard from Mary again, until newspaper reports surfaced in 1944 that she was now working as a private nurse in Hollywood; by 1945, they said she was a nurse in a sanitarium. These reports were false. By 1948, Mary had moved back in with Mabel. On the night of Monday, April 18, 1948, Mary was taken from 4848 Oakwood Ave, where she was still living as Mary Wilson, to the Hollywood Receiving Hospital. When the doctors there recommended hospitalization, she was admitted as a charity patient into Cedars of Lebanon Hospital suffering from malnutrition and a "highly nervous condition." Dr. A.F. Gore said that Mary was showing an encouraging appetite, and resting well, but added that her recovery from years of illness and poverty "may take a long time."[32]

Mary gave an interview in the hospital on Saturday, April 24, where she managed to get out of bed and walk a few steps in a yellow negligee. "How does it feel, Mary?" she was asked. "If you had to do it over again—your life to live over again—would it be like this? Would you change it? Would you have it different?"

"Change it? Why, I've had a beautiful life. I've tumbled into the most beautiful life in the world. I'd never change it!" She was then asked about the last 15 years of bad luck with unpaid bills, court appearances and hospital stays. "I saw it coming," she said. "Luck's all there is to life, I sometimes think. I've had more than my share of good luck. No—maybe I wouldn't change even that."

When asked what the future held for her, she said, "I'd like to write. When I get my strength back. I'm 42 you know. That's not so old. But I don't really know. My life has been so beautiful. I don't think I will ever be completely satisfied with anything again."[33]

She was subsequently released, but was back again at Cedars of Lebanon Hospital in May and then again in mid–August, her fifth admittance since January. It was reported that she was so weak she had to be fed intravenously. After her hospitalization in May, well-known columnist-journalist Jimmie Fidler wrote an article about Mary, part of it reproduced below:

> I knew Mary Nolan at the peak of her success. I realize how much she's thrown away, and how far she's fallen from her one-time state. Reading about her present plight is very much like encountering a ghost. As Imogene Wilson, a headliner in the Ziegfeld Follies, she was acclaimed the most beautiful girl in all America. As Mary Nolan, she became one of Hollywood's most promising stars—not just another "would-be," but an idol to millions of movie-loving fans. And she had real ability, make no mistake about that.
>
> But Mary Nolan had a genius for choosing the wrong kinds of friends and a talent for getting herself into trouble. She lacked the strength of character that she needed to protect herself from the consequences of her own beauty. Fame and success and money, in her case, were not blessings but misfortunes. It wasn't long before she lost out in Hollywood and returned to New York. Gradually she dropped from the limelight, and from the headlines where her escapades had landed her for too often for her own good. I hadn't heard of her in years until I read that recent story.
>
> "I feel sympathy for Mary Nolan. Sure, she made mistakes, but I somehow feel that the people of show business who exploited her beauty, and the fans who fed her too heady a diet of adulation in her heyday, should share the blame. People who administer a poison, no matter how unwittingly they do so, are every bit as responsible, in the event of a tragedy, as is the victim who takes it.[34]

Mary had begun working on her memoirs, *Yesterday's Girl*, with the help of writer John Preston, which was to be an expanded version of the serialized account of her life that had appeared in newspapers in 1941.

On October 31, 1948, weighing a mere 90 pounds, Mary was found dead in her bed in her three-room stucco bungalow court apartment at 1504 South Mansfield Ave. On the morning of the day Mary died, Frank Gallagher, a salesman and roomer at her apartment, said Mary had collapsed around one a.m., and when that happened, he phoned her sister Mabel. Dr. Leo Gelfand was also summoned, but Mary died before he arrived.[35] Dr. Gelfand pronounced her dead but declined to sign a death certificate because he was not familiar with her condition. He told the newspapers that he had treated Mary several weeks prior to her death, when she was hospitalized with a gall bladder ailment. He said he had given her a sedative when she complained of abdominal pains and left an additional supply of sedatives to take if the pain continued.

Gallagher told the police that Mary had been in a sanitarium four times since the beginning of October. The police later learned that Mary had obtained a morphine prescription from a second doctor, who was unaware she had earlier been prescribed sedatives from Dr. Gelfand. Some reports say that Mary had been using the name Mary Wilson, so it would have been quite easy to get multiple subscriptions from multiple doctors.

An autopsy was ordered in November, but because no pathological reason was discovered, a toxicological study of Mary's vital organs was also ordered. Harry Deutsch, the assistant autopsy surgeon from the L.A. Coroner's Office, found that she had a bruise on the right side of her face, probably caused by a fall. They issued a pending certificate so that she could be buried. Coroner Ben Brown reported on November 23 that his final verdict was that Mary had died from an overdose of sleeping tablets. Police said in their official report that she had been hospitalized ten years ago, "for a cure for narcotic addiction." Other information disclosed in the report, the detectives said, was that Mary had also tried to commit suicide twice before—once by an overdose of sleeping tablets, once by slashing her wrists.[36]

At age 42 years, 10 months, and 14 days, Mary Imogene Robertson's flame had finally flickered out.

Around 50 people gathered at three p.m. on Thursday, November 4, in the Utter-McKinley & Strother Hollywood chapel at 6240 Hollywood Boulevard to hear Dr. Walter Raymond, pastor of the Unity Church, give Mary's final sermon. He offered hope that the former star would in the "hereafter find the life that is truly indestructible."[37]

Mabel and Roy attended, as well as actor Richard Denning and his wife, the former Evelyn Ankers. Among Mary's few possessions was the antique piano once owned by Rudolph Valentino, which was later sold in an estate sale. Mabel told reporters that it really was Valentino's piano, and said, "I think she worshiped Rudy's memory. She clung persistently to this piano and always kept Rudy's picture on the music rack. I think somehow it reminded her of her own greatness, and helped her, profoundly, in her discouragement."[38] It was eventually brought by Mrs. Leonie Leach from Detroit.[39]

Mary was interred in Hollywood Memorial Park (now known as Hollywood Forever Cemetery), in the Abbey of the Psalms Mausoleum, Sanctuary of Hope, Corridor D-1, in wall-crypt 594, adjacent to the eventual crypt of Mabel.

When the results of the toxicology test came back in late November, Coroner Braun said that Mary had died due to an overdose of sleeping tablets, either accidentally or on purpose. Her death certificate therefore lists "accidental or suicide" as the cause of death. Some newspapers reported that the sleeping tablets were Seconal. Newspapers also said that Mary had been getting treatment for a chronic gall bladder ailment. Mabel said that what *really* caused her death was: "She didn't stick to her diet."

Mabel died in August 1961, and Ray died in June 1982.

ELEVEN

In Her Own Words

In 1941, Mary sold her life story to *The American Weekly*, which serialized it under the title "Confessions of a Follies Girl." This series is reproduced here.

Chapter 1

The little country girl in the Big City. That was my role when I first set foot in New York. I walked wide-eyed through the jostling crowds of Grand Central Station nervously fingering my nickels and dimes. They added up to exactly thirty-five cents. I didn't know a soul. I had no place to go. I was as green as a 13-year-old girl just out of a convent would be. The next day I was standing partly without clothing beside an artist's easel. It was the first time in my sheltered life that anyone had seen me that way. I wasn't greatly embarrassed. Perhaps I was too much of a child to be.

In my hand was a fifty-dollar bill, my pay for a couple of hours' posing. It was more money than I had ever seen before in my life!

Many more such days as a model followed closely. There were many more bills, with the clothes and finery they could buy to replace the harsh, somber attire I always had known. In a few short weeks, I heard myself acclaimed "Miss America" chosen for the title, not from a bevy of bathing beauties at Atlantic City but selected by the vote of the greatest artists in America to represent the embodiment of all that American girlhood should stand for, physically, morally, and spiritually. It was too high a pedestal.

Therefore, when the first tragic events in my life toppled me from my lofty throne, the spotlight of the country was focused on me to highlight my disaster in bold relief. By the time those first short kaleidoscopic weeks flashed by, I found myself behind the footlights, one flower in the world's greatest garden of feminine beauty, the Ziegfeld Follies.

Yes, you may say, I took New York overnight. But New York took me, too. Perhaps I've paid dearly for the success that swept me to the pinnacle of fame and dropped me just as quickly, but with all the anguish that went with it there were luminous moments that even the darkest days of later dope-ridden years couldn't take from me.

Most vividly, my life with Frank Tinney, the famous comedian, stands out. I cherish those memories and seek no pity. Some may say I am the victim of my own folly—but I've always wondered why life seems to expect so much more of a beautiful woman than it does of her less-favored sisters. What life usually does is to give them much in the beginning, fame, success, adoration, then crashes them with heartaches and tragedy.

Mary Nolan, Ziegfeld Girl and Silent Movie Star

Only one who lived on the Gay White Way, as Broadway of New York used to be called on those hysterical days of the early twenties, can sense the thrills of the life of a Follies girl, the nightly round of fabulous parties, showers of jewels, millionaires scrambling for a smile and a kiss. It's of those days that I want to tell, and of the glamorous figures who stalked through them, some to lasting fame—others to squalor and friendless death.

I doubt if anyone ever was ever more terrified than I was the day I walked out into the bustling streets of New York. The roar of traffic, the incessant mumble of voices, the swish of the crowds, all left me bewildered. A strange spectacle I must have been, if New York had taken pause to look. My plain blue serge suit and square little school cap must have made me conspicuous. But no one noticed me. I almost wished somebody out of the sea of faces would speak—and I probably would have fainted if anyone had. I was alone in the midst of millions of people and scared to death.

I saw a policeman and was frightened, as I had been told a man in police uniform may actually not be a policeman at all. I scurried into a little white front café, thinking I would eat while I tried to decide what I should do next. Two women were seated near me, chattering like magpies. When they spied me, they began to laugh.

"Hello, Rosebud, when did you get in?" one of them asked me. Her voice was coarse, unlike the soft tones of the sisters in the convent. I never had heard anything like it before. Her painted face startled me. Rouge and lipstick were something new. The nuns had always told us that Chinamen would get us in a big city. That danger signal flashed through my mind. Maybe these funny looking women were Chinamen's wives? Maybe they were even Chinamen themselves. I was too frightened to answer.

I grabbed my bag and ran out of the place leaving my food untouched, the laughter of these strange denizens of the city wilderness ringing in my ears. My stomach was empty—but I still had my thirty-five cents. On an impulse to do something, get anywhere, I jumped onto a streetcar, paid my fare and sat down. I rode and rode. Crowds piled on and crowds piled off. I couldn't see anything but faces, more people than I had dreamed were in all the world. It began getting dark. The lights came on. I still sat huddled in my seat, too frightened to move, not knowing what to do. Why the conductor didn't put me off I don't know, but he didn't.

Finally, at midnight, a voice called out.

"Everybody off. End of the line. We're going to the barn"

My decision was made for me. I couldn't sit and ride on the friendly streetcar any longer. I had to take the next step, no matter where it led me. I looked around. There was one other person on the car, a kindly looking man. I thought his nose-glasses were funny but bless his heart. I'll never forget him. He was my first friend in New York and one of my kindliest advisors. Tears were streaming down my face. My eyes were as red as my hair from crying.

"You're in trouble, little girl," the man said. "Are you lost?"

"No-o," I sobbed. "I–I've nowhere to go."

"Well, don't cry," he said, and put an arm gently around my shoulder, "I'll take you home with me."

I looked up at him. He didn't look like what I imagined a Chinaman would be. But by that time, it didn't matter much. I didn't realize it then, but I was already caught in the vortex of New York life. Little did I dream that night where that chance meeting on a streetcar at midnight would lead me.

"You come along with me, and everything will be all right." The man's voice reassured me. Besides I didn't know enough about the ways of the city—and men— to be suspicious. We took a taxi to his house. The man stopped at a doorway and rang the bell. A sweet-faced lady answered. "Look what I've found," the man laughed as we stepped inside. "Just what I've been looking for all over New York. Isn't she a beauty?"

His words startled me. I still didn't see any Chinamen—but I wondered what he wanted with me. And that woman who let us in—was she really his wife, or one of the kind I had heard mentioned vaguely in whispers. That night it didn't matter. I was too tired to care. The lady fixed me something to eat, then led me to a nice clean room and tucked me in. I was safe so far. The morrow would have to take care of itself. That man who took me into his home was Arthur William Brown, the noted illustrator and artist. I never will be able to repay him for his kindness.

The next morning, I got up early and slipped into my clothes, intending to get out before my benefactor discovered I was gone. His remarks about being "just what I've been looking for" still puzzled me. I didn't know who he was. Just as I opened the door Mr. Brown heard me. "And where are you going so early, Mary Imogene?" he smiled. My name was Mary Imogene Wilson then.

Before I could think of anything to say, he went on, "Mrs. Brown is going to take you out and get you some clothes. Then you are going to pose for me." We went into an exclusive gown shop where I was bedecked in finery I had seen before only in my dreams. New York was treating me better on my second day there. Mr. Brown's studio was up a flight of stairs above his home, with a skylight and all cluttered up like most artists' studios are. A painting stood in one corner. Mr. Brown saw me standing before spellbound.

"What is that?" I asked him.

"That, my child, is New York."

It was a painting of the city's skyline. It was my first view of the big city. I had ridden through it all day, but I hadn't seen New York until I gazed upon it on canvas in the artist's studio. It had a spiritual quality I have never forgotten. Things had happened to me so rapidly in this new world that I wasn't shocked when Mr. Brown told me to take off some of my clothes. I stood before him, partly drape, without shame and unafraid. His manner put me at ease. His interest was in his art, not in my body. I can truthfully say that the same was true of the other great artists for whom I posed and exposed for all of the famous ones of the day.

But it was not long before I met other men whose interest in me was distinctly otherwise. That interest and its gratification led to some of the most tragic episodes of my life. I was saddled with an overpowering inferiority complex. I craved the love I never had had, every time I thought it was in my grasp I reached for it like a child seizing a bubble. They called me Bubbles, you know. When the dream ended I had had men in my arms, yes, but I hadn't had love.

Born in Kentucky, fifteen miles from Louisville,[1] I was left motherless at the age of three. My adopted parents placed me in a convent at St. Joseph, Missouri. From that day until the time I left on the trip that took me to New York, my contact with the outside world was confined to one visit to my grandmother's farm at Owensboro, Kentucky, when I was eight years old. All of the other convent girls had relatives and friends who visited them. I had none. When the others received their boxes of candies and cake from home, I ran and hid to hide my feelings of a discrimination I couldn't understand but could resent. I was a charity pupil, but I didn't know why. Second-hand clothes and hand-me-downs were my lot. Instead of feeling grateful, I was resentful. I envied the other girls their bright ribbons. I recall the sweet kindness of one nun who slipped me a quarter so I could get a hair ribbon like the other girls. We were not supposed to touch the nun's habits, but I used to run to them and clutch their skirts, eager for the affection fate had denied me. It seemed as if I grew up clutching at life for something it's said I shouldn't have.

Many showgirls such as I became, were branded as gold diggers. I don't believe I ever deserved that designation, but I was a gold digger once, long before I ever saw Broadway. I asked one of the older girls at the convent how I could get some money to buy candy and apples as the others did. "Oh, there's a pot of gold buried out by the gate," she told me. Early the next morning I was out beside the high-walled fence digging furiously. One of the priests came along.

"Mary Imogene, what are you doing?" he asked in amazement.

"I'm digging for gold."

"I don't believe you'll find any there."

He helped me shovel the dirt back into the hole I had dug. It was just another effort frustrated, but I can view it now as a prophetic incident in my life.

Physically, I developed very early. It had been intended that I should become a nun. Instead I yearned for the outside world. I wanted freedom, but I never found it. I left the confines and rules of the convent, yes, in their place I found the hard bonds of circumstance and later, the merciless shackles of dope which held me helpless in their terrible grip until a will to escape the fetters gave me a new chance at freedom three years ago.

It was arranged for me to return to my grandmother's farm. Before I reached there, an impulse seized me. I had barely enough money for a ticket to New York, but under the wicket it went, and I was on my way to two of the most hectic years a person could live. Each moment brought its new sensation. I was a child in fairy-land, wondering what miracle the next second would unfold. I learned from life and I learned the hard way. I mistook the success and acclaim that came to me for the love I always had been denied. I sought it eagerly. It swept me off my feet. I was wanted for the first time in my life. I thought I was achieving the thing I desired, but in the end, I found myself still empty-handed and fooled.

After posing for Mr. Brown for a few days, he arranged for me to join the Artists and Models Club. I went there to live. The artists called there for their models. Overnight I was posing nine hours a day, three hours in the morning, three in the afternoon, and three in the evening. James Montgomery Flagg. Charles Dana Gibson, Harrison Fisher, Norman Rockwell, Frank Leyendecker and all the other great illustrators employed me as a model. What country kid wouldn't be flattered by such a storm of attention? From an unwanted nobody it seemed I was wanted by everybody. Oh, it was a rosy world in those glorious days. I didn't realize then it was my fresh unspoiled beauty that made me a novelty.

In my free moments, I was taking dance lessons. One day Mr. Flagg said to me, "Is there anything you can do besides look beautiful?" "Yes, I can jog," I said naïvely, and tapped out a few steps that must have looked rather silly. "How would you like to go on the stage?"

"Oh, I'd love it."

"Think I'll give you a note to Flo Ziegfeld. He might use you in the Follies."

I never had seen a theatrical performance.[2] I didn't know the difference between the Follies and *Twelfth Night*.

"Would that mean I could be a dramatic actress?" I asked.

"Not exactly," Mr. Flagg said. "But if you can get on with the Follies, that will be good enough."

I got the note and hurried to Mr. Ziegfeld's office. The place was crowded with beautiful girls, all waiting for their chance. Mr. Ziegfeld was too busy to see any beauties, even with a note from James Montgomery Flagg. But I wasn't disappointed. Life's cup was full anyway. A few days later I was having lunch at the old hermitage. After I left, a big fat man ran up behind me halfway down the block.

"You can walk faster than any person I ever saw," he spluttered. "Come on back with me. Mr. Ziegfeld wants to see you."

"Mr. Ziegfeld? Mr. Ziegfeld doesn't know me. Who are you?" I was getting wise to a few of the city tricks.

"I'm Will Page, his press agent. He wants to talk to you. Come along."

I wouldn't believe the man I met was Mr. Ziegfeld, but it was. That chance incident put me in the Follies. Rehearsals followed immediately. The show was being whipped into shape when I joined it. I was lost in the maze of beauty. I didn't know a cue from a spotlight. About all I did was mix everybody up and mess up their lines. At the first dress rehearsal, I didn't know what to do. Everybody was running around, just as excited as they would have been on an opening night.

"What shall I wear?" I asked one of the other girls.

"Duck into a dressing room, honey, and put on any costume you can find," she said.

I did. I found the most elaborate gown in the place. It was a gorgeous bridal costume. I strutted onto the stage full of confidence and certain I would attract attention. I got it all right, but not the way I had hoped. Ned Wayburn, the stage manager, took one look and started tearing his hair.

"What are you doing out there in that costume?" he screamed. "Get her off the stage."

Crestfallen, I ran for the dressing rooms. Wayburn's anger was mild compared to the fury I encountered there. Vivienne Segal,[3] the prima donna, was just about to tear the place apart. She couldn't find her costume, the gown she was to wear in the big wedding scene. I felt so small I think I crawled out of it under the hem of the train. After that, I was careful whose costume I put on. Another time when the entire cast was on the stage for an ensemble, Wayburn yelled out, "Imogene, where are you?"

"Right back here," I answered, peering around the heads of a score of girls.

"That's fine. That's where you belong. You can help hold up the scenery."

The show went to Atlantic City for the usual two weeks tryout. It was there I attended my first big party. An entire hotel floor was taken over for it. It was strictly a celebration for the cast and entirely theatrical. It wasn't like the parties I came to know later in New York, when the millionaire playboys would invite one of the girls out after the show. Those were the wild parties when each girl found a hundred-dollar bill under her plate or received a jeweled box of candy with a big bill folded under the cover.

But I'll never forget that Atlantic City party because it was my first one as a Follies girl. Of course, Mr. Ziegfeld was there. Sam Harris, Oscar and Arthur Hammerstein, Irving Berlin, Tallulah Bankhead and Pat Somerset were among the other famous ones. And I remember that party for another reason. It was the first night I ever met a real heel. When the party broke up in the early morning hours I went to my room. I slipped off my clothes, put on a negligee and crawled into bed.

I was still thrilled too much by the excitement of meeting so many famous people to sleep. My bedroom door opened and one of the men I had met during the evening stepped in and closed it behind him. He is a man who later became famous in Hollywood, so I will not mention his name. He threw off his dressing gown and started to get into my bed. Yes, I was green, but smart enough by that time to know what his intentions were.

I jumped up and ran screaming into the lounge of the suite. The first person I ran into was Arthur Hammerstein.

"Why, Imogene, you look frightened," he said. "What's the matter?"

"That man," I cried. "He tried to get into bed with me."

"Now, now, don't cry," he said, and then he got me another room.

"Miss America" was a creation of Flo Ziegfeld. Six weeks after I arrived in New York I was preparing to step out behind the footlights, a featured attraction in the greatest musical show on Broadway—and that meant in the world. Named by vote of the illustrators, I was crowned at the first matinee of the *1923 Follies*. Can you imagine a girl of thirteen, who never had seen a show before, being spotlighted at a performance she was able to see only from the wings? That was an unforgettable occasion and moments of that kind were swirling around my bewildered head pretty fast in those mad days.

Will Rogers bless his soul, and Fanny Brice conducted the coronation ceremonies. That day will live forever in my memories, the almost hysterical excitement, people scurrying in and out of the dressing rooms, shouts of the electricians and stage hands, poor Ned Wayburn gnashing his teeth at unforeseen hitches, the hum of voices in the audience, the blood-tingling strains of the orchestra's prelude, the sudden hush from the obscure sea of faces in the darkened rows as the curtain slowly lifted.

My crown was a gorgeous creation of aigrettes. The royal costume, what there was of it, was of sheer crepe de chine. It was white and skintight. Around my shoulders was a beautiful chinchilla wrap, a present from Mr. Ziegfeld. It was so lovely, every other girl in the show was pouting about it. Mr. Ziegfeld called me Emmy. Much as I loved him I hated to have him call me Emmy. But he did and I had to like it. Just before the curtain he came to me.

"Emmy, everyone is jealous of you in that fur," he said. "Maybe you'd better leave it off. Why, even Fanny Brice is in a pout."

I thought that was a good time to show my temperament.

"No, I will not," I said. "I don't care who doesn't like it."

"All right, Emmy, all right. You keep it."

How that great man ever managed to keep such a bunch of prima donnas as we were in the Follies from tearing each other's eyes out at times is more than I can understand. I presume it was because he was a great man.

The stage was dark when the curtain rose. The climaxing crash of the orchestra's number brought the blinding spot sweeping down to highlight me in that gorgeous setting. At first there was a hush. Then came a burst of applause, the first I ever heard, applause really for me. It was almost impossible for me, to whom so many sensations had come in those few short weeks, to realize that the roars of the handclapping were for me. If I hadn't been holding my heart in my mouth, I'm sure it would have pounded right through that thin crepe de chine bodice.

Will Rogers and Fanny Brice stepped into the spotlight. There were a few preliminaries, then Will and Fanny, as the king and queen of the Follies, fitted that cigarette headdress on my brow.

"We crown you Miss America!"

There was more applause. The orchestra struck up. The entire cast, that collection of the most beautiful girls to be found anywhere, was flooded in lights. The show went on.

Will Rogers was the star. He and I had a skit together.[4] At the end of it Will had to kiss me and then back off the stage. Even though it was an act, I believe he always was sincerely embarrassed. I can see him yet as he shifted from one foot to the other, that sheepish grin, the mop of hair over one brow, the ever-present twirling rope.

When he finally mustered up enough courage to kiss me, he ambled up and did it in his usual awkward way. He always knocked his hat off, then backed up, stepped on it and dragged it off on his foot as he shuffled off the stage. Just an act, to be sure, so natural with Will Rogers.

Then there was the irrepressible Fanny Brice, singing "My Man" as only Fanny could. One of her specialties was the egg dance. In it she leaped and cavorted all over the stage in an impersonation of Pavlova's famous swan dance. And what Fanny couldn't do with grimace and gesture. At the end, she stood cackling over a nestful of eggs. Bert and Betty Wheeler were in the cast.[5] I've seen them get so many encores that they were actually exhausted. They would lie down on the stage to still the applause and finish their act after another number came on.

Lina Basquette,[6] twirling around on the tip of her toes, is another bright spot in my memories of those days. Paulette Duval[7] was a beautiful French dancer Mr. Ziegfeld brought over from Paris for the Follies. She came on in a Ziegfeld version of Lady Godiva, riding a white horse, with her pretty black hair streaming down her back. Hilda Ferguson,[8] a beautiful girl, did a breathtaking shimmy dance in an Indian costume that had a gorgeous feathered headdress. Brookie Johns,[9] a banjo artist, picked the strings for her act. How he could make that instrument sing! They always were a hit.

But through even those gay memories there is a note of sadness. When Hilda turned her back on Broadway she had enough diamond bracelets given to her by admirers, to cover both arms to the shoulders. She married and had a child, but staid married life was not for her. She died a few years later, penniless. Hilda, like quite a few of the rest of us, tasted both the bitter and the sweet.

Another famous couple was Edna Leadom and Dave Stamper.[10] Edna was tall. Dave was about half her size. He was her piano player and composed most of her songs. When they walked on the stage, Dave always announced her with a flourish:

"And now, I present Edna Leadom!"

Then, as the applause died down—"Go on, Edna, tell 'em just *where* you lead 'em."

They had their squabbles backstage too, but Edna always came out best.

And there was little Ann Pennington.[11] You couldn't know her without loving her. She used to come out and dance in a little white satin costume that was just right to show her pretty dimpled knees. Banjo Brookie Johns was sweet on Ann. He was a big chap, six feet or more tall. He could pick Ann up in one hand. Many was the time he would wait for her backstage when she had done something he didn't like, grab her in his strong arms, turn her over and spank her. We always knew when Ann was getting spanked. You could hear her screams all over the theater. It happened often, but it was all in fun.

It was a thrill to watch Will Rogers lasso the famous people in the audience. I remember the night he threw his rope around Mary Pickford's head. She was attending the show with Douglas Fairbanks, her husband.

The magazines and papers had given me a lot of publicity by that time as "Miss America." Mary and Doug were in New York taking in the shows. Doug was getting ready to make *The Thief of Bagdad* and was looking for an actress to play opposite him. I was being considered for the part, so Mary and Doug came to the Follies to look me over from a front row seat. Will Rogers lassoed Mary that night, but I didn't get the role.

Scandal was beginning to break into my life and I lost my first big chance to get into pictures. As a Follies Queen, I presume I thought I should have a few eccentricities. I bought a lovely canary. I took it with me to the theater, then back to the apartment when the show was over. Of course, I felt the bird should have more diversion and airing than I could give it. The job of being nursemaid to my pet canary fell to the lot of poor Will Page, Mr. Ziegfeld's press agent, the man who chased me down the street to drag me back to fame in bright lights. For some silly reason, I decided the bird should have a ride each day. I was learning to be temperamental. I knew how to stand up and howl for what I wanted.

"All right, Emmy," Mr. Ziegfeld agreed, "if that's what you want, you'll have it."

How we must have tried his patience. He always was wonderful to me, even through all my troubles. Anyway, each afternoon, Will Page took my canary in a taxi cab and drove for one hour through Central Park to let the bird view the scenery and chirp to its fancy-free feathered friends in the shrubbery. Mr. Page was a big man. Can you imagine anything sillier than a job like that, taking a canary for a daily ride thought the park? But it was one of my fancies at the time and my every whim was being humored then. It was just as well I couldn't see the days ahead, days when I tramped through the same park, branded as too notorious a creature even to be allowed to register in a third-rate hotel.

Great tragedy came into my life. A window was open one morning. My canary, seeking in its way to find the freedom I have sought and never found, flew out. It found its wings unequal to buffet the outside world even as I did when life swept me up in its grasp. It fell, too. A bellboy and a maid found it helpless on a skylight. They brought it to me. Will Page and a friend called in a doctor, but there was nothing he could do. When the bird died, the men gave it a funeral and buried it in a flower pot that held a fern in the living room.

The first big party that was ever given for me as a Follies girl was held in the old Waldorf. It was given by a young New Yorker, the son of a wealthy manufacturer. I was thrilled half to death. To invite one girl to a party didn't mean that your admirer was going to take you to dinner and a nightclub. It was an unwritten rule that a bid to a party meant to bring all your friends. When word went out that someone was giving Soandso a party, we all went.

No particular favors were shown. Each girl got the same gift in money or jewelry as the others. The most favored one, in whose honor the party was being given, got a little something extra. Sometimes it was only a lovely corsage. Other times it might be a diamond bracelet. At my first party, each one of us found a hundred-dollar bill pinned to our place cards. Handfuls of five-dollar gold pieces were tossed out to the entertainers as if they were pennies. Money and feminine beauty were the two cheapest commodities in New York in those days.

One day a man walked into Mr. Ziegfeld's office and announced very formally that he wanted to give Imogene Wilson a party.

"Who are you?" Mr. Ziegfeld asked.

"I am the brother of the King of Spain."

"Well, I don't care if you're the King himself. You're not going to take that kid out on any wild parties. She's too young. There are plenty of other beautiful women in New York. Get them and let Miss Wilson alone."

The man left, but the party was held anyway, and I was the guest of honor. That night this man bought out the first two rows, center aisle, and paid five hundred dollars apiece for them. He filled them with his friends. After the show, we all went to the Waldorf. Our host had taken over an entire floor. It had been turned into a fairyland. Ben Ali Haggan, who was famous for his living statutory creations, was engaged to arrange the setting. Beautiful unclothed girls stood posed in artistic array around the room. It was the most sumptuous scene imaginable.

The host arrived with a coterie of guards, resplendent in gold braid and full-dress uniforms. He, himself, was dressed in attire copied from Tom Mix. Why that, I don't know. Each girl, about twenty of us attended, received a valuable present. Each girl, on turning over her plate, found a pile of gold pieces under it. My present, one of the prettiest I have ever received from anyone, was a pin, made of jewels in the shape of a cluster of forget-me-nots. In the center of each little jeweled flower was a diamond. I have never seen another quite like it. Of course, the champagne flowed like so much water.

They always said a girl sometime had to have a champagne bath before she was really initiated into the night life of those days. One of the girls in the party got hers that night. It was the highlight of the festivities. We filled a bathtub with bubbling champagne. She took off her clothes and stepped in. Then the parade started. We all marched by, dipped in our glasses and drank a toast to her health and success. The cost of that party was tremendous. Naturally I never knew how much and probably didn't give it much though then. At any rate, it was a great many thousand dollars. And the King's brother, that was just a wealthy playboy's whimsical idea.

✤ ✤ ✤

For a time, the life of a Follies girl seemed to be all glamour and glory, champagne parties and jeweled gifts, but I learned all too soon how much heartache could be hidden beneath the glitter and tinsel.

With the Follies, Frank Tinney came into my life, a figure destined to shape it and dominate it for years to come. I speak of it now with no regrets. Frank Tinney is dead. I wouldn't say an unkind word about him even if I felt it and I feel none. Frank was a great man, a great comedian, a great genius. Now that he is gone, I feel a deep love for him much more than I ever felt when we were living together. I didn't love him then. In fact, he bored me. But I did love his genius. I was in love with Frank Tinney, the comedian, not Frank Tinney, the man. I'm not a spiritualist, but he has been closer to me in death than he ever was in life. I can't blame him alone for my troubles. He was at fault, yes, but so was I.

I was not strong. Life was whipping me with every lesson I learned. I, a nobody through the eyes of my own inferiority complex, was captivated by the attentions of the star of the Music Box show, the toast of Broadway. My starved vanity was fed by his favor. My head was in the clouds in those giddy, intoxicating days. I didn't know my feet still were in the common clay. One of the other girls in the Follies had a boyfriend in the cast at Frank's show at the Music Box. She used to meet him after rehearsals. One day she asked me to join several others who were going over with her. That sounded like an interesting idea. I went along. Their rehearsal still was on when we got there. I was standing in the wings looking on when the stage manager yelled.

"Where's Frank Tinney?"

Frank walked on from the back stage.

"Who's that?" I asked my friend.

"Why silly, that's the great Frank Tinney."

"I don't know any more now than I did before you told me. What does he do?"

As far as I knew or cared there wasn't another show in New York then, or in the world, beside the Follies.

"Are you crazy? He's the star of the show. Gee, he's funny. You want to watch him."

The rehearsal ended in a few minutes. Frank walked toward the wings, saw me, and stopped.

"Hello," he said, "Where did you come from?"

I didn't answer.

He turned to the Music Box Stage Manager.

"Hey, where'd you find this? New girl in the show?"

"No, she's not mine," the stage manager said.

"Well, that's good."

Frank walked over and touched my arm. "How about coming down to my dressing room and having a little drink. I'm going to have one."

That was the cue to Frank Tinney's life, but I missed it. Frank wrecked his life. In the years we were together I don't believe I ever saw him entirely sober. He lived on whiskey. Two to three quarts were his daily rations. I think that's the reason I never really knew Frank Tinney, the man.

"No thanks," I told him. "I don't drink."

"You don't? Honey, you don't know what you're missing. Smoke?"

I shook my head.

"No? Swear?"

"No," I told him.

"Well, I'll be—." He stepped back and rested his hands on his hips. He looked me over from head to foot, like I was a freak in a sideshow.

"Well, if that ain't something." He exploded. "A New York show girl who doesn't drink, smoke or swear. I've seen Niagara Falls and the Eiffel Tower, but this. It's can't be real."

He laughed and went to his dressing room.

I didn't realize it but I had sealed my fate, if you want to call it that, that afternoon when I paraded my virtue and innocence. It made me a novelty that Frank Tinney had heard about only in story books. Matinee idol that he was, Frank saw so much of women that they disgusted him. They fell over each other to win his favor or gain admittance to his apartment. They used to stand in line outside the stage entrance, regular mobs of silly creatures to wave a hand or toss a kiss. And society belles were just as bad as the shop girls, all of them throwing themselves at him.

Frank was fed up with women when I met him. He was a man's man and much preferred to spend a night drinking and shooting craps with a bunch of stage hands, then an evening with some fawning aggressive female in her apartment or his. But I didn't know that then, and I didn't know that he was attracted to me because he saw me as an untouched country kid, something that he didn't know existed in a city where it was not uncommon for giddy girls to beg him to pick them up from street corners.

Naturally, I was vain enough and foolish enough to be fascinated to receive the attentions of the great comedian while he spurned the advances of hordes of other women hovering around him. I saw him again a few times soon after that at rehearsals.

A night or two later I was standing in the rain outside the theater waiting for a streetcar to take me to the Artists and Models Club after the show. A car rolled up. Frank and his secretary were in it.

"May I drive you home?" he asked.

I got in.

That short step linked my life with Frank Tinney's from that day on. And no woman ever forgets the first man in her life, whether they be but one of many. No matter what acquiescence or forgiveness I may have shown later, that night was and ever will be a night of horror.

Frank's secretary left us at his stop and we drove on. But instead of taking me home, Frank directed us across to Long Island up the shore to Long Beach. The storm that beat down on us from outside was wild compared to the tempest that raged within my heart and soul. Frank accustomed to having his way, didn't deny himself that night. It wasn't that he couldn't have found plenty of others, and all eager to surrender. My freshness and simplicity were what he craved for the novelty of the moment. I was powerless.

Whatever motivated him that night I don't know, but I do know that he held me in an insanely jealous love from that time on. It was an intense possessive love that I didn't reciprocate. I became his captive. He literally stole me and all that was mine. When the night of anguish ended and we drove back to New York City, he carried me screaming and kicking wrapped in a blanket, into his apartment on Seventy-second street.

I felt the same bewilderment I had known that first day I stepped out of the Grand Central Station. I was lost again. I knew I shouldn't be in his apartment, but I couldn't go back to the Club. I felt that I had the Scarlet Letter branded all over me. For Frank, I must say he was all kindness and tenderness once we reached the confines of his quarters. I was his then, all his in every sense of the word. He couldn't do enough for me.

I was ill. I knew I would not be able to rehearse. Frank wanted to phone Mr. Ziegfeld but I wouldn't let him do that. I felt the whole world would know if he did that. I finally managed to appear for the show that night. Frank's apartment was my home for nearly two years after that until the scandal that broke into the open and ended in driving both of us from Broadway.

But the happenings of those two mad years will have to be told in a later chapter.

Chapter 2

From the night Frank Tinney carried me, screaming and kicking, into his apartment my life was his. A few romantic ones may have called me a love captive. The world at large applied a harsher, uglier term—"Tinney's woman."

That I was a child of fourteen didn't matter. I was a woman in fact and in the eyes of the world. Many whose lives made a mockery of their own respectability perhaps even could visualize the scarlet letter upon my brow. Their scorn was soon to topple me from my throne as Miss America and drive me from Broadway. For me to say I was a victim of circumstances sounds trite and a little cowardly. I'm no coward. I believe the anguish I have faced and the fight I have made to reclaim my life proves that.

And I blame no one. I've languished in the depths of darkest despair, but I've been compensated by moments of unforgettable happiness. I have regrets, yes, but resentment toward none. To Frank Tinney, a truly great comedian, life was just one big laugh. And so was I. That sounds a little incongruous in the light of tragic events that stalked it.

"We're meant to be happy, Bubble," he used to say to me.

His was a grand philosophy. Maybe we tried too hard to live it. Anyway, the more we struggled for happiness the more it seemed as if fights and heartaches ruled us. I don't ever remember ever sitting down to a meal at our apartment when there was a dish left on the table when we finished. Madhouse, you say? Yes—it was the tempo of our lives. We would sit across the table from each other for days without speaking a civil word. Frank usually was drinking. I know I was flighty and quick-tempered. Both of us were insanely jealous. I didn't love the man, but I was infatuated with the realization that I held the love of a man who was the toast of Broadway.

We would sit down to eat in a hostile attitude. Carrie, my Negro maid, and Bobby, Frank's valet, soon learned to keep out of range. One of us would drop a cutting remark and the dishes would begin to fly. Both is us became quite expert at ducking at the right time. We each learned the other's technique and managed to get out of the way of flying chinaware. We broke up hundreds and hundreds of dishes at that pastime but seldom was either of us hit.

Carrie and Bobby would stand in a neutral corner, silent and dumbfounded, as they watched bowls and platters filled with a tasty meal go flying across the table to crash against a wall or chair. It must have been discouraging to them to see the wasted effort that had gone into a nice dinner and contemplate the damage they would have to clean up. Sometimes we had spaghetti. You can imagine what a mess that was after a battle ended. When these dish fights were over we usually both felt better. We surveyed the wreckage with a laugh.

"Come on, Bubbles, get into some clothes," Frank would say. "Let's go out and get a bite. I don't like to eat at home anyway."

Frank's urge for happiness led him on a continuous round of pranks. He would do anything for a joke and I was the butt of most of them. I believe he would have broken his leg for a laugh. One day he did almost drown himself.

We were out on a yacht party on Long Island Sound. A lot of Frank's friends were aboard. Everyone had been drinking cocktails all afternoon, except myself. I wasn't drinking. They were all getting pretty hilarious, but I was used to that. Our apartment always was a gathering place for Frank's friends and I played bartender for them there.

For some reason I was utterly bored by the party that afternoon. I must have shown it. Perhaps Frank was receiving too much attention and not giving any time to me. Finally, he came up to the deck chair where I was sitting. I remember he was dressed in white linen and was wearing a straw hat.

"Bubbles, you look bored," he said.

"I am—dreadfully," I told him.

"Well, precious, what can I do to make you smile?" He danced around in front of me in a silly little jig.

"Jump overboard!" I said and looked the other way.

The next minute I heard a splash.

"Man overboard! Man overboard!" someone began yelling.

The crowd rushed to the rail.

"Why, it's Frank."

Sure enough, the moment the words were out of my mouth he jumped over the rail into the water. Then I was frightened. I didn't know whether he could swim. He pretended he couldn't. He floundered around, sputtering for help, as if he were going down for the last time. I was frantic. When he thought the joke had gone far enough, he struck out for the boat and climbed aboard.

"Did it just to please Bubbles," he explained to his friends.

I didn't appreciate the humor of that one.

Another time I had an engagement to go to Greenwich Village to pose. Bobby, the valet, drove me to the studio and left me. It had been snowing all day and the storm grew worse during the late afternoon. When I was ready to leave I phoned for a taxi, but the streets were so badly clogged I couldn't get one. I called Frank.

"I'm stranded down here, darling. I can't get a taxi. How am I going to get home?"

"Don't worry Bubbles," Frank said. "I'll send Bobby right down for you."

Well, I waited and waited. No Bobby came. I called again. As usual Frank had been drinking. I lost my temper and we had a spat over the phone. I was wondering what to do when three or four cops drove up.

"Miss Wilson?" one barked at me.

"Yes," I said, a bit puzzled.

"Mr. Tinney just called us and—"

"Oh, fine," I smiled. "You're going to take me home."

"Yeh, we're going to take you lady, but not home. You're goin' to the jailhouse."

"Jail? Why, what do you mean?" I was ruffling up again.

"Just that. You're under arrest for annoyin' Mr. Tinney. Call the wagon, Joe." He turned to one of the officers.

In a few minutes the dingy, dirty patrol wagon rolled up. One cop unlocked the grated door at the back.

"Inside, sister," the sergeant growled. He gave me a shove that almost knocked me off my feet. "You're goin' bye-bye now."

I was furious. I started screaming and pounding on the barred sides of the cage.

"You git in with her, Joe," the sergeant said. "If she gits tough, slap the cuffs on her."

I bounced around on the cold, hard seat as the patrol wagon jolted on its way. I couldn't see where we were going. Finally, the machine stopped. The cage was unlocked. We were in front of our Seventy-second street apartment.

"Oh, you did bring me home after all," I beamed.

"Naw, this is just a temporary stop," the sergeant said. "Gotta git Mr. Tinney to sign th' complaint. You sit right where you are."

The policeman went upstairs, while I started fuming again. In a little while he was back.

"Well, Judge Tinney says to release th' prisoner on her own recognizance. He'll handle th' case now."

The cops all roared and drove off. In the apartment I found Frank holding his sides over the fun he had making me ride home in a patrol wagon.

One of the most hectic nights was the time I invited a lot of guests for a party and Frank didn't show up. I had a colored orchestra from Harlem. The place was floating in champagne. I don't remember who was present that night, but W.C. Fields, a great pal of Frank's, Bert and Betty Wheeler,[12] and others from the Follies cast were usually around. When Frank didn't appear, I began to show my temper and jealousy. The longer he stayed away the more furious I got.

At last I got so angry I announced:

"I'm going to commit suicide!"

A newspaperman from one of the theatrical publications was there.

"No, don't do that, Imogene," he said. "Come along with me. I want to take you for a ride."

I threw a fur coat over my shoulders and hurried down to his car. I was so furious at Frank I didn't care where I went or what I did. The man drove me to his office. I followed him blindly into the place. He wrote something on a typewriter and handed it to me.

"Sign that," he said, "then I'll take you back and you can commit suicide."

I signed it, without ever looking at it, and we drove back to the apartment. Still Frank wasn't there. I stomped into my boudoir, put on my prettiest black lace nightgown, swallowed a few sugar-coated pills and got into bed.

My maid, Carrie, came in a few minutes later.

"Why, for lan' sakes, what are you doin' in bed, Miss Imogene?" she asked me.

"I'm committing suicide, Carrie," I said calmly.

"No, now, chile, you cain't do that with all them people out there. You just git right up from that bed this minute."

"No, Carrie, it's too late. I've already done it."

"Whadda you mean, Miss Imogene, whadda you gone an' done?"

"I've taken poison, Carrie, it won't be long now."

Poor Carrie threw up her hands and started to scream.

"Oh, Lawdy, Lawdy, Miss Imogene's done poisoned herself."

She ran crying through the rooms full of guests. "Somebody git a doctor quick."

Nobody believed me but Carrie. The guests, all various by that time, trooped into my room. I might have been dying. They couldn't have told it. They were so used to Frank's pranks that they made one of my supposed suicide. They turned the party into a wake. All of them paraded around my bed. Someone delivered a short tribute. Somebody else poured a hundred-dollar bottle of perfume over me. Others came in with an armful of lilies and arranged them on the bed. All the time I was trying to look as much like a corpse as possible. Carrie was standing in the corner crying her heart out.

While this funeral act was going on, my wandering Frank came in. He arrived just as the mourners were lifting their glasses in a toast to the departed. Carrie was the first to run to him.

"She's done killed herself, Mr. Frank. She's done killed herself."

But it wasn't his joke, so he was furious.

He stormed and raved. Everybody was ordered to leave.

The man who had taken me out stopped him.

"Just a minute, Mr. Tinney," he said. "I have a note Miss Wilson signed just before she did this. Maybe you'd like to see it. Anyway, here it is."

Frank grabbed it out of his hand. I had signed a statement saying I was killing myself because of Frank.

He tore the paper to bits.

"That's all right, Mr. Tinney," the man smiled. "I expected you would do that. I have the original in my office and will publish it any time your conduct warrants it."

At the time I began living with Frank Tinney I didn't know he was married. I didn't know it for a good many months afterward, although I began having my suspicions that there was another woman in his life. His wife, Edna Davenport, was older than Frank. He was twenty years older than I. He depended a lot on his wife. She was steady and a good manager. The first time I ever saw Mrs. Tinney was backstage at the Music Box one night.

"Who is that woman?" I asked him.

"She's my manager," he replied.

"Well, you fire her right now," I ordered.

"All right, Bubbles, she's fired." He waved a dismissing hand at his wife. She merely smiled.

One of my silliest tricks was a habit I had of cutting out all the pictures I could find of Frank and pinning them all over my dress. Being a big star, his pictures were in the papers and theatrical dailies all the time. My cut-out costume pleased him, so I sued to bedeck myself with pictures to greet him when he came backstage.

Mrs. Tinney came into Frank's dressing room one day when I was rigged up like that. She looked at the cut-outs, laughed, and talked about them, but didn't intimate that she was Frank's wife. Frank called her "ED." When I used to get curious about his phone conversations he would dismiss the matter saying:

"Oh, that was Ed."

And I didn't catch on.

They had a country home where Mrs. Tinney lived. Frank frequently went there on week-ends, getting away from me on some sort of pretext, but the rest of the time he lived in our apartment.

A thing that hurt me a lot was the time I thought Frank was buying me a car. He had taken me around to all the showrooms and looked at this limousine and that that one until I finally found one, a gorgeous big town car. I was really bubbling over at the thought of having my own car.

"We'll have your monogram put on the doors," Frank explained.

The next day the car was driven up to the apartment. I flew down to inspect it. The first thing that caught my eye was that monogram. Instead of my initials, the lettering read "EDT." I had spent a week picking out a car I dreamed was to be my own, only to find it was being given to Mrs. Tinney. I still think I had reason to get mad and make a scene that time. Anyway, I did.

That night I went out to Long Island to the Tinney country home. It was the first time I ever had been there when Frank's wife was around and I made it a memorable call. Half of Long Island probably heard the commotion. When that scene ended I left. Frank was with me but I didn't have my car, although he gave me one soon after that to placate my feelings. But I must tell you about the wildest night of our whole mad life.

Frank and I had an agreement. As soon as the curtain fell at the Follies, I would rush over to meet Frank at the Music Box. If his show was over first, he would come to the Follies for me. If we missed each other we were to go straight to the apartment. One night Frank had left the Music Box when I arrived. I thought nothing of that and drove on to the apartment, but Frank wasn't there. Friends always were dropping in. Frank kept continuous open house and open bar. A lot of people came in that night.

Like the time I attempted "suicide," I began getting mad. I was jealous as well as spoiled. I made no attempt to conceal my feelings. Frank's friends knew he had gone to the country to see his wife, but, of course, they didn't want to tell me. It wasn't so much where he was that irritated me. It was the fact he wasn't with me. I finally called Frank's number in the country and that's where he was.

"Well, you just stay right there." I stormed at him. "There's no use coming back here because I'm leaving you. I'm going for good."

Everybody was getting drunk. They all chimed in with me. They said I should leave him. I was having fits after finding him with his wife. I thought it was outrageous that a man should leave me and go home to his wife. Carrie tried to soothe me, but I didn't want anyone to touch me. In my struggles with her, I kicked her in the mouth and knocked a tooth out. That was enough for the guests. They decided it was time to leave.

I ran through the place breaking up everything I could get my hands on. The place was a shambles when Frank finally raced in a little while later. At the sight of him I dealt my final blow of destruction. I struck a match and threw it into a pile of litter on the drawing room floor. As the flames began to leap up toward the ceiling, Carrie grabbed the phone and yelled for the firemen. The drapes and furnishings started to blaze.

"Bubbles, Bubbles!" Frank shouted. "You'll have to get out of here or you'll burn to death."

He moved toward me. My answer was a kick on the shins that made him howl. By that time smoke was pouring out of the windows. The howl of sirens was close. In a few minutes a squad of firemen burst into the suite. It was then that Frank did one of those silly, crazy things that always made me forgive everything.

He flopped down at the piano that already was being scorched by the fire. His fingers rippled over the keys for an instant, then struck the notes of a current hit, and how appropriate, "Won't You Come Back to Our Alley, Sally."

Just as if he had been on the stage he thumped out that rolling tune and sang it at the top of his voice. Firemen were rushing all over the place.

"Sorry, boys, to cause this trouble," Frank turned his head while his hands played on. "One of the guests must have dropped a cigarette."

It was too much for me. By that time, I was sitting on the one chair that wasn't on fire, crying my eyes out. Between myself, the fire, and the firemen, our apartment was worse than an alley, but I went back.

✦ ✦ ✦

The luxurious lives led by the Follies girls of those days seems fantastic and almost unbelievable today. They basked in favors and priceless gifts such as no fabled princess ever received. We had so many beautiful gowns, furs and jewels it always was a problem to decide which to wear. It was part of our business to go on as many parties as possible, to be seen by important people, to meet as many prominent persons as we could. Mr. Ziegfeld encouraged that. The more admirers and suitors a Follies girl had, the more the fame of the Follies spread, the more crowds lined up to see that aggregation of beauties perform. How we lived through that unceasing round of activity is more than I can understand. We were all young. We were overstimulated by the excitement of it all. But we were living too fast a pace. It swept many of us from the spotlight of fame to the obscurity of disaster.

However, there is one thing about those fantastic parties that I want to make clear. The girls never were promiscuous in their conduct.

Oh, of course, those affairs hardly would be called sedate, what with the champagne baths for novitiates, nude models arrayed the walls in the form of living scenery, but they were not the orgies many persons believed. The girls were on their good behavior. Perhaps you might say they were playing a smart game. They were the guests of men of great wealth and influence. They were playing their cards cleverly. They were making acquaintances that they knew would lead to a meeting with other men of prominence.

Naturally, affairs of a more intimate nature developed out of these friendships but our parties were quite decorous.

Likewise, not every man looked upon a Follies girl with lust in his eyes. One of the sweetest episodes in my life was the admiration showered upon me by a man I never met.

He was a wealthy New York banker. He must have been past sixty years of age. I was just a child, perhaps a beautiful one as many were kind enough to say, in his eyes. I received a note from him soon after I joined the Follies as Miss America. It was enclosed in a huge box of candy and merely expressed his appreciation.

Then he began coming to the show every Saturday matinee. Always he occupied the same seat in the front row. I believe he must have bought a reservation for the season. Every Saturday just before the curtain a messenger would appear at my dressing room with a package. It always was a box of candy. Inside each week was a hundred-dollar bill. The container was usually different. Frequently it would be a big doll, just filled with pounds of the finest candies. I remember one gorgeous figure that broke open at the middle. There, as usual, when I opened it was a crisp, new bill.

The notes he used to send with the candy each Saturday were sweet. There never was a hint of anything evil in his mind, nothing vulgar, nothing suggestive. They usually were quite simple:

"Dear Miss Wilson: Please accept this little token of appreciation from an admirer who is made very happy by your loveliness."

Then he began adding:

"Please smile at me."

It was an old man's whim that was almost childish. I always knew where he was sitting. He was very distinguished in his appearance, with snow white hair and high collar. He always got the sweetest smile I could give him. That slight attention was all that he wanted for favors of presents and money that ran into thousands of dollars. He never asked me to meet him and never asked me for a date. I regarded him then as I do now as a kindly old man who gained his own measure of happiness in that way, by bestowing his generosity in exchange for a smile and a nod from a Follies girl. The price seems high but the terms were of his own making and must have pleased him.

After my affair with Frank Tinney broke into an open scandal, I had my only conversation with this man and that was by telephone. He called and extended his sympathy.

"Miss Wilson, I would like to offer you the refuge of my country home," he said, "if it will enable you to get away from this trouble. You will have complete privacy, the use of my stables, servants, everything at my command."

I thanked him and my thanks were from the bottom of my heart. I couldn't accept, but I cherish my memory of that man as one of the utterly selfless persons I have ever known. He wanted so little, only a smile, in return for his remarkable generosity!

Most of the others were so different. They thought their wealth should purchase anyone of their desires, body and soul. And the Follies girls were regarded as fair game in the chase. Life seemed to give us everything for a time, then cast many of us aside. Some, of course, weathered the deluge of adulation and went on to further successes. Others were buffeted into miserable oblivion.

A twinge wrenched my heart some months ago when I read of the tragic death of Jessie Reed[13] in a Chicago charity ward. She was one of us who had everything, unrivaled beauty, millionaire suitors, wealth, great success. Poor Jessie died penniless, her life wrecked by drink, her beauty faded, forgotten by her fair-weather friends of earlier days.

Next week, I will tell you more about my Follies days and about the screaming scandal that hounded me from Broadway and drove from America to seek refuge in a foreign land.

Chapter 3

My life with Frank Tinney was a nonsensical mixture of fights and laughs, about half and half. Those mad, merry days of the Follies—and follies—now seem rather symbolic of my whole life, a contrasting combination of great happiness and acclaim mixed with bitter heartaches and public censure. Frank's jealousy in some matters was almost childish. He and Carrie, my negro maid, used to quarrel constantly over the most trivial things. He always insisted on drawing my bath, a function which Carrie, quite properly, thought she was qualified to perform, but Frank wouldn't have it that way. Not a bit of it. That was one of the little pet attention he wanted to show me.

It was almost a ritual with him. And I can still see Carrie, a good soul, standing aside, her big arms akimbo, with an expression of utter disgust as Frank, humming a tune and tapping his feet, tested the water temperature, selected bath salts of a scent that just suited him, and then announced to "Her Ladyship" that her bath was ready. Perhaps Carrie was annoyed because he did the job so expertly.

Sometimes Frank would shout at her or throw something at her to drive her from her room. At other times he would just whistle or hum, ignoring her, while he went on with his self-assumed duties as lady's maid, combing my hair over his finger and putting on my makeup. He could be the sweetest person in the world one minutes and a little later would do something that made me hate him.

One-day Frank and I had our usual dish-hurling breakfast fight. He left the apartment in a rage. I was in tears. Carrie was still trying to soothe my ruffled feelings a couple hours later when Frank phoned. Carrie answered the call. I was too mad to talk.

"Mister Frank says he's ju' got to talk to you, Miss Imogene," Carrie reported. "Says it's somethin' awful important."

I relented and picked up the phone.

"Listen, Bubbles darling, don't be so angry with me." I never had heard so much sincerity in his voice before.

"One of the greatest things in my life has just happened to me."

Of course, that aroused my curiosity.

"I've just met a very important individual. He has power and position. I've invited him to dinner. You must help me entertain him royally and make a favorable impression. Get flowers. Have Carrie fix her finest dinner. You better hurry to the beauty parlor and dress your best. Promise me, darling, you'll help to make this evening a great success. It means everything to me."

I was won by that time. The morning quarrel was forgotten. I loved to meet important people and we outdid ourselves putting things in order. Carrie called in a florist who almost banked the dining room in flowers.

"This is a great occasion," I told her. "Mr. Tinney is bringing a very important man to dinner. Probably a big politician like a Senator or somebody like that. Fix up the finest dinner you've ever cooked."

I hurried off to the beauty parlor around the corner and went for everything—

massage, rub, manicure and hairdo. A couple of hours later I heard Bobby, Frank's negro valet, running up and down the corridor.

"What booth's she in?" he asked excitedly.

The manager told him. He parted the curtains and stepped in just as the attendant was finishing my hair.

"Mister Frank's home." He said. "You-all better come right up." Bobby's actions showed plainly that something was wrong.

"Is he terribly drunk?" I asked. That always was my first fear.

"No, Miss, not particularly."

"Is his guest with him?"

"Yessum." Bobby rolled the white of his eyes and dropped his head. "I reckon so."

I was in a dither. Here I wasn't dressed. Frank would be angry and there would be a scene with a strange guest present. Bobby knew all the symptoms when a storm was brewing, so it was no wonder he hung his head. I hurried up to the apartment, slipped into my boudoir unseen, and put on my finest gown. With a final glance into the mirror I walked sedately into the living room to be presented.

"I'm so sorry, dear, if I'm late, but—"

The words froze to my lips.

Frank was there, wearing his most engaging smile. In a corner, seated on a chaise lounge, was a donkey! (It was the smallest donkey I ever saw. Its front feet were planted on an ottoman.)

On the floor beside it was a girl from the beauty parlor, busily giving the jackass a manicure. Around its throat was a gorgeous necklace. I almost fainted. I thought I was steeled to most of Frank's pranks, but this was too much.

"It's quite all right, darling. You're not late at all. Miss Wilson, may I present my distinguished friend."

The silly thing brayed and wiggles its long ears. I wanted to tear Frank to pieces. I began throwing ash trays, table lamps, anything I could get my hands on. As usual, his fine footwork kept him out of range of my missiles. The manicure girl swooped up her tray and ran for safety. The donkey just sat.

"But, Bubbles darling, you don't understand." Frank yelled, as he ran behind chairs to keep out of my way. "This is really a very important individual."

I let another ash tray fly.

"You're not showing him proper respect."

At last I ran out of energy and things to throw.

"Now, darling, have Carrie serve the dinner." Frank said something to the donkey. It lumbered to its feet and followed him into the dining room. Poor Carrie had a wonderful dinner spread out on the table. At a word from Frank the donkey squatted on the honored guest's chair that Frank indicated and plopped its manicured front hooves on our finest linen.

Well, of course, I refused to sit down. I was so furious I couldn't speak. I just sputtered. Frank insisted that Carrie serve the dinner. I can laugh about it now, but it was tragic to me at the time. There was that donkey at the table with Frank, seated in the midst of our elegant furnishings, and surrounded by the loveliest flowers I could buy. Frank would talk and the silly animal acted as if it understood him.

"I didn't deceive you when I told you our guest was distinguished," Frank said. "You are being unreasonable and offending your visitor. This is a sacred donkey. It's endowed by the gods. It knows everything and always speaks the truth."

Carrie stopped in her tracks and opened her eyes a little wider than that.

"I'm entertaining his Sacred Highness tonight because there are a few questions I want answered truthfully," Frank went on.

"Are you ready, Your Highness?" The donkey nodded and almost stuck his nose in the caviar.

"Very well. Is Bubbles true to me?"

The donkey shook its head violently, its big ears flopping around its head like a pair of arms.

"All right. Am I true to Bubbles?"

The donkey nodded its head up and down.

"Now, does Bubbles love me?" the donkey shook its head vigorously again.

"Do I love Bubbles?" Another affirmative nod.

"Thank you, Your Highness. That's what I wanted to know."

By this time Carrie's mouth was hanging open. Her eyes were the size of teacups and almost as white. Bobby was trembling. I think they were afraid Frank would ask something about them.

"Now, Carrie, you may serve the champagne."

Carrie brought in a cold bottle. Frank poured half of it in a bowl and sat it before the donkey. The animal sipped it up, then curled its lips in an appreciative gesture. After they left the table, Frank sat down at the piano. As he played, the donkey pranced around over the rug, keeping step to the music. A few minutes later there was a loud bray.

"His Sacred Highness says he would like to go to your bathroom," Frank interrupted.

I screamed.

"No, no, you fool. I've stood for all the rest, but you're not going to take that animal into my bath. You've had your fun. Now get that thing out of here."

I started a fresh barrage of ash trays. That time Frank retreated with his shaggy guest trotting along behind him. He led it downstairs, put it in the back seat of the taxi with him and then drove off. My nerves were shattered and Carrie was in a worse shape than I. It was days before I convinced her that the animal Frank brought home for dinner and a laugh was just a trained donkey that he had picked up and not a sacred creature with supernatural powers.

Frank always brought his check to me. It was $2,000[14] a week and a percentage of the box office. One of our many fights started one day soon after he had given me his check. I stomped out of the apartment and went on a wild shopping spree. I made the rounds of all the expensive shops and bought the most expensive hats I could find—dozens of them.

A couple hours after I started, delivery men began streaming into our apartment, each one with an armful of hat boxes. Frank knew what that meant. He knew his paycheck was going fast. After I had bought all the latest millinery creations on Fifth Avenue, I dropped into a telegraph office and sent Frank this wire:

"Having gorgeous time. Just bought seven hundred dollars' worth of hats. Am in Central Park now spending the rest of your money for peanuts to feed the ducks."

I waited in my car outside the apartment until I saw the messenger boy deliver the telegram and I decided that was a good time to make an entrance. Frank was pacing the floor, the telegram in his hand, when I walked in.

"Whew! Am I glad you're home," he signed. "I was just starting for the park. With delivery boys parading in here with enough hats to stock a store, I though the peanuts business was on the level."

That was one of the few times it was my turn to laugh, but it was a pretty expensive joke with anybody's money. I remembered it, too, in later years when I walked through Central Park without enough money in my pocket to buy a bag of peanuts for myself.

Central Park is a place that holds many memories for me. It was the scene of the sweetest moments Frank and I ever spent together. It was one of the few places we ever were truly alone. Our apartment was like an open bar. Friends trooped in at all hours of the night. Usually something happened that started a fight between Frank and me. But occasionally we would slip out at 2 or 3 o'clock in the morning, get in Frank's touring car and drive until daylight, just the two of us. There were no quarrels, no harsh words, no bitterness then. Those moments were lovely. No grief that overtook me later ever was great enough to rob me of those sweet memories.

But each day always brought back its revive of the constant turmoil that beset our lives. Or of a silly protective notion that I had developed a suicide complex. I have told of the episode when I swallowed some harmless pills and went to bed to die with an apartment full of guests just because Frank was late getting home. After that it became a habit. I used the threat to kill myself as a weapon, thinking it might jolt Frank out of his drinking and abuse. He knew I was fooling better than I did and made a joke of my suicidal tantrums.

Whenever I reached the climax of a quarrel with my threat to end it all, Frank would smile:

"All right, Bubbles, what kind of flowers do you want?"

He cured me of that bad habit one night. He was late, but finally phoned about two o'clock in the morning.

"There's no need of coming home now," I shrieked, "I've taken poison! I'm dying!"

"Oh, darling, that's terrible," he said. "I'll fix everything at once."

I was thoroughly enjoying my pout, hoping I had convinced Frank at last that I was in earnest, when the bell rang, half an hour later. Carrie answered it and hurried into my bedroom wide-eyed.

"Miss Imogene," she stammered, "Miss Imogene, they's two strange gennelmun here."

"Well, what do they want?" I said.

"They got a funny-lookin' basket an' says they's come for the remains."

I jumped up and ran into the reception hall. Sure enough, there stood two sad-faced men, dressed in somber garb, representatives of an undertaking establishment.

"May we extend our condolences?" one said. "Mr. Tinney called. Are you a relative of the deceased?"

"No, you idiots," I screamed. "I'm the corpse. Now get out of here with that hideous thing—and be quick about it."

Of course, Frank stepped in a few minutes later, to appear surprised at finding me alive and to enjoy his ghastly joke. I gave up the suicide idea after that.

Douglas Fairbanks and Mary Pickford were in New York taking in the shows. Naturally, they were receiving a lot of attention. Doug and his attire were the talk of the town. Frank was being crowded out of the limelight as the Beau Brummel of Broadway. Frank was intrigued by a fine pair of shows Doug was wearing, so he phoned to ask Fairbanks where he got them. Doug told him. Frank could hardly wait to get down to the place, a shop that specialized in English-made apparel. The price was thirty-five dollars. Frank paid it cheerfully and hurried home with his shoes, but I don't believe he ever had them on. The first thing, I knew he was shining them with my white ermine evening wrap.

"I'll get you another one, Bubbles, if I spoil it," he tried to calm me. "Nothing's too good for these shoes. Can't take a chance of hurting them."

When he finished polishing them with my expensive fur, he placed them on top of the grand piano, where everyone could see them. He led the guests to them as if they were looking at a rare piece of art. We used to walk down Broadway with Frank and his stocking feet, carrying his fancy shoes in his hands.

"Why make a fool of yourself where everybody can see you?" I would say.

"Darling, they're too expensive to wear, but I want the world to know if Fairbanks can afford thirty-five-dollar shoes I can, too."

※ ※ ※

For a time, my affair with Frank started, it was kept pretty quiet except for the theatrical folks, who knew of our relationship. They regarded some things with a broad view. Our lives were our own business, according to the code of the footlights.

Even Flo Ziegfeld didn't know about it for quite a while. Will Page, his press agent, was delegated to be my good shepherd, scare off the over-amorous playboys, and see that I got in at a respectable hour. Well, poor Will had his troubles. Naturally, he quickly discovered I was living at Frank's apartment. He finally had to tell Mr. Ziegfeld that his "Miss America," so highly acclaimed as a model of girlhood, was being a bit unconventional for such a role. Mr. Ziegfeld was quite annoyed. He called me into his office shortly after that.

"Emmy," he used his pet nickname for Imogene that I so abhorred. "What's this I'm hearing about you and Frank Tinney?"

He didn't wait for me to answer.

"I'm satisfied these stories are true. You're just a child. I'm not going to have you spoiled by running around with that man. It has to stop."

"But, Mr. Ziegfeld—"

"Never mind, Emmy, I'll handle the matter. I'll speak to Mr. Tinney myself."

"Oh, no, Mr. Ziegfeld," I pleaded, "please don't do that. If you do, he'll have you fired!"

Yes, I was still a child. In my eyes Frank Tinney was the greatest man on Broadway. It didn't occur to me that Mr. Ziegfeld was the one who would have the say if any firing was to be done.

"Very well, Emmy," Mr. Ziegfeld smiled. "I'll risk the consequences. You'll be much better off if you end this association."

I didn't need his kindly advice. The merry-go-round was whirling too rapidly then to jump off. I was living for the present, living gloriously, I thought, not consciously doing anything wrong, just following each moment for its pleasures, basking in my popularity and fame as a Follies celebrity. The present suddenly had become so full for me there was no time to think of the morrow, nor head the consequences.

Soon stories began appearing in print. The fights Frank and I were having couldn't remain hidden forever. Our life became tempestuous, our quarrels more bitter. Things were moving swiftly to a climax.

One day in the Spring of 1924 Frank had been drinking more heavily than usual. He was in his bedroom asleep when a friend called to see me. My caller was a young fellow who had shown a kindly interest in me around the Follies. I was new in my career. He was trying to become a reporter, which he did, and a good one, too. I liked him because he was natural and real, but he didn't belong to the silk-stocking, ermine-wrap set in which I was traveling, because he was young and didn't have thousands to throw away on frivolities.

Frank roused from his sleep one day while my friend was still there. Hearing voices, he thought someone of our crowd probably had dropped in for a drink. So, with his usual yearning for a gag, he slipped into Carrie's purple bathrobe, put on her gaudy earrings and walked in, trying for a laugh.

Never had I seen him look so ludicrous as he did in that get-up. Never had I seen him as mad as he got that day. There was nothing wrong, but the sight of my friend and myself sitting together, talking, infuriated him beyond words.

"Soo-o-o, while I rest this goes on—in my own home," he stormed. "Who in h—— is this —— if I may ask?"

"Now, Frank, be reasonable," I tried to explain. "This is Mr. ——, a friend of mine, who just happened to drop in."

"I understand. I understand. That's old stuff. Don't try to explain. Shut my eyes for a minute and I find this whelp in here. I'll break his d—— neck and yours, too."

With that outburst, Frank threw off the bathrobe and made a rush at my friend. My screams for help brought faithful Carrie on the run. In an instant Frank had this poor chap on the floor, beating him unmercifully. Carrie and I pitched in and tried to pry him off, but he brushed us off. Frank wasn't a big man, and with all the drinking he did I don't know where he got his strength, but I never saw so much violence come out of one man. His fists pounded on that fellow's face until the man was limp.

Then Frank grabbed him by the collar and dragged him out of the apartment. As he turned, he flew at me.

We'd had fights before and Frank had struck me before, but never a knock-down and drag-out affair like this one. He was a maniac. He couldn't have known what he was doing. He beat me horribly, with me screaming, kicking and clawing with all my might. But I was powerless against him. Carrie jumped into the battle to help me.

"Lawd-a-massy, Mister Frank, you'all's a-killing that chile."

Frank was too blinded with rage by that time to speak—or hear. His blows kept coming. Carrie hurled her heavy weight against him and knocked him off balance for a moment. When she came at him again, he was on his guard. That time he raised his foot and landed a vicious kick in her stomach. By that time my eyes were swollen and my lips bleeding. His anger spent, I think Frank began to sober up and come to his senses. In a few minutes the police arrived and he was overpowered.

"Take him to jail," I demanded. "Don't ever let him out."

A doctor was called. He ordered an ambulance for Carrie at once and went to work patching me up. Before he had finished the job, the phone rang. It was Frank.

"Bubbles darling. I'm sorry."

With my head bursting I couldn't appreciate his honeyed words.

"Where are you?" I cried.

"I'm at the station, darling. The captain just released me. I'm coming home to make it up to you."

"No, no, don't you dare. I'll kill you if you step into this apartment."

I called back and demanded that he be rearrested. He was but I couldn't keep him in jail. Five times that night we went through that procedure until I finally convinced the entire police force that I wanted him kept in jail. Then, when at last I succeeded, Frank did one of his typical tricks, one of those things that helps explain my attachment for him. When he was languishing behind the bars, he wrote a song which he dedicated to me. It was: "You're in Love with Everyone but the One Who's in Love with You."

And the next morning I had one of my weaker moments too. Of course, after the fight our apartment was overrun with cops, reporters and photographers. Mr. Ziegfeld soon learned what had happened and sent Will Page to keep everybody out. Early the next morning, Bobby, the valet, came in. He had been down to the jail to see Frank.

"Man, you sure has to have a passport to get in this place now," he said. "Miss Imogene, Mister Frank sent me up to get him a clean shirt—and some whiskey—to take to him down in the jailhouse."

That's when I weakened.

"Oh, Bobby," I sobbed, "does he look bad?"

"Yeasum, kinda, but not half as bad as you do, Miss."

That reminder of my own discolored eyes, cut lips and bruised body shook me back to reality and I got mad all over again. As soon as I was able, later that day, I moved out. When I went, I stole all of Frank's clothes. I wore one suit and carried the others.

The whole world knew now and was pointing its accusing finger. Overnight, from a position of envy and admiration, I found myself singled out as an object of abhorrence and contempt. A silly girl, living in a fool's paradise, paying the price for her folly. That, perhaps, was the kindest of the shafts leveled at me. I didn't try to vindicate myself. I didn't try to lay the blame on Frank. I'm glad today that I didn't.

He was at fault, yes. But merely because I didn't know any better than to become his mistress, should I blame him alone? I don't think so. I paid the price, higher than all the jewels and baubles that money could buy, as the subsequent events I am about to relate will show, but my conscious was clear. I am thankful for that when I think of others who came into my life later. The anguish they caused me leaves Frank Tinney in a place of high esteem in my memories of men I have known. Frank went down, too, in the wreckage that tumbled about us. Mothers mentioned our names only in whispers. Clubwomen all over the land took up the hue and cry against us. From headliners, acclaimed by throngs, we became the untouchables, shunned by everybody.

Everybody, that is, but Broadway. The theatrical world was kind to me. Mr. Ziegfeld tried to protect me from the storm in every way he could. The howl of protest rose in a mounting crescendo. Frank saw that he was beaten. He was through as a Broadway star. Thinking the storm might subside during my absence, he sailed for Europe and was promptly engaged at the Empire Theatre in London. Between our flight and Frank's departure, our intimate life was broken, but the night he sailed I went to the boat to see him off.

With Frank gone, I felt the sense of freedom again. I felt a release from the bondage in which I had been held. Once more I reached out for the freedom I've fought for all my life, freedom from the convent's close confines, freedom from poverty, freedom from circumstances that shackled me to misalliances, freedom from the horrors of dope. Even then I didn't realize that the world already had turned its back on me. It was during those Summer months that I met Arnold Rothstein.[15]

He was an intriguing, mysterious character, not handsome but possessed of a quiet, dominating trait that attracted women to him. The men who associated with him were of two classes, those who hated him and those who feared him. There were none who liked him.

The first night I visited Rothstein's place was another revelation to the little country girl, who after two years in the big city still was befuddled by its mysterious ways. The first floor of his establishment was fitted up as a piano store. The place enjoyed a huge patronage, but the piano stock held little interest for the visitors. A stairway led to the floor above. There was one of the most elaborate gambling layouts I have ever seen. Roulette tables and dice tables filled the room. Almost everyone was in evening dress.

I knew Rothstein as a gambler, a cold, unflinching figure whose wagers on the turn of a card, the roll of a dice, or the nose of a horse were counted in hundreds of thousands. But even then he may have been the master mind of a nationwide dope ring, as he was shown to be a few years later when he was shot in a killing that rocked the underworld. That illicit traffic in narcotics, bartered for a stream of dollars from the trembling hands of dope-crazed addicts, netted him millions before he was slain.

That would have meant little to me then, even if I had known of it. Little did I dream when I accepted his hospitality that I too would live to know the day when I would be a victim of that curse on which he attended, a member of the army of the living dead, those poor unfortunate souls who put their blood money to sate an unbearable craving. No, I remember Rothstein chiefly as a most gracious host, a man who loved to be surrounded by beautiful women and willing to pay handsomely for their company.

Through my acquaintance with Rothstein I met a man who lavished more money on me than any other admirer I ever had. He was a retired millionaire, old enough to be my grandfather, but his years didn't keep him from falling madly in love with me. He overwhelmed me with expensive gifts, furs, diamonds, the most gorgeous bracelet I ever owned, and an expensive car. When he learned I was thinking of going to London to rejoin Frank Tinney, he begged me to marry him, offered me anything I could name if I would give up the idea. Frank was drinking heavily again. He refused to rehearse. He wouldn't go on for his act unless I promised to go to him.

My life had been too closely linked with his to ignore Frank's pleas. In spite of all he had done to me, I hated to think that his great genius might die because of me.

At last I relented and made my plans to sail, booking passage as Mary Robertson, the name of my adopted parents. Then, finally I was on my way, embarked on a great new adventure that was destined to bring more thrills, more heartaches with Frank, new love affairs with naïve suitors of the continent, acquaintance with royalty, and success as a film star in Germany. I had cabled Frank I was on my way. He had made every arrangement to expedite my landing. He didn't meet me, but had sent his representative to whisk me to his big flat in West London.

It seemed a little strange that he didn't even greet me at the door, but I understood the minute I stepped inside. My arrival had to be observed with something typical of Tinney originality.

The first thing I saw was an aisle of eggs, two long rows of them, ending at a big chair at the far end of the room. There of course, sat Frank, his feet on a cushion, a scepter in his hand, the king of comedy on his throne, receiving his queen—or his humble servant—as his mood might be. I laughed at the ridiculous setting.

"The eggs? Why the avenue of eggs?"

"Bubbles darling, you always looked to me like you were walking on them. I just wanted to make your entrance a little more realistic."

My hopes that our separation might have changed Frank were in vain. He became more exacting, more dependent on me than ever. I had to play nursemaid to him. Still drinking, he wouldn't put on his makeup at the theater unless I was there. He wouldn't rehearse unless I went with him. I will never forget his first appearance on the stage after I arrived. He demanded that I sit in the front row. As he walked on, his eyes were fixed on me. The spotlight caught him in its glare.

"No, no," he yelled at the operator, pointing his finger at me. "Put the spot on Bubbles!"

The audience was polite. It was English. It had paid its money to see Frank Tinney perform, not to look at me. But that made no difference to Frank. His entire show was directed at me. He wouldn't even look at the others.

"This is for you, Bubbles," he said time and again.

After that experience I kept out of the audience and stayed in the wings, but I had to be there, watching his every move, or Frank wouldn't perform.

I arrived in London on October. By December a new crisis had arisen in our lives. Frank's drinking became worse. My efforts to help him were getting nowhere. I wanted my own career and had a chance to go to work in pictures in Germany. Those circumstances led to our final break. It came in a dramatic setting marked by a foreboding of violent death and ended in a tender New Year's kiss outside a fog-shrouded London window. But that will have to be told next week, with other details of my life in Europe.

Chapter 4

A memorable incident of my first days in London was the night King George V and Queen Mary attended the theater where Frank Tinney was appearing. The royal box was draped with the British flag and the Stars and Stripes. A detachment of brightly uniformed guards stood silently alertly behind the King and Queen. The theater was packed. As the curtain rose, the orchestra burst into the strains of "God Save the King." Everyone was on his feet. It was most impressive and solemn. When the last notes of the music died away, Frank walked to the footlights and turned toward the royal couple.

"Hi, George!"

He grinned and spoke as casually as if he had been addressing a pal from Broadway. A few gasps and restrained titters swept the audience. The English were shocked at such easy familiarity, but that didn't stop Frank.

"You know, George," he went on, "I really like your country, but I'm miserable here. I've been here six weeks now and I haven't been able to get a bath."

There was another scattering of horrified "ohs" from the spectators.

"And it's all your fault, George. Every time I get in a tub and start to sit down, somebody starts playing 'God Save the King' and there I am, standing at attention in my bath."

That's an old gag now, but it was new then—and funny.

The King chuckled, and that broke the tense reserve of the audience. Before the performance was over, Frank had won them all. When he walked off the stage, King George stood and applauded. He had captured the hearts of the aloof Londoners. If all of Frank Tinney's life could only have been of such moments. But that was not to be. Our second try at life together soon was following the same old pattern, ruled by liquor, fights and jealousy. I realized it couldn't go on that way. Besides, I wanted my chance at a career. I couldn't see why Frank wanted to deprive me of that, but he did. He wanted me for himself alone. To try to make me more contented, Frank's manager got me an opportunity to play a role in "Madame Pompadour." When Frank heard about that, he went wild.

"You can't work," he shouted. "I won't let you. I want you with me."

Well, he refused to budge and began drinking more heavily than usual. I gave up that chance. He demanded that I remain constantly at his beck and call. Frank was just as popular in London as he had been on Broadway, if not more so. And as in New York, our flat was overrun with his friends and admirers. Titled celebrities, even the Prince of Wales, were his guests. I felt left out at those affairs. Perhaps I stood too much in awe of Frank's haughty friends. I had been somebody in New York. In London with Frank's associates I was a nobody again. My old inferiority complex came to the fore once more.

I wasn't jealous of Frank, but I felt that I didn't belong in the party. I resented the coolness of those who admired him. Perhaps I was jealous of the attention showered on him by his fine friends. At any rate it heightened my resolve to be somebody in my own right. After giving up my chance on the stage at Frank's demand I was asked by Sidney Drew to take a part in a picture, *Afraid of Love*. That was an appropriate title for me, too. I was afraid of love by that time, but there seemed no way out of the mess.

"I'll burn the studio down if you do it," Frank roared at me. "I'll go out there and shoot everybody. You can't do it."

He kept up that tirade with a bottle of whiskey always by his side, until I gave in.

"All right, Frank," I told him. "You win. I won't do it."

This was the last of December, nearly three months after I had rejoined Frank. By that time, I was ill. Frank was in terrible shape, too. We called in doctors for him and one of them told me I was doomed to break and die if I didn't leave him at once. Our crazy mad life was killing me. Frank was becoming more violent all the time. He got so cruel with his valet, Bobby, who had come over on the boat with me, that I had to send him back to New York to get him out of Frank's sight. I was almost a prisoner in the eight-room flat we had in West London. The Italian valet we engaged after Bobby went home began telling me about a persistent man who kept calling to see me about a picture contract.

I knew I didn't dare see him at the flat. I remembered only too well what had happened in New York when Frank found me talking to a caller. He was watching me even more closely now. But my determination was growing. I was getting frantic to break away from the captive-like life I was leading. I couldn't resist the lure of the offers that were coming to me to build my own career while I had youth and beauty. Finally, I told the valet to make an appointment for me the next time the man called. I would make some excuse to get away. It was arranged for me to meet the caller at the Piccadilly. Two men met me, representatives of the German UFA company. They offered a contract to play in German pictures at a figure equivalent to $1,000 a week. I signed. Then I was too frightened to tell Frank. I was supposed to leave for Germany on New Year's Day. Between Christmas and New Year's, I mustered all my courage.

"Frank, I've signed a contract to go to Germany in pictures," I managed to say. "Isn't that wonderful? You can go on here. We can still see each other."

The words rolled from my lips but Frank had heard only the first few. He looked at me strangely.

"Let me see that contract." His voice was cold and bitter. "I'll tear it up!"

I evaded with some excuse about not having it with me.

"Very well, Bubbles. I've put my foot on the stage for the last time, if you don't tear up that contract."

He turned slowly and walked into the bedroom.

As I've said, I loved Frank Tinney's talent, not the man. We never really knew each other. It's sometimes like that. I could hate him at home, then watch him for five minutes on the stage and forgive everything. I didn't want to see him throw himself away. I followed him to the door. He slipped off his dressing gown and got into bed—with a bottle.

"I'm going to rest, Bubbles," he said. Then coldly, "I'll murder anybody who comes in this bedroom. Fire the servants—all of them. I want you here with me alone."

I hurriedly called the doctors.

"Miss Wilson, it's very dangerous for you to be here alone with that man," they told me. "We have studied him and must tell you he plans to kill you. This is your warning."

I thought they might be right. I knew Frank wasn't in his right mind. The two or three quarts of whiskey he had been drinking were only a starter now. The doctors ordered male nurses. Frank was put on reduced whiskey rations. I believe it started with three ounces every hour. The first nurse failed to give Frank all he wanted and he almost made good his threat to murder the first person who stepped in his room. Where he got the strength to do it in his condition I don't know, but he beat that nurse unmercifully. He was a maniac. He almost tore that man to pieces before he finally hurled him out of the door. I was terrified, but knew from past experience not to interfere. I really thought he would kill the nurse.

The doctors came hurrying back.

"He is planning to do to you just what he did to that nurse," they told me. "You'll be killed the minutes you're alone with him. As his common law wife, we must insist that you have him committed to an institution."

They showed me pictures of the room he would have, and boasted about the care, but no matter how they described the place it still was an asylum.

"No, I won't do that," I told them. "You may call me his common law wife, but we're closer than that. Such a decision will have to be made by his father."

I cabled Frank's father what the doctor wanted me to do. He was irate and threatened dire things if I allowed Frank to be sent to an asylum. With that backing I put my foot down.

"Frank stays here," I told the doctors. "Threats or not I'm going to do my best to take care of him."

"Very well, young lady," they said. "We have been studying Mr. Tinney and know what's wrong with him. Now I think we had better analyze you. None of us can understand why a beautiful girl like you falls in love with a vulgar comedian—"

"You won't be alive tomorrow morning."

"Get out!" I cried. "All of you. You're discharged!"

They went, doctors, nurses and servants, everybody. But as silence settled over the rooms that had been in such a turmoil for days, I couldn't dismiss the doctors' warning no matter how I tried.

"He's going to kill you! He's going to kill you!"

The words dinned through my ears with every step, like some refrain. Then, in the first calm moment I had had all week, came recollection that momentarily had been blotted out—that night was New Year's Eve. The next morning, I was due to leave for Germany.

I was too upset to cry. Perhaps fear of what the night ahead of me might bring made the events of the next day a long ways off. I lived so much in the present I never had much time to think about the future. Frank got up and came to me that evening while we were alone in the big place, now suddenly grown quiet. He seemed strangely changed. He was tender. I was frightened by an unnatural look in his eyes, but I fought hard to conceal my fears.

"Frank darling, do you really want to stop drinking?" I asked him.

"Yes, Bubbles, if you will only stay with me," he said, "but let's not talk of that now. It may be only in eternity," he added, mysteriously.

"Tonight we must be alone, absolutely alone! This is the most important night in our whole lives. First, there are a few things I want you to do."

A plan of some kind was taking form in Frank's disturbed mind.

"All right, darling, what do you want me to do?" I tried to hold my voice steady.

He didn't answer, but took me by the hand and led me into the kitchen. Then he brought a stool.

"Get up on it," he said brusquely.

I obeyed him.

"Now, you can reach that bell. Bend the knocker so it won't ring. Careful, dear, don't fall."

I bent it just a little, but he was watching me closely.

"More than that, Bubbles. I want to be absolutely sure it doesn't ring, that no one gets in here tonight. I must not be disturbed!"

So fearful was I after what the doctors had told me about Frank's murderous scheme that I secretly had made the butler promise to return at 2 o'clock in the morning, even though he had been discharged. When I bent that bell, I felt that I was cutting my last tie with the outside world. The butler might come back too late. In the midst of that great city I was alone with a liquor-crazed man. I couldn't shut out the doctors terrifying words:

"He plans to kill you! You won't be alive in the morning!"

"Now, Bubbles," Frank said after the bell was fixed, "pull out the phone wires."

"But, Frank, we might—"

"No, we won't be needing the phone," he interrupted. "This is our last night."

His voice was sweeter than it had been in weeks. His changed manner was too good to be real. Frank stood close by until the phone was put out of order.

"Now, make me a drink, Bubbles. Then go in the bath and bathe. Make yourself more beautiful than you ever have been before. Don't dress, dear. Just put on a negligee."

I could feel Frank's eyes piercing me, as I stepped into the bathroom. My impulse was to lock the door and start screaming for help. But I was afraid. I was afraid even to lock the door, fearing that act might throw him into a rage. Frank was waiting with that strange smile on his face when I came out.

"We must eat something," he said.

"But I'm not hungry."

"I'll fix it. You sit right here."

A minute later Frank walked out of the kitchen. In his hand was a huge butcher knife. My heart stopped. I was so paralyzed with fear I couldn't speak or move. I felt sure he intended to cut my throat. I tried to eat, but couldn't. Frank kept drinking and soon was very drunk. He drew two chairs close together before the fire in the big drawing room, turned out all the lights and we sat down.

"Hold my hand, Bubbles," he whispered. "This night will remain with me always. You are not going to."

I didn't dare trust my voice to speak.

Frank kept his eyes glued to the clock while he toyed with the point of that gleaming knife. There we sat in silence broken only at intervals when Frank would say:

"I'm waiting for the right time."

I was firmly convinced then that he had some diabolical plan to kill me at a certain time in a hideous, spectacular manner.

Suddenly the thunderous peal of Big Ben rang out. Chimes and bells began ringing everywhere. It was midnight, New Year's Eve. In my terror I had forgotten time and place. Maybe this was the moment Frank had chosen. In the clamor of that New Year's Eve I expected to see him reach for me with that murderous knife. Instead he turned to me and took me in his arms.

"Bubbles darling, tell me you love me."

"I do love you, Frank, with all my heart."

I believe those were the first words I had spoken for hours.

With his arms around me, Frank led me to the windows. There were two, separated by a narrow strip of wall. He threw them open. The sounds of the voices and bells were closer, rising in a roar from the depths of the great fog-shrouded city we couldn't see.

"He intends to throw me out," was the thought that flashed through my mind.

"You put your head out this window," Frank said, "I'll put my head out the other one."

I did. Our eyes met in the misty darkness.

"Lean over, Bubbles—and kiss me. This is different. No one has ever celebrated a New Year this way before."

So there we greeted the start of another year, locked in a strange embrace, hanging half out of the windows of our flat in the heart of London. That was the moment, for which he had kept me in suspense, expecting death, for hours!

Frank was only a boy at heart in his pranks and actions, but there may have been more than a prank in his mind that night. Our midnight kiss there above the hilarious streets of London was symbolic. We were together, yet we were separated by a barrier prophetic of the days to come. I think Frank finally realized I was really going to leave him. He wanted to make our last night dramatic. He did, too dramatic, but I was touched by it. My fears left me. For the first time I felt assured that the doctors' warnings were baseless. When our kiss was over I fell to my knees and murmured a prayer. Frank lifted me to my feet. I was crying in my thankfulness, but Frank didn't know why.

Finally, I said:

"Don't you think I should fix the bell? Some of our friends will be dropping in."

Frank seemed himself again. That reassured me.

I climbed up and fixed the bell. I had hardly turned away before it rang. It was the butler. In a few minutes the other servants were at the door. They had been waiting nearby all night. Frank was so delighted to see them as I was.

"You're hired again," he told them.

In a little while, friends began to stream in. The champagne was brought out and a gay party soon was in full swing. Frank still was drinking heavily, so I slipped out of the room thinking he might not miss me. I wanted to get a little rest before the car came to take me to the station. No sooner has I left than Frank began jumping up and down like a spoiled child, yelling at the top of his voice.

"I want my Bubbles! I want my Bubbles!"

He was frantic. He thought I had slipped away to leave him without saying good-bye. After I convinced him I was merely going to lie down, he got over his hysteria. Our friends left and we went to bed. I couldn't sleep and I knew Frank wasn't asleep, although he pretended to be. When the bell rang at six o'clock I started with the realization that I faced a great decision in my life. I arose, kissed Frank tenderly, and made a last plea to him to take care of himself. Our lives had been too closely intertwined to be broken off easily. He appeared to be asleep. I thought he was. I walked away with tears streaming down my face.

"I can't go. I'm not going to leave him," I sobbed to the film man who was waiting for me.

"You are going," he said sternly, "if I have to drag you all the way to Germany." He gripped me by the arm and started to lead me out. As I stepped through the door, Frank stirred.

"Good-bye Ed," he said.

Knowing every other ruse had failed, he thought he might stop me by arousing jealousy with the feigned farewell to his wife, Edna.

I did stop, but not for long. The agent rushed me out. I cried all the way to the station, but the die was cast. Frank was behind me. I was on my way to a new life and career in Germany. Fortune was kind to me there. The people showed me every consideration. I was given every courtesy at the studios. The public was kind enough to like my pictures. I soon found fame as Mary Robertson, the film star. Imogene Wilson, the "Miss America" of the Ziegfeld Follies, was buried, for a time at least, with the scandals that drove her into exile.

✠ ✠ ✠

But Frank Tinney was not entirely swept out of my life. I kept in touch with him and I sent him half of my check every week for months. Frank lived up to his threat never to set foot on the stage again after I left him. That hurt me, but I felt I had done my share to help him. I had given him more than two full years of my life. I had come to him across the ocean. I had failed to save him from himself, but it was not that I hadn't tried. He didn't lose his hold on me without a struggle. Soon after I arrived in Berlin he sent his valet to see me.[16]

"Mr. Tinney has been divorced from his wife," the servant told me. "He sent me to bring you to him. He wants to marry you."[17]

I told his emissary that I couldn't do that, our lives now had to go their separate ways.

Then a London theater orchestra director, a close friend of Frank's, came to see me to repeat Frank's plea. He had friends in America write, urging me to marry him. They argued that the scandal in our lives would be forgiven if we married. At last, a few months later, Frank himself came to Berlin.

Once, while scolding him for fooling and misleading me about not being married when we first started living together, I told him the day would come when he would beg me to marry him for that deception. That day did come, but it couldn't erase the past. It brought me no feeling of triumph. Frank did fall to his knees and plead with me to marry him when he came to Berlin. He was a changed man but it was too late for me to turn back then. He had come to the tragic realization that everything he had worked for was lost except me. If he lost me there was nothing left. It was pitiful. We both cried like a couple of babies.

"Frank, I don't want to hurt you," I sobbed, "but I don't belong to you. I never did. This is hopeless."

That threw him into a rage. He threw a heavy iron ash tray that luckily missed me and crashed into the wall. He upset furniture and created such a commotion that the manager came running, threatening to call police. That threat with its recollection of such incidents in New York, horrified me. There would be another scandal. I was just getting started on my German picture career.

It was my turn to plead with the apartment manager. I finally succeeded in keeping the fight quiet and got Frank calmed down. The next day Frank called at the studio where I was making a picture. Of course, that was in the days of silents. He watched me go through a love scene. That seemed to make him bitter.

"I would hate to be an actor and have to work in your company," he sneered.

I told him he would have to leave Germany if that was to be his attitude. There was another proposal and another fight, but at last I got him in a car for his train. He was a pathetic figure. That leave-taking was harder than our separation in London. I wish that one at midnight New Year's Eve could have been the last. It was plain to see

105

as I helped Frank on the train that he was a broken man overcome by grief, beaten and alone. I gave him a thousand dollars for his return to America, and kissed him farewell.

His train compartment door was open. After I had left him I had to tiptoe back. I couldn't resist it. Frank didn't see me. He was the most dejected-looking figure I ever have seen, his head was down, tears coursing down his cheeks. My arms instinctively reached out as they would for a child. I cried, but to myself.

"Oh, I can't leave him! I'm going with him! I'll devote my life to him!"

It was an impulse of sentiment. Just as I started to move toward the bowed figure, a stronger power than my own will seized me, turned me around and directed my steps toward the exit. That moment on the train was the last time I ever saw Frank Tinney. It was a sad heart-rending one. How I wish I could have seen him happy and smiling once more.

Frank soon returned to America. After I returned and went to Hollywood he wrote to me. They were rambling letters, but I will never forget them. In each one he described our imaginary marriage, details of the chapel, what I wore, how sweet I looked and always how happy we were. It seemed an obsession with him. A dream of what might have been.

Notwithstanding the happiness and success I was to enjoy in Europe, my life there was not entirely free from tragedy. The specter of scandal never far away it seemed, almost overtook me again.

Chapter 5

Soon after my arrival in Germany I renewed the acquaintance of a man I had met on the boat going from New York to England. He was Dr. Robert Reinhart, one of the most cultured men I have ever known and I thought he was extremely handsome.[18] He was a tall, elderly man, very masculine in appearance, with a dark red goatee and waxed moustache. His eyes were the same color as the sea and looked just that deep.

He taught me a great deal in those few days on board ship. I knew the hurly-burly of show life and I knew the mad frivolities of the New York night life, but I knew nothing of the fine manners and sophistication of which Dr. Reinhart was a master. A brilliant conversationalist, he gave me a foretaste of the life and customs I was to encounter on the Continent. He was a friend of the late Kaiser Wilhelm and very wealthy. One of his prized possessions was a watchchain of platinum and matched pearls that had been given to him by the Kaiser. There was a great deal of mystery about him, too. One night at dinner I had been admiring his pearl watchchain.

"Would you like to see some other jewels?" he asked me.

Of course, I said yes. We went to the stateroom he shared with two companions, one a lawyer, the other a poet. Dr. Reinhart pulled out a small locker trunk and opened it.

I almost fell over. It was filled with jewels of every description, rubies, emeralds, pearls, brilliants, by the handfuls. Never have I seen such a sight. I just gazed at them in amazement. I was trembling too much to touch them. There was no explanation offered for the fabulous collection by my mysterious friend. I asked none.

As I was fleeing from scandal under my adopted name, Dr. Reinhart knew me only as an actress, en route to Europe. He suggested that I come to Germany, that he had many influential friends who could help me. I didn't avail myself of his offer of help, but our acquaintance was resumed as soon as I began appearing in pictures, and that led to my attendance at my most elaborate party.

Dr. Reinhart had a baronial manor at Heidelberg. That's where this party was held. I was merely one of some 300 guests, most of whom were members of the nobility and celebrities from all over Europe. I thought I had known splendor and elegance before, but I hadn't. This setting, the appointments, the jewels, the finery, made everything I had seen before seem trivial and a bit tawdry.

Our host flew to Paris to purchase his gifts for the guests. Mine was a ruby that once had beautified the forehead of an Indian princess. According to legend, great tragedy always had been associated with the gem. Some dire fate overcame its owner. Being so sophisticated and not at all superstitious, I'm sure my host took no stock in these tales when he presented it to me. Frank admired it, so I gave it to him, set in a ring, before he returned to New York. He prized it highly, but I always felt a little unhappy about him having it.

There was a beautiful garden that sloped down to the edge of a small lake. The guests gathered there while groups of gypsies, so picturesque in their gay colors, strolled through the trees and flowers, playing their violins, singing their sweet, plaintive songs, and dancing. That was a scene never forgotten, a sojourn into a land of fantasy.

Before the banquet was served, we went into a room that would be called a cocktail lounge in this country. An incredible sight was unfolded there. Scattered around the room in groups of six were young girls on their hands and knees, their heads pointed outward from each circle. All were entirely nude. Their bodies were lacquered black, so dark they shone like onyx. Resting on the backs of each cluster of the supposed slave girls was a tray, filled with cocktails. As casually as if they were lifting their drinks from a table the guests sauntered through the room, chattering and laughing, picking up their glasses from these human pedestals.

In the huge dining hall where the banquet was served was an all-girl orchestra. They, too, were lacquered black. Each one wore a black lacquered wig. The lighting was amazing in its effects. All was indirect. It was imitation moonlight as well as I can describe it. Fountains played everywhere. The soft music, the mystic light that enveloped everything, the shining bodies of the shapely slave girls transformed it all into a setting from dreamland.

After the sumptuous banquet, served in the height of elegance, the guests retired to Dr. Reinhart's private theater, a small circular playhouse, constructed in his palace. There the opera *Mignon* was presented for our enjoyment. I stood in awe of it all. I was supposed to be sophisticated like all the others, but I wasn't. I was still naïve and spell-bound by glamour. Dr. Reinhart was so charming and gracious. He sensed my feeling and did everything to make me feel at ease. By that time, I had learned to speak German, but even with the language at my command I felt out of place in that throng of titled celebrities.

❖ ❖ ❖

Before I left England, I had met the King of Spain. He came to the theater one night with a party of guests. He was charming, a most interesting man. On a trip to Paris, after I had become quite famous as a star in Germany, I met him again quite by accident, in a boulevard café. Dorothy Gish, then so popular on the Continent, was among others in the party. On that occasion King Alfonso, merely because he regarded me as a pretty girl, gave me a gift that I prized most highly. It was a lovely brooch, an exquisite piece of jewelry, that once belonged to his mother.

I was happy again in those days. The Europeans took me to their hearts just as Broadway had when I first went to New York. The parties they gave were in the best of taste, in fact, the best of everything. The chivalrous conduct of the men fascinated me. They may have been motivated by the same desires, but their suave, genteel manners were quite a contrast to the take-'em-and-leave-'em attitude of the playboys I had known.

An Italian Count proposed to me on bended knee, quite in the approved manner of the storybook knights of old. He was a man I had first met at Dr. Reinhart's party at Heidelberg. I saw him again later in Paris. I accepted his proposal. It seemed the interesting thing to do, but I never entertained any serious thought of marrying him. He may have, I don't know. I wasn't a wealthy American heiress, but I did have fame and considerable wealth. He later married an English lady and took up residence in England.

Notwithstanding the happiness and success I was enjoying, my life in Europe was not entirely free from tragedy. The specter of scandal, never far away it seemed, almost overtook me again. A high German official chanced to be on the same plane I took from Berlin to Vienna. He was little more than a casual friend, met at one of the affairs I had attended in the German capital. Quite naturally, we resumed our acquaintance on the flight to Vienna. We both took suites at the leading hotel when we arrived.

"I have some business matters to attend to," he said, "but please do me the honor to be my guest at dinner tonight."

I accepted and we arranged to meet at a certain time. I went out and returned to the hotel a few hours later to dress. As I opened the door to my suite, a horrifying sight greeted me. Slumped in a chair, dead, a pistol by his side, was my friend. Panic seized me. For a few moments I was too terrified to speak, then I ran screaming from the ghastly scene. I was too frightened to give any thought to the consequences that might come from the news that a man had been found shot to death in my room, that perhaps I might be accused of the crime. Police and hotel officials came hurrying to the suite. I couldn't explain what he was doing in my room. I don't know.

"Was this man in love with you?" the officers asked me.

"No, no," I sobbed. "I barely knew him. We met on the plane and we were going to dinner together. That's all."

"It's very strange that he should be found shot to death in your room. Where were you this afternoon? Is that your pistol? We may have to trouble you for your finger-prints."

On and on the questions went until I was frantic. Finally, they said I would have to go to court. Headlines took form before my eyes. I saw the career I had created for myself besmirched once more with scandal, yet I knew I was innocent of any wrong. A private hearing was held before a magistrate. Just when circumstances looked blackest for me, a telephone operator at the hotel appeared. She told the officers that shortly before I returned to my suite and found the body a telephone call had been made from my phone to Berlin. That was quickly checked. The party to whom the call was made confirmed it and said my friend had expressed great despondency over the outcome of a business matter.

I was cleared. The victim was influential enough that the circumstances of his tragic death were hushed up. That time, at least, Fate was kind to me, but finding a dead man in my room in the heart of gay Vienna was a shock I never could erase from my mind.

Once while I was in Europe I turned gypsy. I must tell of that. It was one of my happiest experiences.

I was making a picture called *Sister Angel*, playing the role of a nun.[19] The character was that of a beautiful woman who had been quite wicked in her younger years. On her death-bed in a hospital when all had despaired of her life, the sisters inspired her to live and become a nun, helping others to avoid the mistakes she had known. That role seemed so appropriate to me.

Exteriors of the picture were being made at San Remo, Italy, a beautiful place, facing the sea and set against a backdrop of mountains. Roving bands of gypsies seemed to be everywhere. It was my custom to get up early every morning, put on my makeup and nun's habit, then go for a stroll through the hotel garden. It was lovely there.

One morning I spied a group of gypsies at the gate. They were singing and dancing and seemed so happy and carefree in the cool morning air that I envied them. At first, they mistook me for a real nun. I walked to the gate and gave them some money. Then they saw the makeup on my face. They began jabbering and laughing. An uncontrollable impulse to be one of these strange people, perhaps to get from them the secret of their perpetual gaiety, swept over me. At last, through a mixture of tongues, I conveyed my wishes to them.

Again, they laughed, threw open the gate and beckoned to me to come on. I gathered up my heavy skirts and ran with them. For three days I was a gypsy. It was wonderful. By day we plodded along through the countryside, stopping at each cottage or little village to play and sing until the householders appeared to toss a few coins. I soon learned some of their old gypsy songs, refrains of the wanderers, and sang with them.

At night we slept out under the stars, in rags, to be sure, but without a worry in the world. I washed off my makeup, discarded some of my somber attire, and took off my shoes, to live as they lived as completely as possible. The gypsy mother was a remarkable person. Her outer garments were rags, but beneath them she wore some beautiful things and had a girdle that was filled with gold pieces.

Mary Nolan, Ziegfeld Girl and Silent Movie Star

The director of the picture was pacing the floor over my disappearance. The papers were full of it. No one knew what had happened to me or where I had gone. The cast was dumbfounded and probably thought I had lost my mind when I wandered in to the hotel grounds leading a band of gypsies, but all was soon forgiven when I explained the fancy that had taken me away.

❖ ❖ ❖

More than two years rolled by. I had played in many pictures. I had proved to myself and the world that I could achieve success on my own merits. But that success wouldn't fill an aching void in my heart. I became homesick for the homeland that had driven me into exile—so homesick that I finally suffered a nervous breakdown and for weeks I lay at the point of death in a Berlin hospital.

After my recovery, I saw European picture stars being signed up all around me by American producers. I was ignored, left behind. That hurt me. I had made a resolve that I wouldn't return to the United States until I could walk down the gangplank on a red carpet. My fight to redeem myself had been successful, I thought. I felt I should be forgiven by my own country. Months rolled by but no offers came.

"Sorry, the public won't have you."

One after another, producers and talent scouts dinned these words into my ears. Then finally one of the biggest men in the Hollywood picture business came to see me.

"I think you've earned your laurels," he said. "You've paid any penalty that is due. You're a star in German films, but your place is in your own country. We want you."

I signed a contract.

Nils Asther, Swedish star who played in a number of picture with me, was signed to come to America at the same time. We sailed together on the *Majestic*, he to a new land, I to my own. Tears of joy ran down my cheeks as the boat came into sight of New York's skyline. I looked upon the upraised torch of the Statue of Liberty as a symbol of my liberation from exile. But that moment of happiness didn't last. Broadway and Main Street hadn't forgotten after all.

The stain of scandal hadn't been erased by my success as a film star in Germany. I was not greeted as an actress home from exploits abroad, but as a notorious creature returning to the scene of her shame. The big film producers who had me under contract hurried me out of New York's bitter atmosphere to Hollywood, where I hopefully awaited the chance to prove that I had reclaimed my life and had something worthwhile to offer the screen.

"Are you really Imogene Wilson?" people would ask me. I must not have looked as wicked as they expected. I couldn't deny my identity, and why should I? But I got more starts than smiles. Oh, there were some kindly friends and civil acquaintances, but for a long time I remained outside the barrier of Hollywood life, shunned by the elite of the film colony. Protests about me poured in. The film producers grew alarmed. They were afraid they had a white elephant on their hands. I had been in Hollywood several months, patiently waiting to be called to work, when I was summoned to the studio.

"We're sorry," I was told, "but we don't seem able to find just the right vehicle for you. How much would you want to cancel your contract and return to Germany?"

"I don't want any money," I replied. "And I'm not going back to Germany. I'm staying here."

"What are you going to do?"

"Make pictures," I said. "If not for you, then for someone else."

"In that case you'll make one for us. However, your name Imogen Wilson is too long for lights. We'll have to have something shorter. How about taking the name Mary Nolan?"

Of course, they were trying to tell me in a polite way that Imogene Wilson and everything associated with that name would be booed from the screen all over the land. They had to give me a new identity, a fresh start, in an effort to bury my past. I agreed. The matter was taken to court and, by the stroke of a judge's pen, Imogene Wilson, "Miss America," once the toast of the Ziegfeld Follies, was legally abolished. Mary Nolan had walked onto the scene. The public relented enough to give me a chance.

Immediately after becoming Mary Nolan I was given my first chance in pictures, the role of Molly in *Sorrell and Son*. It was a good part. I was happy.

A few weeks later I was on my way back to England with the film company on location. Nils Asther, Anna Q. Nilsson, Alice Joyce and H.B. Warner were in the cast.

Just before I left, a pathetic figure out of the old days crossed my path. I had moved into a home in Hollywood. The studio had warned me that I must live quietly and discreetly. I was on probation. One word of unfavorable publicity would ruin me. I was on my way home from the studio when a gorgeous array of flowers at a sidewalk stand attracted me. I asked my chauffeur to stop while I bought some.

Just as I was stepping back into the car with an old-fashioned bouquet in my arms, a girl walked by. I paid no attention to her until she stopped and came back. She was bedraggled and forlorn-looking but gave me a nod of recognition.

"Hello, Imogene," she said in a flat-toned voice. "Read where you were out here. Back from Europe, eh? And making food in the movies. Well, ain't life grand to some people? But how are you anyway?"

"Just fine, thank you," I replied. "but I don't believe I know you, do I?"

"Oh, gone high hat, huh? Well listen, kid, don't try to pull that stuff on me. I knew you when."

Her voice was cold and hard. Her eyes shone in a glassy stare.

"How do you rate a chauffeur? Well, just don't forget I knew you in the days you were living with Frank Tinney."

"I'm sorry, but who are you?" I asked.

"You really don't know me? Then don't tell anybody. I wouldn't have stopped if I'd known I've really changed that much. I'm Helen Lee Worthing."[20]

Recognition came to me then, but I was so shocked I could hardly believe my eyes. She had changed so much. But I'm glad to say that since that chance meeting, Helen has gone a long way toward reclaiming herself. She has completed a voluntary jail term, fought off the curse of drugs, regained her health and now has found employment. And

I sincerely hope that the future will repay her in deserved kindness for the cruel blows of the past.

"Helen!" I said. "Please forgive me. I didn't know you for an instant. It has been so long."

I tried hard to make amends for my unintentional slight.

"But, dear, you look ill. You fooled me completely. Come, get in the car, and let me drive you home."

With her eyes staring straight ahead, Helen stepped into the car and sat down beside me. We drove the rest of the distance to my home scarcely a word spoken between us. Just what was in Helen's thoughts I can only imagine. My mind was racing back some five years to the bright lights of Broadway. I could see a beautiful, tall, statuesque girl, proudly and naturally graceful. She was a lady by birth and training. Her rare beauty and lovely bearing quickly earned her a place of prominence in the front ranks of the Ziegfeld Follies. She was acclaimed as one of the world's ten most beautiful women.

As we drove silently through the Hollywood streets I wanted to look at this girl beside me again to make sure I wasn't dreaming, but I don't want her to see me watching her. Could this girl be the same beautiful creature I had known in New York? What could have happened to her? Questions I couldn't answer and didn't dare ask tumbled though my thoughts.

Timid and shy, Helen had seldom joined the rest of us on the gay champagne suppers and hilarious parties staged by the millionaire playboys. When she did attend, it was one of the more decorous affairs. Her escort usually was some socialite. The last I heard of her she was engaged to a young man whose family was in the blue book. Now this? I couldn't believe it.

When we reached my home, I got out. I had guests coming to dinner and had to hurry but I didn't want to offend Helen again. I explained, took her address and told the chauffeur to drive to her apartment.

"O.K. Emmy." She used Mr. Ziegfeld's pet name for me in that flat, metallic voice. "But I'll be seeing you."

I was a poor hostess that night. I was in a daze. I couldn't get that girl off my mind.

The guests left about one o'clock and I retired, but not to sleep. I was wrestling again with that baffling question I've never had answered: why the world gives many beautiful women so much, so quickly, then robs them of everything and casts them aside.

About three o'clock in the morning the doorbell began ringing frantically. The housekeeper answered it. As she opened the door a taxi driver pushed in, half carrying a screaming blonde woman. Blood was streaming from a gash in her wrist. Her nightgown was streaked with crimson. Her eyes glared.

"Where's Imogene?" Her cry shrieked through the night stillness as the driver and the housekeeper tried to quiet her. It was Helen.

I couldn't imagine who it was until I heard that unmistakable voice call my name. I still was in my bedroom, horrified over the terrible commotion going on downstairs.

Again, I had visions of another scandal. Those piercing screams seemed to reach for miles. There would be police. Too well I now knew the price of notoriety. That I was blameless wouldn't matter.

I was in tears when I rushed downstairs. There was poor Helen, eyes wild, hair flying, holding her bleeding wrist. I paid the taxi driver and sent the housekeeper for something before I spoke.[21]

"For heaven's sake, Helen, why pick on me? I've had my troubles, plenty of them, but I'm playing straight now. Why come to my home in this condition and create a scene? Why didn't you call someone who could help you, a doctor?"

"I did," she sobbed, "but he wouldn't come. That's why I did this."

"I don't understand. There are lots of doctors."

"No, no, Imogene. You don't understand. You see I'm in love with him. I can't help it. Please call him and make him come and save my life."

She gave me a number. A soft, cultured voice answered the phone.

"Please come at once," I pleaded. "Miss Worthing has cut her wrist. She is bleeding to death."

"I'll be right over," he answered, "but she must understand my call is strictly on a professional basis."

"Certainly, but hurry."

The bell rang a few minutes later. I opened the door. The man who stood there was a Negro!

"I'm Doctor Nelson," he said politely. "You called for Miss Worthing?"

I pointed to the couch on which she was lying. A strange light of happiness came into Helen's eyes. A plaintive cry of joy escaped her lips.

"Oh, I'm glad you came. You've made me so happy."

I stood by while Doctor Nelson carefully stopped the flow of blood and took several stitches in Helen's wrist. Out of his kit came a hypodermic. In an instant the needle slipped under the skin of her thin white arm. She smiled at him with a look of relief that I didn't understand then. I did later.

"There," he said, "that will quiet her nerves and take care of her until morning. I'll call back then."

"No, no!" Helen had lost a lot of blood but she had enough strength to utter a scream that echoed through the house. She seized his hand and held it tightly until he knelt beside her.

"Don't leave me until I fall asleep," she whispered drowsily. The hypodermic needle was taking effect. I tiptoed from the room. When I stepped in later, Doctor Nelson was gone. Helen was sleeping soundly.

Soon after that, Helen and Doctor Nelson were married at Tia Juana, Mexico, and took up their residence together in the doctor's home. Eventually the whole world knew of their strange alliance. Trouble was inevitable. There were separations and reconciliations and at last divorce, five years after their marriage. But the end of the trial was not yet. For a time Helen was committed to a sanitarium by court order. It was said she had hallucinations and insomnia.

Then came arrests on dope charges. Poor Helen was caught in the grip of that horrible curse. She worked for a time as a seamstress but the pittance that was paid was not enough to satisfy the craving. She was held for forging narcotic prescriptions, the ruse of any addict who will resort to any means to "get a shot." There was another attempt to escape her bonds with suicide. It failed and kindly care gave her hope. But new misfortunes soon hurled her back into the clutches of the dope. Eagerly she threw herself on the mercy of the court, hoping that confinement in jail might bolster her courage to win her fight.

"I'm an addict, I guess I can't fall any lower," she sobbed. "I thought I could break the habit and I still believe I can. I want to go back to jail because I am sure I can make a new start in life from there."

The judge granted her request and, as I said, she has completed her voluntary jail term and is now well along the road of rehabilitation. Poor Helen! I know from my own experience the agony she has gone through. Yes, there's a high price on beauty and fame and folly. Too soon came a day when Mary Nolan sank to depths far below any ever touched by Imogene Wilson, lived through an era of bitter degradation, and experienced the deepest anguish a human can know, "living death" as a dope addict.

Real friends were few, but men again came into my life. There always were men. They were the luring flame. I was the silly creature that invariably got its wings singed. With them, as I will tell next week, came new sorrows, affairs that were fated to overshadow my entire life as my relationship with Frank Tinney had rules and ruined my earlier years.

Chapter 6

My screen debut in *Sorrell and Son* was very favorably received. My new career in Hollywood seemed safely launched. The public was accepting Mary Nolan. It was even kind enough to say she was beautiful and talented. Of course, I was intensely happy. It looked as if the unfortunate events of my past were forgotten. Other picture assignments followed. Associates in the film world relented, too. Doors that once had been closed were opened to me. I was privileged to enjoy a certain measure of the social life of Hollywood. Living was sweet for a few memorable months.

There was one unforgettable birthday party given for me at Agua Caliente in Mexico. That was a famous rendezvous then. Almost everyone in Hollywood attended. I felt flattered and thrilled. It was a gorgeous setting, a gay night in the casino, reminiscent of the revelries of the Follies days in New York. There were eighty couples at the party. At the height of the festivities, two bellboys walked in carrying an enormous basket of orchids.

I lost my voice and my breath both when they lifted it onto the table in front of me. Rising out of the center of the mass of delicate blooms was a three-foot doll, a replica of myself as I appeared in my latest picture. All stood to drink my health. Never was I happier than that night.

Soon after that, Tom Mix gave me a New Year's party. Tom was always kind to me.

The first time I met him he asked me to marry him. Of course, he was joking but it took me by surprise.

"You don't even know me," I replied. "Why would you propose to me?"

"Oh, just because it seemed like a nice thing to do," he laughed. "People probably expect it of me." It was his way of flattering.

There were Hollywood premieres with all the stars present, football games, happy afternoons at the Riviera polo matches. With all of it, of course, went lovely dresses, clothes that every woman adores, attentions from admirers, flowers by the armloads. I paid $750 for the gown I wore at my Caliente party, a gorgeous satin creation, studded with ruby-like brilliants. I wouldn't think of wearing the same outfit in public twice. It couldn't be done. That was the cost of maintaining prestige. But with all the happiness there were saddening moments to mar the glamour, too.

One of my closest friends was a beautiful girl who had been a showgirl like myself and whom I had admired from the first time I saw her on the screen, long before I came to Hollywood. I don't want to tell her name so I'll call her—well, Casalda.[22]

Her lovely deep dark eyes intrigued me in her pictures. They positively fascinated me when I came to know her in life. Of course, I was not an addict then and although she was, I didn't know it for a long time after we became acquainted. I saw her only as a lovely, sweet character. She was that until her death. I didn't know the outward characteristics of that fiendish craving that became so familiar to me later.

But as I look back now it seems strange that so many of my friends should have fallen victims to that affliction. Visitors I didn't know used to slip in and out of my hotel apartment when Casalda was visiting me, and later when I moved into a home in Beverly Hills. She always made some plausible excuse for their calls—they were delivering a message or conferring on business. I wasn't suspicious then but I learned later they were dope peddlers.

One morning at my home Casalda began acting quite strangely at the breakfast table. Her eyes and nose were streaming. Yawns wracked her in gasps. Then she lost her voice. The doorbell rang. She jumped up without waiting for a maid to answer. A man I never had seen before was there. I didn't see what went on between them, but the caller left in a moment and Casalda hurried to her room. A minute later she walked out a changed person, as serene and demure as ever.

"Why, dear, what was wrong with you?" I asked.

"Oh, some hot coffee went down the wrong way," she laughed. "It strangled me."

That telltale incident passed without arousing my suspicions. Not long after that, Casalda was taken to a sanitarium near Los Angeles for a "nervous breakdown." I went to see her.

"I'm sorry," an attendant said when I walked in, "we'll have to search you before you can see her."

"Search me?" I protested. "Why what do you mean? I'm one of her best friends."

"Can't help it. Those are orders."

I didn't see Casalda, but before I left the place I had learned why she was there, why her visitors were searched. The terrible truth staggered me. Casalda was in a straitjacket, or restraining sheet, as they sometimes called it on polite occasions. She was being forcibly held in the torture that only an addict knows. All morphine was withheld from her. I left the place sobbing at the awful discovery I had made. I wanted to do something to help that poor, suffering girl but I didn't know how.

A very wise and very brilliant man, a famous wit and writer, was one of my friends. I went to him that night and cried out my story of finding Casalda strapped to her bed, screaming piteously for a shot she couldn't have.

"Isn't anyone allowed to see here without submitting to search?" he asked me, when I finished.

"Only members of her immediate family."

His agile mind never was at a loss for an answer, whether it be a witticism or a solution to a knotty problem.

"Don't you think it would be nice if her father called to see her?" he asked.

"Yes, but I don't know where her father is or whether he is living."

"Of course, my dear, I understand that."

A few days later a friend of the family called me on the telephone.

"Do you know, Mary, the strangest thing has happened." she said. "Somebody has been getting dope to Casalda. They can't understand how."

"Is that so?" I was as much astounded as my informant, knowing how strict they were at the sanitarium.

"Yes, and there hasn't been a soul to see her except the family. The sweetest thing, though, her father has been coming to see her every day and spends a few minutes visiting with her."

"Her father? Oh! Of course. That is sweet," I answered and the face of a man lined with a deep understanding of the frailties of human kind took form before my eyes.

"I know he does make her very happy."

Casalda never was cured, but she was released. I don't believe she ever mustered the will that it takes to throw off dope's strangling hold. Narcotics affect different persons in different ways. It thrills some, depresses others. Its powerful effect thrilled Casalda, but its grip was more the fault of designing persons than hers. It first was given to her to relieve recurring pains. Before she knew it, she was caught in its meshes. My new knowledge of her addiction didn't affect our friendship. We were together a lot. There were other dope fiends around her. They like the companionship of fellow sufferers, but in all the time I knew her, never once did she suggest that I join in her "thrill."

However, the habit became an obsession with her. She worshiped morphine. The poor girl was the victim of a lot of misunderstanding, too, on the part of the public. She was arrested once for disturbing the peace at her apartment. They said she was annoying other occupants by peeping in their windows late at night. She had an apartment in a big place in the Hollywood hills. A number of other well-known motion picture people lived there, too. That meant a party was going on in somebody's apartment every night.

There was a continuous round of gaiety. That was a day when Lew Cody, Norman

Kerry, Jack Pickford, Wilson Mizener and Owen Moore were in the forefront of Hollywood night life. There was a continuous ring of laughing voices and sounds of revelry. Poor Casalda was simply fascinated by the seeming perpetual mirth of the revelers. Seldom was she a part of it. She did peep into the windows at these affairs, but the world never knew the real reason. When she was arrested, the public scoffed and simply put it down as the morbid curiosity of a Polly Pry.

But that wasn't her reason, and perhaps the world today will laugh at her reason. "I only wanted to find out why, to learn their secret, that's all."

Casalda didn't find the key to happiness spying on other people's joyous moments or any other way. Dope kept tightening its hold on her. A girl friend, an unknown who used to take it with her, took an overdose intentionally one night and never woke up. But before she slipped off into her sleep she whispered her last words to Casalda.

"Life is too hard for me," she murmured, "just as it's too hard for you. This is our only companionship. I'm leaving this world, but I'm coming back for you."

A few months later Casalda was in New York. One night, she told me, a vivid figure came into the room while she was sleeping, under the numbing influence of her hypo. Before her in a dream stood the figure of her friend who had killed herself.

"Remember, Casalda, I said I'd return for you," came a voice in the dream. "I'm here for you now."[23]

That incident made a lasting impression on Casalda. Death did come to her soon. She returned to Los Angeles and a short time later was arrested on a dope charge in San Diego. Hidden on her person and sewed in the hems of her dresses were narcotics worth $5,000. Hounded by the fear of being deprived of the one thing that gave her surcease from her lonely agony, she was trying to flee from what she knew not what.

I believe the saddest moment of my life was the day I stood beside her casket and looked down at her marble-like hands. She always was beautiful to me, too lovely for the harsh realities she found in the world, and I remember her as more beautiful in death than she had been in life.

�֍ �֍ ✗

Disaster stalked into my life again, too, at a time when I thought my mistakes were behind me, my screen career assured, and happiness safely mine. Yes, it came in the person of a man, a man who was everything I wanted.[24] Why men and misfortune have gone hand in hand through my life I don't know, but they have. And I can say it without rancor in my heart. Someday I hope to know why some men will be kind and sweet to one woman and so cruel and mean to others. I seem to attract that kind. I am always the one who gets kicked around. They recall the lines of Oscar Wilde:

> And all men kill the thing they love,
> By all let this be heard,
> Some do it with a bitter look,
> Some with a flattering word,
> The coward does it with a kiss,
> The brave man with a sword!
> I've known too many cowards.

Mary Nolan, Ziegfeld Girl and Silent Movie Star

I don't believe I ever have been truly in love, but the feeling I had for this man was close to it, probably as close as it ever will be. He fascinated me, but he had a dual personality as most men have. One I loved. The other I hated. I endured one to hold the other. There were times when no one could have been sweeter to me. Flowers, lovely orchids, came every day, always with a note expressing some sentiment like this: "To the sweetest girl in the world."

He was a man's man, masculine in very sense of the word. That's the only kind that ever has appealed to me. I've had no time for sissy, slick-haired Romeos. At any rate I fell, and hard: I was foolish again.

From the day he whispered, "I'm in love with you, I'll be true to you," I gave myself to him as completely as I ever had to Frank Tinney, but the consequences of that affair left my health shattered, my pride humbled. Like Frank, he, too, was married. My association with him naturally led to domestic trouble, so one day when a crisis arose I called his wife and told her she could have him, that I was giving him up. But I didn't mean it. I wanted him and meant to have him.

Yes, that was wrong. That he encouraged my affection may explain, if not excuse, my conduct. He was seeking new love. I gave it to him. However, out of that association came an accident that sent me to a Los Angeles hospital, seriously injured. There were long months of painful suffering, recurring operations that kept me constantly under the care of doctors and nurses. I didn't dare bare my private life to the world again, so I nursed my secret, and my agony. I struggled on in pictures. Only my closest associated knew I was ill. It was a struggle, too.

I went on the set on crutches and in a wheelchair. During those months I played in *Undertow, Shanghai Lady, Outside the Law* and *Carnival Girl*.[25] How appropriate those titles sound when I write them now. I had to steel myself to summon strength to leave my chair or discard my crutches to go through my part before the camera when the director called: "Action!" A nurse was with me constantly. I had been given hypodermics to ease my excruciating pain in the hospital. The nurse always was at hand to give me a relieving shot when the torture became unbearable after I had finished a scene.

I seemed to forget myself and my agony when I stepped into character before the camera. I think it must have been the same mental process that makes fright obliterate pain. In the last scene made in *Carnival Girl*, I was supposed to commit suicide by jumping from a high platform. My double had performed the more dangerous episodes, but I had to do this one, a close-up, myself. I leaped off. The hidden net was only a few feet below me, but that short fall wrenched my injuries and almost killed me. I was in a state of collapse when I was taken down.

Again my nurse was waiting with a hypo that brought relief. I thought nothing of it. I had been told the injections I was taking were to normalize me. I didn't know that I had been given up as incurable by the doctors, that they were pampering my wishes to continue my screen work. No one was to blame. I felt that I had to carry on while my talents were in demand. At night, when a day's work was over, I went back to the hospital, which was my home for nearly two years. Few knew my whereabouts or my condition.

118

At the end, when my doctors had given up hope of my eventual recovery, I was discharged from the hospital and their care. They had done all they could. I was thought to be suffering from an inoperable cancer. I was able to walk again without crutches, but I was still in constant pain. I was given but months, or, at most, a few years of life. The day I left the hospital, the most damning words a person can hear were uttered to me.

"Miss Nolan," I was told, "there is something you must know. Your condition and painful nature of your injury and the treatment has required the use of heavy dosages of morphine. The pain you suffer will require continuation of its use."

They didn't tell me I had only a short time to live. I was a dope addict, but I didn't realize the significance of those fatal words then. As a matter of fact I laughed at the idea. I had known others but it was silly to think that I was hopelessly caught in the merciless grip. I thought dope was taken only for a thrill, that most of the addicts were poor unfortunates who just didn't know better.

Me an addict? I laughed at them.

But I don't know how soon I was to invade that fantastic half-world of fitful dreams and agonizing torture. I kept a nurse with me and moved into a home in Beverly Hills. The first night I was there I took the nurse's hypodermic kit while she was out of the room, broke the needles, smashed the syringe and threw them away. They were crazy to imagine I had to depend on that stuff. I would show them how stupid it was. I felt better. I was sure I was getting well. I went to bed and quickly fell asleep with a free mind and conscience.

A few hours later I awakened out of a nightmare in terrible agony. Every nerve in my body felt like a thread of scaring flame. Every fiber in me throbbed with pain. My frantic screams brought the nurse running. She rushed for her kit. Of course, it was gone.

"Did you—what in the world did you do with it?" she asked.

I told her.

"You can't do that. You have to have it. You can only suffer now until the doctor gets here."

She called him immediately.

In the half hour it took him to get there I did suffer. Tortures I never had known before. I lived days, it seemed, before he came. He quickly prepared a hypo. The instant the needle penetrated my arm I felt relief, but, with a relief came the most sickening realization I ever have experienced.

"It's true! I am one! I'm lost!"

Hospital bills, nurses, doctor's fees, operating costs had taken all my salary and more. I finally discharged my nurse, determined to fight this thing out alone. Perhaps I was becoming reconciled to fate. I held a certificate from my doctor authorizing me to obtain narcotics. I was registered in Washington as a hopeless addict, an incurable sufferer who had to have it because of my physical condition. Any doctor to whom my credentials were presented had to supply me. After my nurse left I faced the task of giving myself my first shot. I had been taught how to do it, but the thought of giving myself a hypo terrified me.

I boiled the needle as directed, but I trembled while I did it.

When I finally got the solution prepared I sat looking at the needle. My hand was trembling so I could hardly see it. Several times I touched my arm with it, then drew it away. Something within me, even in my pain, revolted. But at last the screaming urge of my body overcame whatever reluctance may have been in my mind at taking the first step alone. I jabbed the needle into my skin and pressed down the plunger. It was done.

Almost instantly the quieting, deadening drug began spreading its allaying effects over my twitching nerves. There was physical relief, but with it something hardened in me.

"O.K., then I am a hop-head," was my thought. "Fair enough. I don't give a damn!"

With that surrender I had another skeleton that had to be kept hidden in the closet.

✤ ✤ ✤

The country was becoming more and more critical of the lives of the movie stars. Scandals and tales of Hollywood orgies had brought the entire film industry under the lash of rebuke. Rumors of dope addiction were prevalent. Filmland was warned to mend its ways. Clauses went into contracts to curb scandalous conduct. Private lives must be free from stain. There was I, my career in the balance, saddled with an illicit affair with a married man and now—a slave to dope.

I tried hard to keep my secrets covered. One word and my world was shattered. My life became an existence of terror, fear of exposure alternated with a dope-fed craving that brooked no denial. Caught in the mesh of circumstances, I stumbled on, "normalizing" myself with relieving "shots" keeping up a front to safeguard my work. During those harrowing days I met the man I later married, Wallace McCreery.

He was just a boy then, handsome and inexperienced. Oh, perhaps he was as old as I in years, but he was just a child and immature through the eyes of my worldly knowledge. I had seen too much of older men. Wealthy, of a fine New York family, Wallace had come to Hollywood for a lark, hoping he might meet some of the glamorous beauties he had seen on the screen. He made the acquaintance of the Beverly Hills police and began spending a lot of his time hanging around the station.

The police made it their duty to guard my home and me. The strange alliance in which I lived frequently made it imperative for an officer to remain in the house overnight as a bodyguard. There was one there nearly all the time. Wallace got in the habit of playing cards with the men at the police station to while away the long night hours. Naturally he learned of the frequent calls that were made at my home.

"I'd certainly like to meet her," he said one night. "I've seen her in every picture she's made. If she's really that sweet, she must be wonderful."

"Well, I'll tell you what I'll do," a policeman said. "We'll deal a hand of show-down poker. If you get the high hand I'll take you up the next time I go."

The cards were dealt. Wallace won.

"O.K., kid. That settles it," the policeman said, "but you'll have to pretend you're a cop."

They hunted up an old uniform that was about three sizes too big for him and drove up. I was alone.

"This is a new officer," the policeman said. "He's going to be your guard tonight."

I started to laugh.

There stood this boy, draped in oversize clothes, a cop's cap on his head, and a gun in his hand.

"Why, officer," I smiled, "he's just a child. Take that gun away from him before he hurts himself."

"Oh, no, Miss Nolan. It's on the level. You'll find he knows his business."

He was back the next night.

"My name's Wallace McCreery," he explained. "You know I am no cop, so there's no use kidding ourselves. I was crazy to meet you, I've seen you so many times in pictures, so I played cards with the fellows at the station for a chance to come up."

While we were talking, my protector walked in. Always suspicious, he started to get ugly.

"Who is this?" he demanded.

I was panicky. I had to say something quick. I lied.

"Oh, why this is my brother," I stammered, not very convincingly.

"Is that so? I never heard you mention him."

"Well, he dropped in very expectantly."

"Are you her brother?" he turned sharply to Wallace, who caught the cue and said yes.

"Sit down, son. It's funny Mary didn't say anything about you coming."

"Oh, you see," it was Wallace's turn to lie, "she didn't know I was coming. I really didn't either until I got here. Anyway., I thought it would be nice to surprise her."

"I see. Well, now that I get a good look at you I can see a family resemblance. Tell me about yourself."

I was fidgeting all over the place. Questions kept popping at Wallace and myself both. We were in deep water and I didn't know when one of us would trip ourselves. I wanted to avoid a fight and after starting with a lie, I tried to make it stick. One of the officers from the police station dropped in to see that everything was all right. Of course, he knew Wallace and spoke to him.

That upset the brother story.

My friend took Wallace out for a ride. Before the ride was over he had forced the truth out of the boy. Wallace was warned to stay away from me, but he didn't do it and that brought more trouble. The freedom I wanted so much was getting farther away each day. I was a prisoner, chained to two masters—dope and a man I thought I loved, a man who ruled every moment of my life, selected my friends, directed my activities, and even told me where I might go for dinner. Perhaps a stronger person would have broken the spell under which I lived, but the ravages of narcotics already were weakening my will. My greatest desire was to protect my career, I would yield to any pressure to hold my place in pictures.

That ambition placed a powerful weapon in the hands of my master. The threat of exposing my addiction to dope constantly was held over my head. I knew that step would bar me from the screen overnight. So, on down the fateful road I trudged, bowing to every whim, locked again in circumstances that were bearing me swiftly to the brink of despair.

Next week I will tell of my banishment from Hollywood, my strange loveless marriage, and the rapid downward strides that soon dropped me back on the sidewalks of New York, a lonely, furtive outcast, combing the lowest dives of the city for a pittance to buy the only thing that life held for me—dope.

Chapter 7

It seems absurd that a man would force a woman he loves to marry someone else, but that is just what happened to me. I drank a cocktail that was a strange mixture of spite, fear and pride. Although I had success in pictures, my life no longer was my own. My every action was governed by two relentless forces, a forbidden love affair that I tried to keep secret, and the tightening clutches of dope.

The climax in my Hollywood came with dramatic swiftness. I was compelled to give up my home in Beverly Hills and move to a place at Santa Monica beach. A bodyguard, hired by the man I thought I loved, was assigned to watch me. I lived a constant nightmare. I was told where I could go and when I could go. My bodyguard was my escort.

Once I disobeyed my orders. Instead of going to dinner at a place selected, my escort and I went to Fatty Arbuckle's nightclub. For a few minutes I felt free. I was following my own desires for once, but it was not for long. My suitor, who always checked every move I made, discovered my deception, if deception it was. He traced my whereabouts and hurried to the scene. He was furious. There was a terrible scene.

"You're making a fool of me," he shouted.

I was sent back to my captive retreat like a whipped child.

The friends I had made shunned me. I was an outcast and a lonely one. I had fine cars, servants, lovely clothes, everything a movie star's public expects her to have, but I had nothing else, except loneliness. Night after night I sat alone, surrounded by my finery, waiting for a telephone that never rang, watching for visitors who knew my plight and didn't dare come to see me. My hypodermic became my closest companion in those days. I soon was turning to it every four hours for the only moments of tranquility I knew.

Wallace McCreery, the wealthy New Yorker who fell in love with my image on the screen and worked a ruse to meet me by playing cop, had been forbidden to visit me. Foolishly perhaps, he ignored the warnings. He called to see me one day in my prison on the beach. It was all very innocent but the consequences were nearly fatal. Wallace always wore a slouch cap and gloves. He took them off when he walked in, threw them into a chair in the corner, and sat down. My sister was with me.

The three of us had been chatting for a few minutes when I heard footsteps that I recognized coming down the hall. My sister, whose presence with me was resented by my suitor, scurried out a back way. In desperation I pushed Wallace into my clothes closet. It locked automatically and could be opened from the outside only with a key. The entrance door opened and my master walked in. Naturally I must have betrayed my extreme nervousness.

"What's wrong? Who's here?" Scowls and questions foretold the coming storm.

"Why, you're here, dear," I tried my best to be nonchalant.

"Don't give me that. There's somebody in here. Who is it?"

"You're just imagining things, always suspicious of me."

He started to look around, into every room, under the beds. While the search was on I was quaking. Wallace's cap and gloves still were in plain sight on the chair. I didn't dare try to hide them. That would have been disastrous. At last he came to the closet door. Maybe the lock hadn't caught. He tried the knob, then gave it a yank. It wouldn't budge.

"Who's in the closet?"

"My evening clothes and furs. It's always locked."

"You're lying. Where's the key?"

I fumbled through my purse and handed him two keys. I knew they wouldn't work and they didn't.

"You know I can get a key downstairs."

"Of course. I must have misplaced mine." I was praying he would go for a master key. It would give me a chance to slip Wallace out.

"But I have a better idea." he went on, walking into another room. He came out an instant later with a revolver in his hand.

"I think this will open it quicker."

My heart stopped.

"Come out of there, whoever you are, before I shoot."

There wasn't a sound. I wanted to scream. I didn't know what to do. I give Wallace a lot of credit, because he knew the man's temper. The gun came up level with the closet door. The hammer clicked back.

"Are you coming out?"

Still not a sound.

"All right," my suitor said, finally, "I guess you win." He put up the revolver and sat down.

A short time later the bodyguard came into the apartment. He spied the telltale cap and gloves at once. He gathered them up under his coat and was starting to hide them when my jealous admirer caught him. That sent him into a new rage.

"I knew that kid was here," he stormed.

"How do you know they belong to him?" I was fighting for time.

"You don't wear a man's cap and gloves, do you?" he shouted.

"Oh, I might." I didn't know what I was saying.

At last the bodyguard lured the man out on some pretext. The instant they were safely gone, I flew to the closet.

"For heaven's sake, open the door and get out of here quick," I whispered.

"They'll be back as soon as they get a key. Slip out the back way and hide in the boiler room. If they find you here, you'll be killed."

Wallace knew what a close call he had had. He did as I told him. The critical moment was past, but the bodyguard did find Wallace before he could escape from the boiler room and gave him a horrible beating. The next morning, I was handed my ultimatum.

"I'm through letting you make a fool of me." I was told. "If that kid's in love with you, that is just swell. I'll see that you marry him. California isn't big enough for both of us. So you're leaving."

"No, I am not!" I put my foot down. "You can't do that to me. My work is here, too. I'm not going!"

A hard look came into his eyes.

"You are leaving tonight!"

The grim, set faces of the bodyguard and the man to whom I had surrendered my life, told me all too well that my fate was cast. I had no choice. I was too weak to fight. The threat of exposing my dope addiction, a step I knew would drive me from pictures overnight, was a powerful weapon. That was one thing I couldn't ward off. I would have preferred to die then rather than to have the world know I was an addict. I felt that way not just for myself but for the entire profession. Exposure would have hurt not only me, but would have cast reflection on every actress on the screen.

"See that she's on that train tonight."

With those words to the bodyguard, the man slammed the door on a terrible episode in my life. The bodyguard followed orders. He was with me constantly to see that I made no phone calls and sent no telegrams. I packed a few bags and that night I was put on the Santa Fe Chief, bound for New York, my back turned reluctantly on Hollywood and on my career. I even was watched on the train.

"You are not to leave your compartment," I was told. "Your meals will be served here."

At Chicago a man met me. He was pleasant, but he made sure I didn't get out of his sight until I was safely on the Twentieth Century Limited for New York. I was lost and befuddled again in the Big City almost as completely as I was the first day I walked out of Grand Central Station as a little convent girl, but an offer came from a Philadelphia theater where one of my pictures was showing. I accepted and went there for two weeks, the first of a long series of personal appearances that carried me through every field of entertainment until I hit rock bottom, doing my feeble best with song and dance to earn a few dollars in the toughest dives around New York.

Poor Wallace, perhaps thinking he was to blame for my banishment from Hollywood, followed me to New York. He was quite innocent through it. He was just madly in love with the Mary Nolan he saw on the screen, but that infatuation made him a pawn in the events that were shaping my life. Without knowing it, he was caught in the same vise of circumstances that was closing around me. He asked me to marry him, but I had laughed it off.

One day the bodyguard who had been assigned to watch me in Hollywood, came to see me. He was armed. He had the same look of determination I had seen in Los Angeles the night I was put on the train. I knew he meant business.

"I've a telegram I want you to send," he said politely but firmly.

It was handed to me to read. It was addressed to the man I once thought I loved.

"Have I your consent to marry Wallace?" the message read. "He is a nice boy and I'm in love with him."

"No, no," I protested. "I can't send that. I have no intention of marrying Wallace. What is the idea of this ridiculous telegram?"

"It will be much healthier for you, if you send it," the visitor said coldly.

My tears meant nothing. The message was finally sent. The next morning, stories came chattering over the wires from Los Angeles that Mary Nolan had found romance, was in love with a wealthy New Yorker, planned an early marriage. I was stunned at the news put out in Los Angeles as a result of the telegram I was forced to send. But in the lucid moments that my growing need for morphine allowed me, I began to see the pattern of the scheme laid out for me. My being in love and marrying another man would do much to still the ugly tales. My trip to the altar would go far to discredit the scandalous gossip.

Wallace, innocently enough, fell in with the plan. My wedding, an event which should be the climax of a girl's dreams, was as coldly planned as a business deal. I had nothing to say about it. A woman was sent to stay with me until I was married. She came in the guise of a maid, but her chief object was to keep an eye on me. My wedding gown even was selected for me and sent to my hotel.

Instead of being a gay, happy occasion, my wedding was a nightmare. The ceremony was performed at 8 o'clock in the evening at a church in Brooklyn. Even the elements seemed to cry out in story protest. An hour or two before the ceremony, a violent storm came up, with thunder, lightning and sheets of rain. I thought it would never end. Only a few people were invited to attend the wedding. The reporters and photographers outnumbered the guests. As I started to walk down the aisle, it seemed as though I would never reach the altar. It seemed so far away, as if I had been walking toward it for hours.

When the words, "Do you take this man to be your husband" were spoken, they sounded far away. I couldn't realize they were addressed to me. I didn't answer. A prompting jarred me back to reality and I murmured, "I do." It was my wedding—but I wasn't there. When the time came to hold out my hand to receive the ring I stood numbed. Wallace finally lifted my hand to receive the golden circlet, symbolizing my truth.

I didn't feel as sorry for myself as I did for Wallace that night. He was sincere and honest and sweet about it all. I was just a human automation, stalking through a sacred rite. It was mockery but I felt I was blameless. Our entire married life was a mockery. We lived together, but never as man and wife. We had our separate bedrooms and respected each other's privacy. Wallace was finely bred and well educated. He was highly sensitive to the feelings of others and respected mine. That is more than I can say of most men I have known. He realized our position and gallantly took it as a matter of course.

Naturally we were not happy. We pretended to be gay when our friends were around and when we appeared in public. He always was tender and considerate, but the sham of it all drove me home in tears every night we went out. In our apartment we sat in silence with our thoughts of what might have been. We used to drive through Central Park in the old horse-drawn cabs, but always silently and alone. Then we would go to a good show, with a dance and supper afterward. We tried, but there was a barrier too wide for love to bridge.

My life already was wrecked. The disillusionment of marriage left Wallace shaken. It was unkindly said that Wallace followed me into the pitfall of dope. I would like to spike that falsehood. It is entirely untrue. But he did become cynical. Life swept him off his feet just as it had me. My past was largely an open book, so Wallace knew all about my affair with Frank Tinney in my earlier years in New York. We had discussed it frankly. Besides, it didn't matter since our life was a sham.

Perhaps out of curiosity, Wallace went to see Frank Tinney once at a sanitarium in Philadelphia where he was living. Maybe it is unfortunate that he didn't make that call the day before he fell in love with me. Frank looked at him blankly and uttered one sentence but it spoke volumes: "Son, don't ever go near a stage door!"

I went on with all the personal appearances an agent could book for me, but week after week, more and more doors were closed on me.

"Sorry, Miss Nolan, we can't use you," came to be the standard reply. They were too polite to say, "We can't use addicts."

Besides, I never liked personal appearances. I couldn't sing well enough to be a hit. My talents showed to their best advantage in dramatizations with a stage cast or before a camera. When the first-class theaters began turning a cold shoulder, I took any bookings I could get. Most people would say, "I had to eat." That was unimportant to me. My cry was, "I have to have morphine."

I wired to Los Angeles and sold what personal effects I had left there. One by one, bit by bit, expensive furs and precious jewelry began going over the counter for whatever I could get. Financial reverses had hit Wallace. He was beginning to feel the pinch too.

At last, when I saw that our mis-mated marriage must come to an end I was filled with an urge to fight my back to Hollywood, to make another attempt to regain my place as an actress. My life and addition threw me a contact with a good many people who certainly weren't to be found in the Blue Book. One was Dutch Schultz.[26] That he was a kingpin of the racketeers and chieftain of a ruthless gang of New York mobsters didn't matter to me. I was hard then too. I was disillusioned about all mankind. I was heartsick over my broken screen career.

The demand of my body for dope had me at its mercy. I could look any man in the eye, whether he be a killer or a jabbering idiot in the gutter, and feel a current of understanding. Dutch Schultz was introduced to me by a police lieutenant when I was appearing at the Place Theatre in New York. Dope had not yet robbed me of my beauty. Schultz became interested in me. I never felt I deserved to be called a gunman's moll, but in those days, it wouldn't have mattered much. My toboggan was pitched pretty steep.

At any rate I did go out with him a few times, but to give the devil his due his conduct always was quite proper with me. We went to some pretty terrible places. Every waiter and attendant in them was a gangster. They were tough, but naturally none of them bothered me as long as I was Schultz's guest. On one of my black days, and there were many of them, Schultz wanted to know what was troubling me, if there was anything he could do for me. I opened my heart to him.

"I would like to go back to make another start in pictures before the world forgets me." I told him.

He had power. I had none. I had no scruples about using any advantage he could give me. He said nothing and I forgot the incident. A few weeks later he called me.

"Be at my apartment at 2 o'clock sharp tomorrow afternoon," he said brusquely.

"Why? What's up?" I asked.

"You want to go back to Hollywood, don't you?"

"Yes, but what does that have to do with it?"

"Plenty! If you want to go, be here."

"Well, I do, but I don't understand."

"You will tomorrow." He hung up the receiver.

I was in Dutch Schultz's apartment half an hour early. All I could pry out of him was that I would get a phone call. Exactly at 2 o'clock the phone rang.

"Answer it," Schultz ordered. "It's for you."

I lifted the receiver in curious wonderment.

"Miss Nolan?" the operator asked. "Hold the wire please, Los Angeles is calling."

It was an invitation to come out and go to work! I could hardly wait to get started, but once on the train the terror seized me again. The heavy amounts of dope I was taking by that time may have contributed to my feelings, but nevertheless they were very real. Now that what I wanted was in my grasp I shrank from it. Perhaps it was fear of other ordeals such as I had known before. Hollywood was a place of mixed memories, some sweet, but most filled with heartaches. At times I was tempted to get off the train. I actually hoped that something would happen to prevent its arrival. But nothing did. I finally had to step off the train not wanting to.

A man met me. He was a representative of Dutch Schultz. Reporters and photographers were on hand to take pictures and interview me. Schultz's man had rented a home for me. I sat in it alone for a week with just my thoughts and my hypodermic. No one came near me. No one called.

Finally, I was signed for a part in a picture, *The Big Shot*. Like the titles of most of the other pictures I made, that one was appropriate of my life, too! Hollywood in general shunned me like poison. I knew no social life, very little companionship. But there were two other lonely souls in the picture world who shared my desolation with me. They were big men and they're still big today, so I'll leave them unnamed.

We had only our loneliness in common but that was great enough to encompass us. The three of us began to pal around together, going to the fights, the Cocoanut Grove, out-of-the-way gambling places for dinner, but the best times we ever had were after the night's outing was over. We would go to the home of one of the men, take over the kitchen, sit down on the floor, eat caviar sandwiches and drink champagne.

It all sounds very silly, but it gave each of us a chance to cry on the other's shoulder. Many a night we went through the same routine, talking until morning with the champagne and caviar on the floor beside us. The companionship of these kindly men filled a void in my lonely life that kept me from going stark mad. Maybe they didn't know they were doing me a favor. Maybe I gave some small measure of happiness to them. I hope so, because I've no other way to repay them. But like every sweet thing that happened to me in Hollywood there was a bitter sequel.

My picture was finished, and I was negotiating for another contract when a story about Wallace came out of New York. It was something about a scene he was supposed to have created at our former honeymoon suite at a New York hotel. They said he was carrying a torch for me. It was still blamed on the fact that I had left him and returned to Hollywood. Of course, that put my name in the headlines again. The contract offer was withdrawn. The door was closed on me in Hollywood.

For the second time in my life I had no choice but to turn my back on my chosen career and retrace my weary footsteps back to New York, the scene of my first triumph as a Follies girl, the backdrop of my deepest heartaches. I was bitter. I was hard. The downward steps were taken in swift strides. My whole life soon revolved entirely around one thing. That was dope. Nothing else mattered.

My existence was divided into two recurring periods, rushing some place to take a shot, then waiting a few hours living in agony, knowing that the inevitable craving soon would return, to be relieved only by more of the deadening drug. It was a vicious cycle, lucid moments of mental anguish, born of awareness that other moments of physical torture soon were to follow. I came to know the day when my frenzy would drive me to jab the needle into my leg right through my clothing.

Yes, I had gone a long way from the day I gave myself the first hypodermic in my fine home in Beverly Hills, when I carefully boiled the needle to sterilize it and sat shaking for ever so long before I could bring myself to inject it into my arm. An addict doesn't stop to worry about a sterilized instrument when a thousand demons are tearing at every nerve in his body. The last of the film star's fine furs, the final jewel of the bountiful days of Miss America went for whatever was offered to satisfy the desperate demands of the curse that held me.

Dozens of evening gowns, for which I had paid hundreds of dollars apiece during those days in Hollywood, went for a pittance to the first person who would heed my pleas. It was not long before my attire exactly fitted my station, a terror-ridden addict slinking furiously through the streets of New York. Hotels refused to admit me. It was hard to realize I had fallen so low that places where once I had wined and dined would call the police if I set foot inside the entrance. Of course, I didn't try to approach those scenes of former glory. I can see the irony of it all now, but I didn't think about it then.

I had a greater problem, a master that demanded obeisance every four hours. It was enough that I was being kicked out of a third-rate rooming house every few days for non-payment of rent. Theaters were turning a deaf ear to my entreaties for an engagement. For a short time, I managed to get a few bookings with the better class nightclubs, but every dismissal left me a rung further down the ladder. And dismissals were frequent. The shabbier I grew in appearance and dress, the shabbier the club that would give me a chance. I soon was reduced to spots in the lowest dives in New York.

[The next two paragraphs are illegible in the newspaper.]

My very presence seemed an open invitation to insults. Beggars can't be choosers. Yes, I drank deeply of the dregs of the cup that once overflowed with the clear effervescence of beauty and youth. There were times when my purse held nothing but cab fare to carry me to an underworld nightclub, where more times than not, I was turned away with a blunt "No crowd, can't use you tonight, sister."

Those were the agonizing times when I thought of the thousands of dollars that had slipped through my fingers, of the seven hundred dollars' worth of hats that I brought on a moment of pique with Frank Tinney's money, of the fabulous suits that had been thrown away at playboy's parties when I was the toast of the great city that knew me now only as a denizen of the streets.

There was only one bright spark in my life, of those tragic days. That was a dog, my Pomeranian, Toy. I had bought the pet on my last exile from Hollywood. Toy was the sweetest thing in the world ... his loyalty....

[The last three paragraphs are illegible.]

Chapter 8

Just when life was blackest a helping hand was stretched out to me one day in New York. I had slipped out of my squalid hotel room, taking care to dodge the landlady with her inevitable questions about room rent, and turned off a side street into Eighth Avenue. My teeth were chattering. A cold wind stabbed through my thin clothes to the bone. I had reached the level about one step above the gutter.

An examination of my purse brought back a memory of the first day I stepped timidly out of the Grand Central Station into the streets of the big city. I had thirty-five cents in my pocket that day when I was a simple little convent girl of thirteen, bewildered by the labyrinth around me. Ten years and more had passed. I had just thirty-five cents now. Fame and success, disillusionment and heartaches had come to me in that span of time. I was back on the sidewalks of New York, still bewildered, but haggard and hard, a dope fiend.

A well-dressed man stepped up and caught my arm. I scarcely turned. To be approached by a strange man on the street was commonplace. I pulled my arm away to shake off his hand.

"Pardon me but aren't you Imogene Wilson?" The man had a kindly voice. He even tipped his hat, a courtesy I no longer expected.

"I used to be," I said coldly and started to walk on.

"Wait a moment," he said. "I've admired you ever since you were in the Follies. Isn't there something I can do to help you?"

"No, thanks."

"Now, come on up to my hotel and have a drink. You look as if you need it."

Clothes were of little concern then. They came only after more urgent things were provided, but at mention of my appearance my eyes dropped to the shabby coat and rumpled skirt I was wearing. They weren't much like the satins and silks Miss America wore.

"No, I don't drink."

Liquor and dope don't mix.

"But I sincerely would like to help you," he went on. "This is my birthday. Suppose I celebrate by getting you a present."

"O.K. You win." I managed a smile. I didn't have much to lose. My craving left me a few scruples.

A few blocks away we turned into a dress shop.

"Let this lady select anything she wants, a complete outfit, and send the bill to me," the man said, handing the manager an engraved card.

"I'll be back shortly," he said to me.

Half an hour later, when I had finished picking out the first respectable garments I had worn in months, my benefactor stepped in.

"Here is a key to your suite," he said. "It is ready for you."

I was too grateful even to offer a polite thank you.

The suite was in my new friend's hotel. There were no strings tied to his generosity. Frankly, I expected some, but this man seemed to find his happiness in an unselfish act—in helping an unfortunate. It was a great change from the sordid environment of third-rate hotels and tawdry rooming houses. I lived there for several months, concealed for a time from the outside world under a mask of respectability, but it was only a mask. I was not happy. Demands of my body for dope made my physical existence a constant torture, whether rags or fine raiment covered me. When my efforts to get work in New York failed, my friend suggested I might do better in London. I welcomed any opportunity.

He arranged my transportation and bought me a new wardrobe. A few days later I once again saw the lights of New York twinkle out behind me as my boat steamed down the harbor and out to sea. In London I took the same flat that Frank Tinney and I had occupied—so long ago, it seemed. A doctor was the first person I contacted to arrange for my morphine. Then I obtained an agent who got an engagement for me at the Piccadilly Theatre.[27]

I tried hard to make a comeback, but my vitality was so low it was hopeless. The cold and fog, which addicts feel so much more than others, made me miserable. I managed to get to the theater for rehearsals, but I caught a cold. The night I was to open, I had a raging fever. My voice was gone. I couldn't even speak. The manager insisted that I appear on the stage and take a bow. After all his efforts to put me on, he wanted the audience to see me at last.

I hurried back to my flat and went right to bed where I stayed for weeks, desperately ill with double pneumonia. When I finally began to convalesce, I had my nurse cable my friend in New York. He didn't fail me. Transportation for my return came on the next mail. As soon as I was able to travel, I started for home. It was not like my first return, when I came with high hopes from my screen success in Germany. This time I dreaded it. I had failed completely.

With the last bit of will, my all-consuming habit had left me. I made a firm resolve on that trip to New York. If I salvaged my life, I knew I would have to do it on my own courage, alone. I would have to fight this thing out by myself. The kindness and charity of friends couldn't do it for me. My benefactor met me at the boat.

"Your old suite is waiting for you," he said. "You have been so terribly ill, I want to go on helping you."

It was a big temptation to revoke the decision I had made. I knew the comforts he could provide. He knew of my addiction and had offered to finance a cure, but I knew that wouldn't work. I would be pampered too much. If I won, I would have to do it the hard way.

"No thanks," I told him and explained my reason.

"I wish you luck and if I ever can help, call on me."

I went back to the cheap rooming houses and offered the few talents dope had left me to any kind of club that would give me a night's booking. In the days that followed, I believe I met or saw about every gangster in New York, Legs Diamond, Owney Madden and all the rest. The only places that would permit me to appear were the dives that harbored the underworld. Occasionally these men would do me a favor, perhaps out of pity, because I had lost all physical attractiveness. One would walk up to a table where I was waiting my turn to go on.

"You're lucky, kid. Your horse won," he would say. A hand would drop something in front of me. "Here's what you got back."

I hadn't bet, but there usually was a twenty-dollar bill or two, charity in gangster fashion. Some of the managers weren't so considerate. More than one tried to pay me for my poor efforts in drinks. I didn't want that. If they had offered me morphine, I would have accepted gladly. As the hypodermics of dope I was taking became larger and larger, I began living in a ghost world, a realm of fantastic creatures of my imagination. At times it seemed as if I were two or three different persons, each with a separate personality, each wanting to do a different thing. Mary Nolan was completely detached from them.

There was one specter, a little girl, that used to come into my room often at night. Sometimes I would waken with a start to find this ghostly little figure leaning over me or hovering over my bed in a misty cloud. I probably didn't really wake up at all. I just dreamed the whole thing in that distorted half-world of aberration. But the child came to me time and again in my dope-born land of fantasy. Its presence was as vivid as any experience in my life. There were times when I even heard its imaginary footsteps pattering around the room or down the hall.

Locked doors and windows were no barrier to my ethereal visitors. The ghost child used to take me by the hand and lead me off into the strangest places, all awesome and grotesque. On those jaunts into dreamland I became one of the personalities that detached itself completely from my weary body. I could look at myself as much to say: "Poor Mary Nolan, I'm glad I'm not in her shoes."

Mary Nolan, Ziegfeld Girl and Silent Movie Star

There were other ghost-like figures that harassed and tortured me. They would glide noiselessly around me, their long, thin fingers reaching closer and closer to my body. Some of them seemed to have dozens of arms. Each spot they touched burned as if I had been touched with a searing needle. That was just my body setting up its cry for morphine, my aching physical being trying to arouse a sodden mentality to supply its need—another shot. When the pain of the torturing fingers finally brought me out of my troubled sleep I would jump in agony. I would be frantic for morphine.

Addicts get a lot of strange obsessions. The commonest one is that they have a supply of dope hidden in their clothes or round their room. It probably is born of the addict's greatest fear, the terrible dread of not being able to get the next shot.

I woke up one morning in a frenzy, in my back-hall room after a night spent with my torturing ghosts. It was just dawn. My body was on fire. I had that idea that I had some morphine hidden in the room. I rolled back the thin mattress. Cotton spilled out of a gaping hole on the underside. Into the opening went my hand to search and poke into every wad of the matted filler.

There was nothing there. I had gone through the same search many times before. Each time more cotton spilled out, the hole got bigger, but there is no reasoning in an addict's mind. The place and circumstances all are swept away and one's body screams for relief. They always are in the same obvious places, for something that I put there only in a dream. By the time I had ransacked everything in my room, and that wasn't much, I had become rattled enough to realize that I had to get to my dealer to get my morphine. I frantically counted my money. I had enough to buy a day's supply.

I hurried out into the street. It was before six o'clock. I would be there hours before the doctor's office opened. I knew I would have to stand the agony that wracked me until that time. I had learned from experience that he would appear early. He was used to people who cried and begged and even threatened to get their fix at all hours of the night. I thought of walking to his office just to pass the time, but I couldn't do it. The cold morning air pierced my body. I was sneezing. My nose and eyes were streaming as an addict's do. My face was twitching with grimaces I couldn't control.

I scurried into a subway station, hoping I could find a seat on an early-morning train where I could sit alone to hide my face. In the subway station, I found a seat in a corner where I must have waited two hours or more as trains shuttled in and out a fantastic new idea seized me. What if there should be a wreck, to have me tied up, and I would be delayed? That thought frightened me to such proportions that I almost went mad. When my train pulled in I hurried towards the end car. Then I was afraid I might get shut out. As the train slowed down I raced abreast of a door to be sure I wouldn't miss it. When it opened I lunged through.

My rush caused such a commotion that passengers dropped their papers and stared at me. My disheveled appearance must have been frightening. I slumped in a corner seat and turned my head toward the window. My three-station ride on the subway that morning took on the proportions of a trip to the North Pole in my distorted mind. Everything that might happened to stop us, and a lot that couldn't happen, flashed before me. By the time the train started, people around me had gone back to their morning papers or resumed conversations.

A man and a girl sat near me. They were talking and laughing in the highest of spirits. The girl's merry laughter seemed to fill the car. The agony I had known for the last three years came back to me with all its bitterness. I cried a prayer as that girl's laugh beat against my ears.

"Oh, God please, I want to be happy like these people! I have the right to live normally, enjoy normal things, do the ordinary things that ordinary people do. I want my own life, not this nightmare."

I think I knew then how poor Helen Worthing felt in her misery.

At last the train reached my stop. I hurried out, half running, toward the doctor's office. Every sound was magnified a hundredfold. Even my own heels tapping on the pavement reverberated through the top of my head like a hammer blow. The nurse checked my permit, brought out the morphine and counted my money. I stumbled out as quickly as I could. The doctor didn't want my kind hanging round his office.

I rushed into a public rest room, fixed my hypo with trembling hands, and jabbed the needle into my flesh. Relief came instantly. I washed my face and made a gesture of combing my stringy hair. A few hours of calm now lay ahead of me. I rode back to my dismal room, hoping to sleep until the time came for my next shot. I turned the key and pushed against the door, but it didn't open. Then, in the semi-darkness I saw why.

A hasp and padlock had been placed on the door. The landlady had grown tired of my evasive answers. I was locked out. My scanty belongings were inside. I truly was at the end of my string. My purse contained fifteen cents and a day's supply of morphine. Slowly I trudged up to Central Park. It was noon when I reached there, and the sun was warm. I dropped to the first secluded bench I found and curled up on it for a few moments of sleep. I was too exhausted then to indulge in reveries and it probably was just as well. Memories can bring nothing but pain, recollections of days of affluence when I had ridden through the park, swathed in furs and nestled in comfort in Frank Tinney's arm. Now I was back there, a derelict, in rags, my last place of refuge barred to me.

One nickel went for a cup of coffee. I started to use another for a phone call to try to get work for the night, but I knew that was useless. I was too weak. Instead, I used a nickel for a call to the Actors Fund. I was desperate. I couldn't go on this way. The Fund was wonderful. No one has a more generous heart than theatrical people. They proved it to me.

A modest apartment was provided for me and a nurse was sent to look after my wants. She didn't try to interfere with my dope but began telling me of plans that were being made to send me to a hospital. The idea appealed to me when the nurse told me about it. Then a policeman came, and I was frightened. Fear that I would be deprived of morphine swept over me. With a hop-head's cunning I watched my chance and slipped out of the apartment in the middle of the night. I had nothing on but a nightgown. I must have been out of my head. It was such a crazy thing to do. I was just running away from something. I didn't know what.

I hadn't gone far before I heard a siren. An ambulance rolled up, a man grabbed me, and I was whisked to Bellevue. But I couldn't stay there, so I soon found myself in a narcotic hospital, committed for a cure. After four months I realized my condition was worse instead of better. One morning I got into the office and confronted the nurse on duty.

"I'm leaving," I announced.

"Why, you are in no condition to do that," she said. "I can't sign you out."

"That's too bad. I'm going anyway."

I bolted for the door.

I had lost all track of time. The passage of day and night meant nothing to me, because I was kept in a constant stupor. I didn't even know the season or month. When I stepped outside, the ground was covered in snow. The nurse hurried after me.

"Come back, come back," she called. "I'll give you a hypo right away."

"Thanks. I've just had one," I cried over my shoulder.

"Well, come back and I'll give you another one."

"That's just what I'm afraid of and that's the reason I'm not coming back."

Some way I managed to elude her. I made my escape. A short time later I slipped into a little café to try to gather my thoughts. A radio was going. The first thing I heard was a broadcast telling of my escape and asking police to pick me up. I hurried on with no idea where my steps were leading me. I just wanted to get as far from that hospital as I could. Probably I didn't get very far. The next thing I knew a car pulled up beside me. A policeman, a doctor and a nurse jumped out.

"No, no, let me go!" I screamed as they grabbed me. "I'm not going back to that place."

"Now, just take it easy," the doctor said, "you're not going there. We're taking you to a new place."

There was nothing I could do to prevent it. The four of us rode in silence. It seemed like hours. At last we stopped, and I was led into another institution. While the doctor and nurse were talking to the superintendent, I wandered aimlessly into an adjoining room. The first object that caught my eye was a beautiful Christmas tree. It jarred me back to reality, fixed time in my mind again. Tears came into my eyes as I edged over to the tree and touched one of the glistening ornaments with a trembling hand. My senses played so many tricks on me I didn't trust my eyes.

Then I looked around the room. Above a desk was a daily calendar. The big figure read: "Dec. 24." It was the day before Christmas. I had forgotten there was such a thing. My Christmas present was being arranged in the front office—commitment to a state hospital for narcotic addicts. I broke into a hysterical laugh as I stood gazing at the beautiful tinseled tree, symbolic of the sweetest memories of mankind.

My mind is confused about the next few months, but the doctors were gentle and kind. They and the nurses nurtured my feeble will to get better, to throw off the chains that had dragged me down. I was kept asleep most of the time. The amount of morphine I was taking was gradually reduced, with a milder narcotic sub-stituted to make me sleep. In that period which is largely a blank in my mind I was actually taken back to infancy and all but reborn through the kindness and skill of my doctor.

My hair grew brittle. Most of it came out. My fingernails dropped off. My teeth became so loose they almost fell out, too. My body shriveled. Skin and calluses peeled off in layers. I really grew a new body, free from the pains and taunts of dope that the old one demanded. The doctors had to teach me to talk. Nurses taught me to walk all over again. The first time I looked in a mirror after I began to improve, I was horrified. I couldn't believe the wizened creature whose image I saw could really be me.

I was allowed to see myself for a purpose. I wouldn't eat.

"You see how badly you need nourishment," I was told after the peek into the mirror. "If you eat as we want you to, you will regain the beauty you have lost."

I didn't believe it, but I tried. They used to stuff me with food. The doctor begged and coaxed until he got me to eating nine slices of heavily buttered bread each day, three slices a meal besides my other food. Slowly I began to grow stronger, I learned to walk alone. One day a sudden realization came to me as my mind revived the past. I wasn't living in terror of four-hour periods that marked the moments when I had scurried furtively into a rest room to take a shot to relieve my jumping nerves. There were no pains, no yawns, no jerking muscles. I was free! The desire was gone!

It was the most wonderful sensation of my whole life. I knew then that I had won my fight. As soon as I was able, the nurses took me for drives along the Long Island shore. Occasionally, later, we would go to a picture show. It all seemed too good to be true, like walking fresh and clean into a Spring garden.

In October 1938, I was told that my cure was complete, that I was well again. I could go any time I wished. The Actors Fund came to my aid as before. I wanted to return to Los Angeles, even though I had been told I never could go there again. My sister lived there, I had no one else, no other place to go. Before my train left, I was taken to a luncheon in a large New York hotel. It had been so long since I had dared to step into such a place with my head up. I walked in that day proudly. It brought back memories. There had been a time in the Follies days when I had led a fashion parade in that very place, the magnet of all eyes.

I recalled that as we walked in and sat down in the mirrored dining room, I took a look at myself in my new attire and tried to smile. I didn't look so bad.

"Maybe I'm not Miss America," I thought to myself, "but I've come a long way since the days in the gutter."

As I turned from the mirror I glimpsed a man at a nearby table looking at me. I didn't know him. He didn't know me, but I'm grateful to him for his attention that day. He gave me a confidence I hadn't felt before, a feeling that I had not lost all attractiveness.

As my train bore me toward Los Angeles, my mind was filled with mixed emotions. I was happy with my freedom from physical pain, but naturally I was worried about the future. I couldn't go on accepting the aid of the Actors Fund forever. I wondered if the ban still barred my course in Los Angeles.

My sister and niece met me at the station and took me to their home. There was no crowd of movie fans, reporters and photographers waiting that day. I walked through the station throng unnoticed. Then I became ill again. Another wonderful organization, the Motion Picture Relief Fund, came to my assistance and made the hospital arrangements. For five days I remained in a coma. As soon as I got on my feet again I wanted to be alone. I knew I was close to that freedom I had hunted all my life. I didn't want to be dependent. The Relief Fund wanted to arrange for me to enter a rest home, but I didn't want charity.

My whole life had been spent at the whim and direction of someone else. It had been governed by routine, controlled by others. Hospitals, lovers, studios had told me what to do and what not to do. I determined to follow my own will. I called on a number of agents. They all tried to find something for me, but all came back with the same answer.

"Sorry, nothing doing. You understand how it is?"

I did understand, too well. I was hurt at finding I couldn't go back to the screen. I had been cured of my dope habit. My health was fine. I thought I had earned a chance. I always had been a failure at personal appearances. I was not good at appearing on a stage with a smile, some pretty clothes and nothing to do. With the studios closed to me, the next step was not easy. Few chances are open to a woman untrained to gain a livelihood except in a field that was barred to me. There was not even "anything that would pay a few dollars a week."

Of course, I knew I could hang around bars, meet plenty of men who would buy drinks and supper. I could do that—and live. That was the easy way.

My other choice was to be decent, even if I had to go out and hoe in the ground. I had my health. I had been given back some of my beauty. I would have been false to myself, untrue to friends who had helped me out of the gutter if I had taken the easy path. A kindly couple engaged me to manage their bungalow court. It was a place to eat and sleep and food to eat. That's all. I was working for room and board and gladly. There was not much to do. My identity was unknown except to the couple who hired me. I spent my leisure time working in their garden. I was truly down to earth for the first time in my life.

One day a lady tenant stopped to watch me as I was digging among the flowers. I was wearing slacks and a big floppy hat. I couldn't have been more glamorous.

"My dear, you're wasting your time," the lady said, "you should be in pictures."

"Thank you, you're very flattering," I told her, "but that's not for me."

"I don't know why not," she went on. "You know, you remind me a great deal of an actress who used to be very famous."

"Really?"

"Yes, her name was Imogene Wilson. She was a star in the Ziegfeld Follies. Oh, she was famous. She was the girl who broke up Frank Tinney's home. Surely you must have heard of her."

I was grateful for that hat that spared me an answer.

"She came to Hollywood and changed her name to Mary Nolan. She made a hit in pictures, but the poor thing became a dope fiend and just threw her life away. It was too bad."

"Yes—it was—too bad."

I sat among the flowers for a long time. There was so much to remember, so much to forget. As I ran over my life in retrospect, I realized that I had too much, too young. It spoiled all natural instincts. It has been said that beauty is a gift, money a blessing, and success a crowning glory, but success robbed me of happiness. I didn't misuse these things that were given to me. They misused me. But I don't believe anything bad will ever happen to me again. I hope the rest of my life will be normal and nice. I don't know what the future holds for me, but whatever it is I will face it with faith and courage. I owe that to those that had faith in me.

Three years have passed. Already I have learned how much joy there is in just being a plan, normal person, free to gaze untroubled at the stars at night or walk alone beside the rolling seas, unguarded and unwatched. God has been good to me. The cynical may scoff at that. Let them.

I know my own heart.

✛ ✛ ✛

Filmography

1925

Wenn die Liebe nicht wär! *Production-Distribution Company:* Phoebus-Film AG. *Director:* Robert Dinesen. *Writers:* Robert Dinesen, Walter Jonas; Emil Scholl (from his novel). *Composer:* Willy Schmidt-Gentner. *Cinematographer:* Julius Balting. *Art Director:* Willi Herrmann. *Production Manager:* Alfred Kern. *Cast:* MARY NOLAN (as Imogene Robertson), Fritz Alberti, Harry Halm, Antonie Jaeckel, Jenny Jugo, Frieda Lehndorf, Karl Platen, Hans Adalbert Schlettow, Daisy Torrens, Elsa Wagner. Silent. Black and White. Released on February 8, 1925.

Die Feuertänzerin. *Production-Distribution Company:* Phoebus-Film AG. *Director:* Robert Dinesen. *Writers:* Robert Dinesen, Walter Jonas, Ernest Klein. *Cinematographer:* Julius Balting. *Art Director:* Willi Herrmann. *Production Manager:* Alfred Kern. *Cast: Die Feuertänzerin*—MARY NOLAN (as Imogene Robertson), *Generaldirektor Godenberg*—Alfred Abel, *Malanie*—Ruth Weyher, *Holland*—Carl Auen, *Bartos*—Hans Heinrich von Twardowski, *Untersuchungsrichter*—Erich Kaiser-Titz, *Portiersfrau*—Roas Valetti, *Gertrude Berliner*—Trude Berliner, and Harry Halm, Jenny Jugo. Silent. Black and White. Released in July 1925.

Das Parfüm der Mrs. Worrington (Mrs. Worrington's Perfume). *Production Company:* Emelka. *Distribution Company:* Bayerische Film. *Director:* Franz Seitz. *Producer:* Ernst Reichner. *Writer:* Hendrik Kerdon. *Cinematographer:* Toni Frenguelli. *Art Directors:* Ludwig Reiber, Otto Völckers. *Cast: Stuart Webbs*—Ernst Reicher, *Mabel Christians*—Maria Mindzenty, *Dr. Harry Edwards*—John Mylong, *Philipp Worrington*—Otto Wernicke, *Charles Taylor*—Karl Falkenberg, *Bob Trum*—Ferdinand Martini, *Hubert Mills*—Manfred Koempel-Pilot, and MARY NOLAN, Claire Kronburger. Silent. Black and White. Released on July 10, 1925.

Die unberührte Frau. *Production Company:* Greenbaum-Film. *Distribution Company:* Bayerische Film. *Director-Writer:* Constantin J. David. *Cinematographer:* Mutz Greenbaum. *Art Director:* Karl Görge. *Cast: Marcelle Vautier*—MARY NOLAN, *Jane*—Tamara Geva, *Roger Clermont*—Alf Blütecher, *Lucien*—Harry Halm, *Colette Duflos*—Jeanne de Balzac, *Casimir Lebrun*—Hans Junkermann, *Andre*—Hans Behrendt, *Jasmin Potfin*—Ulrich Bettac, and Constantin J. David. Silent. Black and White. Released on December 10, 1925.

Verborgene Gluten (Hidden Fires). *Production-Distribution Company:* Emelka. *Director:* Einar Bruun. *Writer:* Patrick Macgnil. *Cinematographers:* Toni Frenguelli, Franz Koch. *Cast: Ias, Jack's Wife*—MARY NOLAN (as Imogene Robertson), *Jack Bruce*—Alphons Fryland, *Dickie, their son*—Lisa Deihle, *The Maid*—Mary Hainlin, *Danham*—Ferdinand Martini, *Olive Clayton*—Gertrude McCoy, *Guipe Golding*—Georg H. Schnell, *Estela*—Gloria Sved. Silent. Black and White. Released on December 31, 1925.

Filmography

1926

Fünf-Uhr-Tee in der Ackerstraße (Tea Time in the Ackerstrasse). Production Company: Domo-Film GmbH. *Distribution Company:* Domo-Strauß-Film GmbH. *Director:* Paul Ludwig Stein. *Writers:* Alfred Schirokauer, Reinhold Schünzel. *Cinematographer:* Franz Planer. *Art Directors:* Otto Erdmann, Hans Sohnle. *Production Manager:* Willy Morree. *Still Photographer:* Walter Lichtenstein. *Cast:* MARY NOLAN (as Imogene Robertson), Reinhold Schünzel, Maria Kamradek, Fritz Kampers, Heinrich Schroth, Angelo Ferrari, Frigga Braut, Rosa Valetti. Silent. Black and White. Released on March 29, 1926.

Unser täglich Brot (Our Daily Bread). Production Company: Greenbaum-Film. *Distribution Company:* Veritas–Film GmbH. *Director:* Constantin J. David. *Executive Producer:* Herman Millakowsky. *Writers:* Hans Behrendt, Mutz Greenbaum. *Composer:* Hansheinrich Dransmann. *Cinematographer:* Mutz Greenbaum. Art *Director:* Karl Machus. *Cast: The School Teacher*—MARY NOLAN (as Imogene Robertson), *Overseer*—Paul Hartmann, *Tagger*—Hans Mierendorff, and Fritz Kampers, Dina Gralla, Elza Temary, Harry Nestor, Leonia Bergere, Paul Rehkopf. Silent. Black and White. Released on March 30, 1926. *Synopsis:* When he runs out of money, one of Tagger's factory workers goes on a strike. The supervisor is jealous of Tagger's son and fuels the conflict.

Eleven Who Were Loyal. Production Company: Internationale Film AG (IFA). *Distribution Company:* UFA Film Company. *Director-Producer:* Rudolf Meinert. *Writers:* Max Jungk, Julius Urgiss. *Cinematographer:* Ludwig Lippert. *Art Director:* Gustav A. Knauer. *Cast: Mary Von Wedel*—MARY NOLAN (as Imogene Robertson), *Major von Schill*—Rudolf Meinert, *King Wilhelm III*—Gustav Adolf Semler, *Königin Luise*—Grete Reinwald, *Freiherr von Wedel*—Leopold von Ledebur, *Fritz von Wedel*—Ernst Rückert, *Udo von Reckenthin*—Werner Pittschau, *Freiherr von Mallwitz*—Fritz Greiner, *French Commander*—Albert Steinrück, *Französischer Offizier*—Charles Willy Kayser, *Minne*—Camilla von Hollay, *Franz*—Henri Peters-Arnolds, *Freischärler*—John Mylong, *Herr Von Malwitz*—Fritz Alberti, and Else Reval, Aruth Wartan, Fred Immler, Edgar Hellwald, Jaro Fürth, Mark Asarow, Clementine Plessner, Emmerich Hanus, Rudolf Del Zopp, Kurt Thormann, Bobbie Bender. Silent. Black and White. 60 minutes. Released on August 27, 1926.

Wien, wie es weint und lacht (Vienna, How It Cries and Laughs). Production-Distribution Company: Aafa-Film AG. *Directors:* Rudolf Walther-Fein, Rudolf Dworsky. *Producers:* Rudolf Dworsky. *Writers:* Ludwig Anzengruber, Alfred Halm. *Composer:* Felix Bartsch. *Cinematographer:* Carl Drews. *Art Director:* Jacek Rotmil. *Production Manager:* Arno Winkler. *Cast: Adele*—MARY NOLAN (as Imogene Robertson), *Leopold Gruber*—Fritz Greiner, *Martin*—John Mylong, *Sefi*—Mady Christians, *Die Großmutter*—Frida Richard, *Pepi Gschwandtner*—Hans Brausewetter, *General Albrecht V. Wagher*—Erich Kaiser-Titz, *Hofrat Anton Hutter*—Hermann Picha, *Leutenant Otto Hutter*—Werner Pittschau, *Rittmeister Graf Kollodat*—Julius Falkenstein, *Schöllerer*—*Wagenwäscher*—Paul Biensfeldt, *Der Bursche des Generals*—Max Menden, *Ein dicker Gast*—Wilhelm Diegelmann. Silent. Black and White. Released on September 16, 1926.

Das süße Mädel (The Sweet Girl). Production Company: Noa-Film GmbH. *Distribution Company:* Süd-Film. *Director:* Manfred Noa. *Writers:* Leo Stein, Joseph Than, Ludwig von Wohl. *Composers:* Hans May, Heinrich Reinhardt. *Cinematographer:* Otto Kanturek. *Art Directors:* Gustav A. Knauer, Hermann Warm. *Cast: The Prince's Son*—Nils Asther, *Dancer*—Manfred Noa, and MARY NOLAN (as Imogene Robertson), Paul Heidemann, Mary Parker, Eugen Burg, Hanni Reinwald, Loo Hady, Ernst Pröckl, Karl Platen, Henry Bender, Sophie Pagay, Bobbie Bender, Alex Angelo, Ernst Morgan, Geza L. Weiss, Max Hiller. Silent. Black and White. Released on October 8, 1926.

Die Welt will belogen sein (***The World Wants to Be Deceived***). *Production Company:* Nero-Film AG. *Distribution Company:* Bayerische Film. *Director:* Peter Paul Felner. *Producer:* Heinrich Nebenzahl. *Writer:* Peter Paul Feiner. *Cinematographers:* Curt Courant, Sophus Wangøe. *Art Director:* Ernst Stern. *Cast: Ly, dessen Tochter*—MARY NOLAN (as Imogene Robertson), *Robert Cors*—Harry Liedtke, *Charles Barcknell*—Georg Alexander, *Mery*—Mady Christians, *Dr. Stone*—Walter Rilla, *Hutten*—Paul Biensfeldt, *Albert Cors*—Henri De Vries, *Jones-Journalist*—Eugen Rex, *Ein Professor*—Paul Morgan, *Dr. Sixtus*—Carl Geppert, *Actress*—Else Reval. Silent. Black and White. Released on October 28, 1926.

Die Abenteuer eines Zehnmarkscheins (***The Adventures of a Ten Mark Note***) (AKA ***Uneasy Money***). *Production Company:* Deutsche Vereins-Film AG. *Distribution Company:* Fox Film Corporation. *Director:* Berthold Viertel. *Producer–Production Supervisor:* Karl Freund. *Writer:* Béla Balázs. *Composer:* Guiseppe Becce. *Cinematographers:* Robert Baberske, Helmar Lerski. *Assistant Director:* Herbert Selpin. *Still Photographer:* Walter Lichtenstein. *Art Directors:* Robert Basilice, Walter Reimann. *Cast: Anna*—MARY NOLAN (as Imogene Robertson), *Die Mutter*—Agnes Mueller, *Robert*—Walter Franck, *Andreas*—Werner Fietterer, *Fritz*—Harald Paulsen, *Frieda*—Iwa Wanja, *Direktor Haniel*—Oskar Homolka, *Frau Hamel*—Ressel Orla, *Ein* — Francesco von Mendelssohn, *Herr Fischer*—Otto Wallburg, *Eine Zimmervermieterin*—Luise Morland, *Ein Chauffeur*—Karl Etlinger, *Ein Lumpensammler*—Vladimir Sokoloff, *Ein Bierjunge*—Geza L. Weiss, *Der Hauswirt*—Julius E. Herrmann, *Eine Bufettdame*—Margo Lion, *Eine Bettlerin*—Frieda Blumenthal, and Hans Brausewetter. Silent. 60 minutes. Black and White. Released on October 28, 1926.

Mary in a publicity still for *Das süße Mädel*.

Die Königin des Weltbades (***The Queen of the Baths***). *Production Company:* Alfred Sittzarz. *Distribution Company:* National-Film. *Director:* Victor Janson. *Producer:* Alfred Sittarz. *Production Manager:* Heinrich Lisson. *Writers:* Edward Stilgebauer, Jane Bess, Adolf Lantz. *Composer:* Austin Egen. *Cinematographer:* Otto Kanturek. *Art Director:* Jacek Rotmil. *Cast: Micheline Bonnard*—MARY NOLAN (as Imogene Robertson), *Lord Arthur Blythe*—

Walter Rilla, *Marquis*—Livio Pavanelli, *Mme. Richemond*—Camilla von Hollay, *Fürstin Wolkonski*—Ida Wüst, *Lady Blythe*—Gertrud Arnold, *Maler Tschakoff*—Ferdinand Hart, *Mannequin*—Lissy Arna, *Direktrice*—Eva Speyer, *Gibson*—Alf Blutecher, *Spieler*—Paul Morgan, *Spieler*—Siegfried Berisch, *Spieler*—Oreste Bilancia. Silent. Black and White. Released on December 10, 1926.

Das Panzergewolbe (The Armored Vault). *Production Company:* Rex-Film GmbH. *Distributor:* Universum Film (UFA). *Director-Producer:* Lupu Pick. *Writers:* Curt J. Braun, Lupu Pick. *Composer:* Jos von Streletzky. *Cinematographer:* Gustave Preiss. *Set Decorator:* Rudi Field. *Cast: Ellen, Frau Elgin*—MARY NOLAN (as Imogene Robertson), *Stuart Webbs*—Ernst Reicher, *Elgin*—Johannes Riemann, *Cracker*—Heinrich George, *Ronna*—Aud Egede-Nissen, *Sandy*—Sig Arno, *Craigh*—Max Gulstorff, *Bobby*—Hugo Fischer-Koppe, *Der Dicke*—Julius E. Herrmann, *Der Elegante*—Hadrian Maria Netto, *Der Brutale*—Erich Kaiser-Titz, *Der Künstler*—Paul Rehkopf, *Der Ingenieur*—Fritz Rulard, *Der Chauffeur*—Louis Brody, *Diener*—Ernst Behmer, *Untersuchungsrichter 1*—Artur Retzbach, *Untersuchungsrichter 2*—Julius Falkenstein, *Untersuchungsrichter 3*—Jakob Tiedtke, *Radfahrer*—Geza L. Weiss. Silent. Black and White. Released on December 30, 1926.

1927

Die Mädchen von Paris (The Girl of Paris). *Distribution Company:* British Independent Exhibitors' Distributors. *Director:* Victor Janson. *Cast:* MARY NOLAN (as Imogene Robertson), Livio Pavanelli. Silent. Black and White. Released in 1927.

Erinnerungen einer Nonne (Memoirs of a Nun). *Production Company:* Münchner Lichtspielkunst. *Distribution Company:* Süd-Film. *Director:* Arthur Bergen (Bergen died at the Auschwitz concentration camp during the Holocaust in 1943). *Writers:* Arthur Bergen, Ernst Iros. *Art Director:* Ludwig Reiber. *Cinematography:* Franz Koch. *Music:* Hans May. *Cast:* MARY NOLAN (as Imogene Robertson), Camilla von Hollay, Werner Pittschau, Ellen Kürti, Georg John. Silent. Black and White. Released on February 24, 1927.

Halloh—Caesar! (Hello Caesar!). *Production Company:* Reinhold Schünzel Film. *Distribution Company:* UFA. *Director-Producer:* Reinhold Schünzel. *Writers:* Reinhold Schünzel, S.Z. Sakall. *Cinematography:* Ludwig Lippert. *Art Direction:* Otto Erdmann, Hans Sohnle. *Production Manager:* Fritz Grossman. *Cast: Girl*—MARY NOLAN (as Imogene Robertson), *Caesar*—Reinhold Schünzel, *Willard*—Wilhem Diegelmann, *Baron von Glatzenstein*—Julius Falkenstein, *Frau Svoboda*—Ilka Gruning, *Zwillingsbrüder*—Paul Kretschmar, *Zwillingsbrüder*—Richard Kretschmar, *Rosi*—Toni Philippi. Silent. Black and White. 90 minutes. Released on May 5, 1927.

Topsy and Eva. *Production Company:* Features Productions. *Distribution Company:* United Artists. *Directors:* Del Lord and (uncredited) D.W. Griffith, Lois Weber. *Production Consultant:* Myron Selznick. *Writers:* Harriet Beecher Stowe (novel *Uncle Tom's Cabin*), Catherine Chisholm Cushing (play), Scott Darling, Dudley Early, Lois Weber. *Cinematographer:* John W. Boyle. *Art Director:* William Cameron Menzies. *Cast: Topsy*—Rosetta Duncan, *Eva*—Vivian Duncan, *Simon Leegree*—Gibson Gowland, *Uncle Tom*—Noble Johnson, *Marietta*—Marjorie Daw, *Aunt Ophelia*—Myrtle Ferguson, *George Shelby*—Nils Asther, *St. Claire*—Henry Victor, *Angel*—Carla Laemmle, and MARY NOLAN (footage deleted), Lionel Belmore, Dot Farley. Silent. Black and White. 80 minutes. Released on July 24, 1927. *Synopsis:* Based on the stage show of the same name, which was a musical adaptation inspired by Uncle Tom's Cabin, this is the story of a friendship between two girls, who become inseparable and then ultimately save each other. Little Topsy, portrayed by a white girl in black face, is offered for sale by Simon Legree at auction. She is then bought for a nickel by Eva

St. Claire. When Eva is unable to payback Legree, he comes to reclaim Topsy, but she escapes. Later, learning that Eva is gravely ill, Topsy prays for her recovery, returns to see her. Ultimately Eva revives, and the two friends are happily reunited.

Sorrell and Son. *Production Company:* Feature Productions. *Distribution Company:* United Artists. *Director:* Herbert Brenon. *Assistant Director:* Ray Lissner. *Writer:* George Warwick Deeping (novel), Elizabeth Meehan. *Photography:* James Wong Howe. *Art Director:* William Cameron Menzies. *Editor:* Marie Halvey. *Set Decorator:* Julian Boone Fleming. *Makeup:* Fred C. Ryle. *Cast: Molly Roland (as a woman)*—MARY NOLAN, *Stephen Sorrell*—H.B. Warner, *Dora Sorrell*—Anna Q. Nilsson, *Kit Sorrell (as a child)*—Mickey McBan, *Flo Palfrey*—Carmel Myers, *John Palfrey*—Lionel Belmore, *Thomas Roland*—Norman Trevoe, *Molly Roland (as a child)*—Betsy Ann Hisle, *Buck*—Louis Wolheim, *Dr. Orange*—Paul McAllister, *Fanny Garland*—Alice Joyce, *Kit Sorrell (as a man)*—Nils Asther, *Young Woman*—Florence Fair. Silent. Black and White. 100 minutes. Released on November 13, 1927. Based on George Warwick Deeping's 1925 novel *Sorrell and Son*. Director Herbert Brenon's only onscreen credit appears above the title and reads "A Herbert Brenon Production." As part of the first Academy Awards in 1929, Brenon was nominated for Best Director, Dramatic Picture. The film was also voted one of the Top Best Features of 1928 by the 1929 *Film Daily Year Book*. The film was presumed lost until an incomplete print was discovered. The final reel is still lost. There was a real Sorrell: Named Moxley Sorrel, he too was considered a war hero, serving for most of the war as staff officer for Lt. Gen. James Longstreet, who mainly operated as corps commander for Lee's Army of Northern Virginia. *Synopsis:* The film tells the story of returning WWI soldier Captain Sorrell, who returns home to find that his wife has left him for another man. As he has a young son to take care of, he takes a low-level job as a hotel porter. His son Kit then grows up to become a successful surgeon and worships the ground his father walks on. When Sorrel gets cancer, Kit is unable to watch him die a painful death, and he reluctantly euthanizes hm. Although the overriding theme is a father's love for his son, it is also about a WWI veteran's difficulties reestablishing his pre-war position in society.

1928

Good Morning, Judge. *Production-Distribution Company:* Universal. *Director:* William A. Seiter. *Assistant Director:* Nate Watt. *Writers:* Earle Snell, Harry O. Hoyt, Beatrice Van, Joseph Franklin Poland, Tom Reed. *Photography:* Arthur L. Todd. *Editors:* Edward

Poster for *Good Morning Judge*.

143

M. McDermott, John Rawlins. *Cast: Julia Harrington*—MARY NOLAN, *Freddie Grey*—Reginald Denny, *Jerry Snoot*—Otis Harlan, *Ruth Grey*—Dorothy Gulliver, *Elton*—William B. Davidson, *First Crook*—Bull Montana, *Second Crook*—Sailor Sharkey, *Mr. Grey Sr.*—William Worthington, *Butler*—Charles Coleman, *Judge*—William H. Tooker. Silent. Black and White. 60 minutes. Released on April 29, 1928. *Synopsis:* After a street brawl, Freddie Gray, a wealthy young man, finds himself in court the next day, and is amazed to find that the man he was in a fight with, is the Judge presiding over his case. It is there that he then meets Julia Harrington, a wealthy social service worker who runs a mission for reformed criminals, and she ultimately pays his fine. He then starts working at her mission as part of his supposed rehabilitation. Julia then tries to reform him, and he keeps resisting telling her he is a hardened criminal. ion. She then takes him and several other "reformed" guests to a charity benefit. It provides too much temptation for some of the men, and Freddie uncovers that some of them are stealing jewelry from the guests at the event. Freddie then reveals his true nature by capturing the men, recovering the stolen goods and then wins Julia's heart.

The Foreign Legion. *Production-Distribution Company:* Universal. *Director:* Edward Sloman. *Writers:* Ida Alexa Ross Wylie (novel), Charles Kenyon, Jack Jarmuth, I.A.R. Wylie. *Cinematographer:* Jackson Rose. *Editor:* Ted J. Kent. *Cast: Sylvia Omney*—MARY NOLAN, *Richard Farquhar*—Norman Kerry, *Col. Destinn*—Lewis Stone, *Capt. Arnaud*—Crauford Kent, *Gabrielle*—June Marlowe, *Corp. Gotz*—Walter Perry. Silent. Black and White. 80 minutes. Released on June 23, 1928. Based on the 1913 novel *The Red Mirage* by Ida Alexa Ross Wylie. The working title of this film was *The Red Mirage,* and *Variety* reviewed the film simply as *Foreign Legion.* An earlier adaptation of Wylie's novel was produced by the Jesse L. Lasky Co. in 1915. That film, entitled *The Unknown,* was directed by George Melford and starred Lou Tellegen and Theodore Roberts. *Synopsis:* A father and a son, a Colonel and Private respectively, are both duped by a beautiful woman who finds pleasure in crushing the spirit and love of men. The son, Richard Farquhar, and the father, Colonel Destinn, being unaware of each other's identity, fight out for the affection of the woman, until Farquhar is brought to appear in a court-martial, where Destinn sits in judgment on him. It is here that Destinn learns that Farquhar is actually his son, and helps him escape, thereby condemning himself to death, allowing his son to be with the woman he loves, the beautiful woman's sister.

West of Zanzibar. *Production-Distribution Company:* MGM. *Director:* Tod Browning. *Assistant Director:* Harry Sharrock. *Producer:* Irving Thalberg. *Writers:* Elliott J. Clawson, Chester De Vonde, Kilbourn Gordon, Joseph White Farnham, Waldemar Young. *Photography:* Percy Hilburn. *Still Photographer:* Bob Bonner. *Art Directors:* Cedric Gibbons, Richard Day. *Editor:* Harry Reynolds. *Costumes:* David Cox. *Composers:* William Axt, Wayne Allen, Maurice Baron, Irenee Berge, Jack Feinberg, Sam Feinberg, Fritz Stahlberg. *Presenter:* Louis B. Mayer. *Voodoo Mask Maker:* William Mortensen. *Cast: Maizie*—MARY NOLAN, *Phroso*—Lon Chaney, *Crane*—Lionel Barrymore, *Doc*—Warner Baxter, *Anna*—Jacquelin Gadsdon, *Tiny*—Roscoe "Tiny" Ward, *Babe*—Kalla Pasha, *Bumbo*—Curtis Nero, *Music Hall Performer*—Chaz Chase, *Zanzibar Club Owner*—Rose Dione, *Old Woman on Street*—Louise Emmons, *Vaudeville Comedian*—Fred Gamble, *Stage Manager*—Emmett King, *Cannibal*—Dick Sutherland, *Dancing Girl*—Edna Tichenor, *Stagehand*—Art Winkler, *Zanzibar Club Customer*—San Wolheim, *Woman in Zanzibar Bar*—Zalla Zarana. Silent with some sound. Black and White. 65 minutes. Released on November 24, 1928. Estimated Budget $259,000. Gross $921,000. *Synopsis:* Flint is a crippled self-proclaimed King on an East African island. He came to the island after a man named Crane stole his wife and left him a paraplegic. Crane has a nearby ivory business, and Flint plots his revenge on Crane for 18 years, concentrating his hatred on Crane's daughter Anna. After secretly paying for her convent education, Flint brings Anna to his island, where he gets her hooked-on drugs and forces her into a life of prostitution. As a final humiliation, he intends to allow Anna to be sacrificed in a native ritual, but when he finds out that Anna is his own daughter, he does an abrupt about-face and rescues Anna and her sweetheart, from the natives.

1929

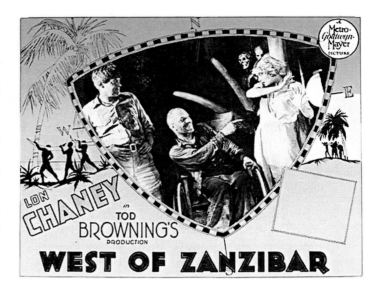

Poster for *West of Zanzibar*.

Silks and Saddles. *Production-Distribution Company:* Universal. *Director:* Robert F. Hill. *Writers:* Edward Clark, James Gruen, Gerald Beaumont, Paul Gangelin, Faith Thomas, J.G. Hawks, Albert De Mond. *Photography:* Joseph Brotherton. *Editor:* Daniel Mandell. *Presenter:* Carl Laemmle. *Cast: Sybil Morrissey*—MARY NOLAN, *Johnny Spencer*—Richard Walling, *Lucy Calhoun*—Marian Nixon, *William Morrissey*—Sam De Grasse, *Walter Sinclair*—Montagu Love, *Jimmy McKee*—Otis Harlan, *Judge Clifford*—David Torrence, *Mrs. Calhoun*—Claire McDowell, *Ellis*—John Fox, Jr., *Trainer*—Hayden Stevenson. Silent. Black and White. Released on January 20, 1929. UCLA Film Archives has a viewable print of this film. *Synopsis:* Jockey Johnny Spencer loves both Lady Courageous, the racehorse owned by Mrs. Calhoun, as well as her daughter Lucy. When he goes to New York to race for the Morrissey racing combine, he falls under the spell of Sybil, a blonde vamp who persuades him to throw the race. The racing judges however, uncover this plot, bar him from the track, and Sybil flees to Cuba with Morrissey. Johnny then becomes a racetrack bum, but when Lady Courageous' new jockey is unable to work with her, Mrs. Calhoun reluctantly agrees to have Johnny ride her again and he wins the race. This causes him to gain the respect of Mrs. Calhoun and regain the love of Lucy.

Desert Nights. *Production-Distribution Company:* MGM. *Director-Producer:* William Nigh. *Writers:* Lenore Coffee, Willis Goldbeck, Endre Bohem, John Thomas Neville, Dale Van Every, Marian Ainslee, Ruth Cummings. *Photography:* James Wong Howe. *Art Director:* Cedric Gibbons. *Editor:* Harry Reynolds. *Costumes:* Henrietta Frazer. *Music:* William Axt. *Cast: Lady Diana*—MARY NOLAN, *Hugh Rand*—John Gilbert, *Lord Stonehill*—Ernest Torrence, *The Real Lord Stonehill*—Claude King. Silent. Black and White. 72 minutes. Released on March 9, 1929. Production started on October 30, 1928, under the working title *Thirst*. Exterior scenes were shot in the Mojave Desert, California. *Synopsis:* Hugh Rand, the Manager of a South African diamond mine gets news that two visitors are coming, Lord Stonehill and his daughter Diana. They arrive ahead of schedule, and against Rand's own predictions, Lady Diana turns out to be a beautiful woman. However, the two are imposters, and are found out by Rand before he can let the authorities know. The pair of thieves, along with their other companions, take off into the desert with their stolen diamond, bringing Rand along as hostage. Things begin to go wrong for the thieves, and soon it is just Rand and the two imposters on foot, lost in the desert, searching for water. Realizing that Rand is the only person to lead them out of the desert, they untie him, and he leads them to safety. Along the way Diana and Rand fall in love and she repents her shady past. The fake Lord Stonehill is then arrested, leaving Rand and Diana to be together.

Charming Sinners. *Production-Distribution Company:* Paramount. *Director:* Robert Milton. *Writer:* Doris Anderson, based on the play *The Constant Wife* by W. Somerset Maugham. *Music:* Karl Hajos, W. Franke Harling. *Cinematographer:* Victor Milner. *Editor:* Verna Willis. *Sound Engineer:* Earl S. Hayman. *Costume Design:* Travis Banton. *Cast: Anne-Marie Whitley*—MARY NOLAN, *Kathryn Miles*—Ruth Chatterton, *Robert Miles*—Clive Brook, *Karl Kraley*—William Powell, *Mrs. Carr*—Laura Hope Crews, *Hellen Carr*—Florence Eldridge, *George Whitley*—Montagu Love, *Margaret*—Juliette Crosby, *Alice*—Lorraine MacLean, *Gregson*—Claud Allister, *Waiter*—Tenen Holtz. Sound. Black and White. 66 minutes. Released on August 17, 1929. Filming started on March 9, 1929. A nitrate print of this film survives in the UCLA Film and Television Archives. *Synopsis:* When Kathryn Miles discovers that her neglectful husband, Robert, a wealthy doctor is having an affair with her best friend, Anne-Marie Witley, she takes matters into her own hands and pretends to be in love with an old boyfriend, Karl Kraley, to make her husband jealous and come back to her. After much verbal shenanigans, Robert and Kathryn are reunited.

Shanghai Lady. *Production-Distribution Company:* Universal. *Director:* John S. Robertson. *Producer:* Carl Laemmle. *Writers:* Houston Branch, Winifred Reeve; based on the play *Drifting* by John Colton and Daisy H. Andrews. *Cinematography:* Hal Mohr. *Editor:* Milton Carruth. *Music:* Sam Perry. *Presenter:* Carl Laemmle. *Cast: Cassie Cook*—MARY NOLAN, *"Badlands" McKinney*—James Murray, *Polly Voo*—Lydia Yeamans Titus, *Repen*—Wheeler Oakman, *Mandarin*—Anders Randolf, *Lizzi*—Yola d'Avril, *Rose*—Mona Rico, *Counselor*—James B. Leong, *Golden Almond*—Irma Lowe, *Young Woman*—Wanna Lidwell, *Bill Collector*—Willie Fung, *Shanghai Pay-Off Man*—Philip Sieeman. Sound. Black and White. 66 minutes. Released on November 17, 1929. The silent version of this film survives in the UCLA film archives. The soundtrack had one song, "I Wonder If It's Really Love," written by Bernie Grossman and Arthur Sizemore. An earlier film adaptation of the play, *Drifting* (Universal, 1923), was directed by Tod Browning and starred Priscilla Dean and Matt Moore. *Synopsis:* After being evicted from a Shanghai opium den for constantly disobeying the rules, Cassie Cook yearns to start a new life, and decides to become a respectable lady to help find a man who will take care of her. Ex-convict Badlands McKinney is also wanting to go straight and live a more respectable life. McKinney escapes from Chinese detective Repen, and on boarding a train, meets Cassie and they fall in love, each not knowing the true background about each other. Unfortunately, Repen comes back onto the scene after their train is attacked by bandits. Although McKinney offers to turn himself into him in exchange for Repen not telling Cassie about his past, this is not needed, as Repen is killed by a Chines gangster, and this allows Cassie and McKinney to be free to start a new life together.

1930

Undertow. *Production-Distribution Company:* Universal. *Director:* Harry A. "Snub" Pollard. *Producer:* Carl Laemmle. *Writers:* Edward T. Lowe, Winifred Reeve, Wilbur Daniel Steele. *Editor:* Daniel Mandell. *Cinematographer:* Jerome Ash. *Sound:* C. Roy Hunter. *Music:* Sam Perry, David Broekman, Heinz Roemheld. *Cast: Sally Blake*—MARY NOLAN, *Paul Whelan*—Johnny Mack Brown, *Jim Paine*—Robert Ellis, *Lindy*—Churchill Ross, *Kitty*—Audrey

Ferris, *Child's Mother*—Ann Brody, *Beach Vendor*—Jack "Tiny" Lipson. Sound. Black and White. 65 minutes. Released on February 23, 1930. *Synopsis:* Lighthouse keeper Paul Whalen marries Sally Blake and she lives in virtual isolation with him for five years, during which time they have a child. Paul then loses his sight, just before Sally's former fiancée Jim Paine comes to do an inspection of the lighthouse. Sally is lonely and takes up Jim's offer to come ashore with him and experience life there, going to various parties and dances, leaving Paul alone. She feels guilty however and always returns to the lighthouse. When Paul gets his eyesight back, he surprises Jim trying to kiss Sally and they get into a fight. Realizing however that Sally was only with Jim out of loneliness, they realize they love each other, reconcile and return to the lighthouse.

Young Desire. *Production Company:* Universal Pictures. *Distribution Company:* Universal Pictures. *Director:* Lewis D. Collins. *Producer:* Carl Laemmle. *Writers:* William R. Doyle, Winifred Reeve, C. Gardner Sullivan, Matt Taylor. *Cinematographer:* Roy F. Overbaugh. *Editor:* Charles Craft. *Supervising Editor:* Maurice Pivar. *Costume Design:* Johanna Mathieson. *Recording Supervisor:* C. Roy Hunter. *Composer:* Sam Perry. *Music:* David Broekman, Bernie Grossman, Heinz Roemheld. *Presenter:* Carl Laemmle. *Cast: Helen Herbert*—MARY NOLAN, *Bobby Spencer*—William Janney, *Blackie*—Ralf Harolde, *May Roberts*—Mae Busch, *Mr. Spencer*—George Irving, *Mrs. Spencer*—Claire McDowell, *Dancer*—Alice Lake, *Dancer*—Gretchen Thomas. Sound. Black and White. 68 minutes. Released on 8 June 1930. Based on the play *Carnival* by William R. Doyle. Filmed in May/June 1930 at Universal Studios, 100 Universal City Plaza, California. *Synopsis:* Helen Herbert, is a bored sideshow dancer in a carnival. Hoping for a better life she leaves and meets a handsome wealthy playboy, Bobby Spenser. They fall in love, but after be confronted by his father, Helen breaks off the romance, and flees back to the carnival. Undaunted, Bobby tries to find her there, but her friends make sure she is hidden away. Realizing the only way to stop Bobby from searching for her is to disappear permanently, Helen takes a balloon ride and jumps to her death.

Outside the Law. *Production Company:* Universal Pictures. *Distribution Company:* Universal Pictures. *Director:* Director Tod Browning. *Producers:* Tod Browning, E.M. Asher, Carl Laemmle, Jr. *Associate Producer:* E.M. Asher. *Writers:* Tod Browning, Garrett Ford. *Cinematographer:* Roy F. Overbaugh. *Editor:* Milton Carruth. *Supervising Editor:* Maurice Pivar. *Art Director:* William R. Schmidt. *Costume Design:* Johanna Mathieson. *Recording Supervisor:* C. Roy Hunter. *Sound Technician:* William Hedgcock. *Music:* David Broekman, Sam Perry, Cecil Arnold, Heinz Roemheld. *Cast: Connie Madden*—MARY NOLAN, *Cobra Collins*—Edward G. Robinson, *Harry 'Fingers' O'Dell*—Owen Moore, *Fred O'Reilly*—Rockliffe Fellowes, *The Kid*—Delmar Watson, *Jake*—Eddie Sturgis, *Humpy*—John George, *Judy*—Louise Beavers, *Mr. Sparks*—Matthew Betz, *Assistant D.A.*—Sidney Bracey, *District Attorney*—Frederick Burt, *Messenger*—Wong Chung, *Police Sergeant*—Rodney Hildebrand, *Police Chief Kennedy*—DeWitt Jennings, *Party Guest*—Clarence Muse, *Onlooker*—Rose Plumer, *Cigar Clerk*—Charley Rogers. Sound. Black and White. 79 minutes. Released on 18 September 1930. *Outside the Law* was a remake of a 1920 silent film that producer-director Tod Browning made for Universal Pictures, starring Lon Chaney. Chaney, who had recently remade another of his silent films, *The Unholy Three*, was too ill from throat cancer to reprise his role in *Outside the Law and* died 26 Aug 1930. *Synopsis:* Fingers O'Dell is an enterprising bank robber who plans to rob the City National Bank. However, Cobra Collins, a gang leader, finds out about it, and demands a 50 percent cut of the spoils. Finger's girlfriend Connie tries to thwart this by giving Collins the wrong date of the robbery, but it does not work, and Fingers blows up the bank's safe, and with Connie in tow, hides out in an apartment, which happens to be next door to where a policeman lives. Collins finds out where they are hiding and turns up wanting his share of the takings. However, Fingers had already called the police, and when they show up a gun fight ensues, with the policeman, Cobra and Fingers being critically wounded. Connie calls for some medical help, but Cobra dies trying to escape. When Connie and Fingers are arrested, they are given light sentences for having saved the life of the policeman.

1931

Enemies of the Law. *Production Company:* Regal Talking Pictures Corp. *Distribution Company:* State Rights. *Director:* Lawrence C. Windom. *Producer:* Samuel S. Krelberg. *Writer:* Charles Reed Jones. *Photographer:* Frank Zucker. *Editor:* Russell G. Shields. *Sound Engineers:* Bob Oshman, John Dolan. *Cast: Florence Vinton*—MARY NOLAN, *Larry Marsh*—Johnnie Walker, *Eddie Swan*—Lou Tellegen, *Jack*—Harold Healy, *Lefty*—Alan Brooks, *Big Tony Catello*—Dewey Robinson, *The Big Shot*—John Dunsmuir, *Joey Regan*—Danny Hardin, *Babe Ricardo*—Bert West, *Blackie*—Gordon Westcott, *Booker T*—Doe Doe Green, Barry Townley, and Robert Pitkin, Jack Renault. Sound. Black and White. 76 minutes. Released on 21 July 1931. *Synopsis:* Gang leaders Larry Marsh and Eddie Swan are rivals, and hoping to get evidence against Marsh, the government sends in undercover agent Florence Vinton to try to obtain enough evidence to put Marsh away. Swan decides to kill a boy that Marsh is helping by putting him through school, thus escalating their hatred while Tony Catello, a Chicago gangster, tries to muscle in on their territory. Meanwhile, Marsh takes his revenge on Swan by killing one of his henchmen. At one of Marsh's nightclubs, Florence meets Catello and he falls in love with her, but against her better judgment, she has already fallen in love with Marsh, and tries to make him see the error of his ways and go straight. At the same time, she is setting a trap for Catello, but her plans backfire, when Marsh and Catello get into a gunfight and both die.

X Marks the Spot. *Production Company:* Tiffany Productions of California, Inc. *Distribution Company:* Tiffany Productions of California, Inc. *Director:* Erle C. Kenton. *Producers:* Sam Bischoff, William Saal. *Writers:* Warren B. Duff, Gordon Kahn, F. Hugh Herber. *Photographer:* Gilbert Warrenton. *Art Director (Settings):* Ralph De Lacy. *Editors:* Arthur Huffsmith, Martin G. Cohn. *Sound Engineer:* Carson Jowett. *Cast: Vivyan Parker*—MARY NOLAN, *George Howard*—Lew Cody, *Sue*—Sally Blane, *Ted Lloyd*—Wallace Ford, *Edward P. Riggs*—Fred Kohler, *Hortense*—Virginia Lee Corbin, *Gloria*—Joyce Coad, *Gloria as a child*—Helen Parrish, *Prosecutor Walter*—Richard Tucker, *Detective Kirby*—Charles Middleton, *Eustace Brown*—Clarence Muse, *City Editor Martin*—Henry

Lobby card for *Enemies of the Law.*

Hall, *Defense Attorney Harris*—Lloyd Ingraham, *Solly Mintz*—Hank Mann, *D.A. Harry B. Miles*—Bradley Page, *Gloria (as a child)*—Helen Parrish. Sound. Black and White. 72 minutes. Released on December 13, 1931. *Synopsis:* When a showgirl tries to sue a newspaper for libel, a columnist, Ted Lloyd shows up at her apartment to get her to sign a release to drop the case, but she refuses. Shortly after that she is found murdered, and he is considered the prime suspect. He manages to find the true killer, but it happens to be a man from his past, Riggs who had lent him money when he was desperate eight years before. He promises Riggs not to testify against him, but double crosses him in court and the police charge Riggs with murder. However, a final battle in the courtroom ensues and Lloyd shoots Riggs.

The Big Shot. *Production Company:* RKO Pathe Pictures, Inc. *Distribution Company:* RKO Pathe Pictures, Inc. *Director:* Ralph F. Murphy. *Producer:* Harry Joe Brown. *Writers:* George Dromgold, Hal Conklin, Earl Baldwin, Joseph Fields. *Photographer:* Arthur C. Miller. *Art Director:* Carroll Clark. *Editor:* Charles Craft. *Costumes:* Gwen Wakeling. *Music Director:* Arthur Lange. *Sound Engineer:* Earl A. Wolcott. *Cast: Fay Turner*—MARY NOLAN, *Ray Smith*—Eddie Quillan, *Doris Thompson*—Maureen O'Sullivan, *Rusty*—Roscoe Ates, *Mrs. Isabel Thompson*—Belle Bennett, *Old Timer*—Arthur Stone, *Mr. Howell*—Louis John Bartels, *Dr. Teasley*—Otis Harlan, *Jack Spencer*—William Eugene, *Uncle Ira*—Edward McWade, *Mr. Hartman*—Harvey Clark, *Mr. Potts*—A.S. "Pop" Byron, *Herb, the Postmaster*—Frank Darien, *Minor Role*—Phyllis Fraser, *Butch*—Ralph Ince, *Rodney, the Garage Boy*—Hilliard Karr, *Townswoman at Dance*—Lillian Lawrence, *Mr. Tuttle*—Gus Leonard, *Town Marshal*—Charles Thurston. Sound. Black and White. 66 minutes. Released on December 31, 1931. *Synopsis:* Ray Smith is a young hotel clerk in a small town as well as a part-time hustler. He borrows money from girlfriend Doris Thompson's mother, to buy some land which after as few twists and mishaps, turns out to contain a valuable sulphur spring, which he uncovers by mistake after he takes a sample of water on the land to be tested. Ray and Doris then turn the land into a swanky health resort.

1932

Docks of San Francisco. *Production Companies:* Action Pictures, Inc., Ralph M. Like, Ltd. *Distribution Company:* Action Pictures, Inc. *Director:* George B. Seitz. *Producer:* Ralph M. Like. *Production Supervisor:* Cliff P. Broughton. *Writer:* H.H. Van Loan. *Cinematographer:* Jules Cronjager. *Editors:* Ralph Dixon, Byron Robinson. *Sound:* James Stanley. *Cast: Belle*—MARY NOLAN, *John Banning*—Jason Robards, Sr., *Rose Gillen*—Marjorie Beebe, *Vance*—John Davidson, *Reggie*—William Haynes, *Max Ranovich*—Max Davidson, *Cookie*—Ernie Adams, *Vance's Henchman*—George Chesebro, *Phony Café Waiter*—Walter James, *Policeman*—Charles McAvoy, *Plainclothesman*—Frank Meredith, *Police Chief Dafferty*—Arthur Millett, *Café Waiter*—Paul Panzer, *Vance's Henchman*—Hal Price, *Nick a.k.a. King Pin*—Sam Rice. Black and White. 60 minutes. Released on 1 February 1932. *Synopsis:* Belle is a waitress in a café, but also the mistress of gangster Vance. She wants to go straight, and Vance agrees and also makes a promise to marry her. One night she meets novelist John Banning after he takes exception to Vance manhandling Belle in a restaurant. Vance then tells Belle is he quitting his life of crime and arranges to meet her at a restaurant and they will then go to a JP to get married. Unknown to Belle, he and his gang then rob a bank. Vance is chased by the police and meets Belle at the restaurant, and gives her the bag of stolen goods, advising her to hide. John Banning is also at the restaurant, and Belle forces John at gunpoint to take her to his mountain cabin. Belle falls asleep on the way there, and he grabs the gun, after seeing that the bag she has contains a large amount of cash. At the cabin Banning offers to help her as they make a meal. However, Vance and his gang have followed them to the cabin, and during a gunfight, both Belle and John are shot, with Belle mortally wounded. The police arrive in time to save John, and all the gangsters are subsequently killed.

The Midnight Patrol. *Production Company:* Monogram Pictures Corp. *Distribution Companies:* Monogram Pictures Corp. *Director:* Christy Cabanne. *Producer:* C.C. Burr. *Writers:* Arthur Hoerl (story), George Jeske (screenplay), Barry Barringer (adaption), C. Carrington (adaption). *Dialogue:* Barry Barringer, C.C. Carrington, Charles E. Roberts. *Camera Operator:* Victor Scheurich. *Assistant Camera:* Irving Glassberg, Lewis Physioc Jr. *Editor:* Tom Persons. *Sound:* Homer C. Ellmaker. *Still Photographer:* Edward Tanner. *Cast: Miss Willing*—MARY NOLAN, *John Martin*—Regis Toomey, *Ellen Gray*—Betty Bronson, *Joyce Greeley*—Edwina Booth, *Judson*—Earle Fox, *Howard Brady*—Robert Elliott, *Stuart*—Eddie Kane, *Powers*—William Norton Bailey, *Dummy Black*—Mischa Auer, *'Snub' Pollard*—Snub Pollard, *James J. Jeffries*—James J. Jeffries, and Ray Cooke, Franklin Pangborn, Wilfred Lucas, Mack Swain, Jack Mower, J.C. Fowler, Tod Sloan, Barrie Oliver. Sound. Black and White. 67 minutes. Released on April 10, 1932. *Synopsis:* Joyce Greeley, a former showgirl is released from prison, as arranged by her shady at-

Poster for *Docks of San Francisco.*

torney, Arthur Judson. While riding in a taxi after her release she is shot and her body is thrown from the vehicle, which is witnessed by was reporter John Martin. Martin meets Joyce's sister, Ellen, who does not know about the murder. Arthur Judson arranges for his accomplice, Miss Willing, to impersonate Joyce in dealings with Ellen, and Ellen is tricked into giving them the keys to Joyce's safe deposit box, which holds valuable papers. Finally, Martin and a detective friend find Joyce's killer.

Beautiful and Dumb. *Production Company:* Van Beuren Studios. *Distributor:* RKO Radio Pictures. *Director:* Emmett J. Flynn. *Associate Producer:* Nat Ross. *Writers:* Emmet J. Flynn, Richard Smith, Ruth Todd. *Editor:* Vera Wade. *Cast:* MARY NOLAN, Lew Cody, Dot Farley. Black and White. Short. Released on 16 April 1932. Also known as Liberty Short Stories #6: Beautiful and Dumb.

Broadway Gossip No. 3. *Production Company:* Educational Films Corporation of America. *Director:* Raymond Kane. *Writer:* Leo Donnelly. *Cinematographer:* George Webber. *Presenter:* E.W. Hammons. *Cast: Movie Star*—MARY NOLAN, *Columnist*—Leo Donnelly, *Former Screen Star*—Lillian Walker, *Beautician*—Madame Sylvia. Sound. Black and White. 9 minutes. Released on 27 December 1932. *Synopsis:* Columnist Leo Donnelly, in the third of his series interviewing Hollywood stars, starts off first with former movie star Lillian Walker, a prominent move star, and then interviews current movie star Mary Nolan. The short film finishes with an interview with Madame Sylvia, a former movie-studio beautician.

1933

File 113. *Production Company:* Allied Pictures Corporation. *Distribution Companies:* State Rights, Allied Pictures Corp. *Director:* Chester M. Franklin. *Assistant Director:* Wilbur McGaugh. *Producers:* M.H. Hoffman, M.H. Hoffman Jr. *Screenplay:* Jack Natteford, Emile Gaboriau. *Cinematographers:* Tom Galligan and Harry Neumann. *Asst. Camera:* James Higgins, Monty Steadman. *Still Photographer:* Otto Benniger. *Art Director (Settings):* Mack D'Agostino. *Production Manager:* Sidney Algier. *Sounds:* L.E. Tope. *Camera Operator:* Tom Galligan. *Assistant Cameras:* James Higgins. Monte Steadman. *Cast: Mlle. Adoree*—MARY NOLAN, *M. Gaston Le Coq*—Lew Cody, *Mme. Fauvel*—Clara Kimball Young, *Verduet*—George E. Stone, *Prosper Botomy*—William Collier, Jr., *Madeline Fauvel*—June Clyde, *Fauvel*—Herbert Bunston, *De Clameran*—Roy D'Arcy, *Lagors*—Irving Bacon, *Michele*—Harry Cording, *Ottoman*—Crauford Kent. Sound. Black and White. 53 minutes. Released on February 19, 1932. Based on the short story "Le Dossier #113" by Emile Gaboriau (Paris, 1867), as translated into English by George Burnham Ives. A film based on the same source entitled *Thou Shalt Not Steal* was made in 1917 by William Fox (see *AFI Catalog of Feature Films, 1911–20;* F1.4446). In addition, a two-reel film entitled *File No. 113* was produced by the Biograph Co. in 1915. This film is believed to be lost. *Synopsis:* Madame Fauvel, the owner of a bank, is being blackmailed by her cousin, de Clameran, because he knows her daughter Madeline is not her natural child. Fauvel fires her daughter's boyfriend, Prosper, from the bank, because he was planning to elope with Madeline, and shortly after that the bank is robbed. Both Prosper and Madame Fauvel confess to the crime, but Detective Le Coq does not believe them, and during his investigation, finds out that Madeline is actually de Clameran's daughter, and that he had forced Madame Fauvel to give him the keys to the bank. LeCoq starts to suspect de Clameran of both the bank robbery and a prior jewel theft, so hires someone to break into his rooms, resulting in de Clameran getting killed. The money is then recovered and Madeline and Prosper are reunited.

Chapter Notes

One

1. Some sources state that Mary was born in 1905, but Mary's passport application and various other formal records all say 1902.

2. In an interview Mary had with Will A. Page she said her mother was Mary Covington, and her grandfather was General Covington.

3. There is some confusion here as to which orphanage Mary went to. There was an orphanage in St. Joseph, Missouri called Home for Little Wanderers, and then there was the St. Joseph's Orphan Asylum in Louisville. Mary always referred to the orphanage as St. Joseph's, hence many books and articles refer to it as just St. Joseph's. Given St. Josephs in Louisville was over 200 miles closer, this would seem to be where Mary went.

4. *The Kentucky Explorer*, November 2013.

5. *Motion Picture Classic*, September 1928.

6. Michael Ankerich, *Dangerous Curves Atop Hollywood Heels*.

7. *The Kentucky Explorer*, November 1913.

8. Michael Ankerich, *Dangerous Curves Atop Hollywood Heels*.

9. Bodeen DeWitt, "Mary Nolan: The Hard Luck Girl," *Films in Review*, Vol 31, #5, 1980.

10. Harold Koda, *The Model as Muse: Embodying Fashion*.

11. Oscar Hammerstein, *Hammerstein's: A Musical Theatre Family*.

12. James Leve, *American Musical Theatre*.

13. *Star-Tribune*, October 18 1931.

14. Buster Keaton, *My Wonderful World of Slapstick*.

15. *Detroit Free Press*, October 18, 1931.

Two

1. *Brooklyn Daily Eagle*, 1 April 1923.

2. *Motion Picture*, February 1932.

3. *Pittsburgh Post-Gazette*, 28 October 1923.

4. Arthur Frank Wertheim, *Will Rogers at the Ziegfeld Follies*.

5. Ethan Mordden, *Ziegfeld: The Man Who Invented Show Business*.

6. *St. Louis Dispatch*, 30 November 1923.

7. Margaret Reid, "A Girl Who Had No Childhood," *Picture-Play Magazine*, May 1929.

Three

1. Marjorie Farnsworth, *The Ziegfeld Follies*.

2. *Ibid.*

3. *The Jacksonville Daily Journal*, 25 May 1924.

4. *The Tribune*, 26 May 1924.

5. Marjorie Farnsworth, *The Ziegfeld Follies*.

6. *Times-Herald*, 29 May 1924. The Diamond Brothers refers to Morris and Joseph Diamond and John Farina who were subsequently executed at Sing Sing in 1925 for the murder of two bank messengers, William Barlow and William McLaughlin who were killed as they stepped from a subway station in Brooklyn with a sack containing $43,607. The Hoffman Frank was referring to was Harry Hoffman who was arrested on suspicion of murdering Maude Bauer, found guilty and was sent to Sing Sing. He appealed the sentence and after a number of trials that ended either in a hung jury or in one case, his lawyer had a heart attack, Hoffman was finally was acquitted after six years in jail. But the murder was never officially solved. After Maude's murder, Hoffman changed his looks, reupholstered his car and mailed away his gun. But this was all circumstantial evidence and he was acquitted.

7. *Oakland Tribune*, 29 May 1924.

8. *The St. Louis Star and Times*, 25 February 1929.

9. *The Baltimore Sun*, 1 June 1924.

10. *The Cincinnati Enquirer*, 5 June 1924.

11. *The News-Herald*, 31 May 1924.

12. *Detroit Free Press*, 9 June 1924.

13. *Lincoln Evening Journal*, 11 June 1924.

14. *Medford Mail Tribune*, 12 June 1924.

15. Roscoe "Fatty" Arbuckle was a famous silent actor and comedian who was the defendant in three widely publicized trials for the rape and manslaughter of actress Virginia Rappe in September 1921. He was finally acquitted after the third trial, but he never fully recovered from the pub-

licity and he was publicly ostracized. He died in his sleep of a heart attack in 1933, aged 46.

16. *The Morning Call*, 28 June 1924.

17. Frank was referring to being the best man for Johnny Dooley, another comedian who married musical comedy actress Maria Fruscella, known professionally as Constance Madison on June 21. It was Dooley's third marriage. Dooley died on 7 June 1928 aged 38 from complications from an operation.

18. "Jake" meant everything will be all right.

19. *The Springfield News-Leader*, 29 June 1924.

20. *The Brooklyn Daily Eagle*, 5 August 1924.

21. *The Detroit Free Press*, 16 August 1924.

22. *Bridgeport Telegram*, 20 August 1924.

23. *Fitchburg Sentinel*, 25 August 1924.

24. No reference was found of Mary's appearing in a show in Paris at this time.

25. Charles Robert Rondeau, Mabel's son, went on to become a well-known director and producer who died in August 1996.

26. *Times Herald*, 27 September 1924.

27. In reality she was 22.

28. *Times-Herald*, 29 September 1924.

29. *Times Herald*, 8 October 1924.

Four

1. *Picture Play Magazine*, July 1930.

2. *The Decatur Daily Review,* 25 October 1927.

3. The musical *Sometime* ran in London from February 5th for twenty-eight performances before it went on the road. It finished early as it was considered distasteful. It was originally on Broadway in 1918 staring Mae West.

4. *The Pittsburgh Press*, 21 March 1925.

5. *The Brooklyn Daily Eagle*, 2 April 1925.

6. *Times Herald*, 4 April 1925.

7. *The Miami News*, 24 June 1925.

8. *The Brooklyn Daily Eagle*, 10 July 1925.

9. *Pittsburgh Press*, 13 September 1925.

10. *Delaware County Daily Times*, 14 September 1925.

11. *Springfield Missouri Republican,* 13 September 1925.

12. Ronald L. Smith., *Comedy Stars at 70 Rpm*.

13. *Variety*, 12 December 1928.

14. *Decatur Daily Review*, 25 October 1927.

15. *The Los Angeles Times*, 18 February 1927.

Five

1. *Pittsburgh Daily Post*, 19 January 1927.

2. *The Waco News Tribune*, 31 January 1927.

3. *Pittsburgh Press*, 19 January 1927.

4. Hans J. Wollstein., *Strangers in Hollywood.*.

5. *The Los Angeles Times*, 18 February 1927.

6. *The Pittsburgh Press*, 21 February 1927.

7. Australian-born artist Henry Clive started out as a vaudeville magician, became a silent film performer, and then found fame as an artist. Ziegfeld used him to illustrate the *Follies* showgirls, and he went on to be the cover artist for William Randolph Heart's, *The American Weekly*.

8. Hudovernick, Robert, *Jazz Age Beauties*.

9. A "mash note" is a letter that expresses infatuation with or gushing appreciation of someone.

10. "Copper the Bet" was a phrase used in gambling, meaning it will not be a winning hand or card, so only put down a penny as you will probably lose.

11. Will A. Page, *Behind the Curtains of Broadway's Beauty Trust*.

12. Slide, Anthony, *A Special Relationship: Britain Comes to Hollywood and Hollywood Comes to Britain*.

13. *Chicago Tribune*, 4 September 1927.

14. Scott Eyman, *The Lion of Hollywood: The Life and Legend of Louis B. Mayer*.

15. *Moving Picture World*, 19 November 1927.

16. *Moving Picture World*, 20 August 1927.

Six

1. *Variety*, 27 June 1928.

2. *New York Times*, 26 June 1928.

3. Lee Grieveson and Peter Kramers (eds), *The Silent Cinema Reader*.

4. *Variety*, 17 June 1928.

5. *The New York Times*, 25 June 1929.

6. Brett Wood, "West of Zanzibar," *Filmax: The Magazine of Film and Television*, Feb/March 1991.

7. Fleming, E.J., *The Fixers: Eddie Mannix, Howard Strickling and the M-G-M. Publicity Machine*.

8. *The Los Angeles Times*, 16 January 1929.

9. *Universal Weekly*, 26 January 1929.

10. Eve Golden, *John Gilbert: The Last of the Silent Film Stars*.

11. *Motion Picture News*, 19 January 1929.

12. *Variety*, 8 May 1929.

13. E.J. Fleming, *The Fixers*.

14. *Hollywood Filmograph*, June 1929.

15. *The New Movie Magazine*, December 1929.

16. *The Film Mercury*, 26 July 1929.

17. *The Morning Call*, 15 September 1929.

18. It was very popular for actors and actresses to make themselves appear younger than they were, especially for women. In this case Mary made herself 3 years younger as she was born in 1902.

19. Mary was born Robertson, not Robinson so either the journalist transcribed this incorrectly or for reasons unknown, Mary did not give her real surname.

20. Now Mary is introducing a third location for the orphanage she did indeed go to, as previously she said it was in St. Joseph Missouri or Kansas City. And she did not go there after she was born, but only after her mother had died. But a story of being an orphan was either fabricated and encouraged by the studios or by Mary herself to add some drama to her childhood

21. It is doubtful she went to school, but the studios did provide teaching for child actors.

22. This would have been Worcester, where Mabel was living with her husband Charles. I am sure Mabel would not have been pleased to read this, but there may be some truth in Mabel not wanting Mary to live with her.

23. In later versions of this story, Mary said it was the man itself, who in this case was Frank Tinney, that offered her a lift. There was no mention of a secretary.

24. Mary was known as "Bubbles" when she was with Frank Tinney, so she may have gotten that name at the orphanage or indeed when she was appearing on the stage in New York.

25. There is no evidence Mary made movies anywhere else but in Germany.

26. There is no evidence or any further reference by Mary to having a heart attack and being in hospital.

27. *The Los Angeles Times*, 14 November 1929.

28. *The New York Times*, 11 November 1929.

29. *Photoplay*, January 1930.

30. *Exhibitor's Herald*, January 1930.

31. *Screenland*, January 1920.

32. *The New Movie Magazine*, December 1929.

Seven

1. *The Film Daily*, 30 August 1931.
2. *Variety*, 5 March 1930.
3. *Talking Screen*, July 1930.
4. E.J. Fleming, *The Fixers*.
5. *The Oakland Tribune*, 14 March 1930.
6. *Exhibitor's Daily Review*, 17 March 1930.
7. *Exhibitor's Herald*, 29 March 1930.
8. *The Cincinnati Enquirer*, 19 May 1930.
9. Michael G. Ankerich, *The Sound of Silence*.
10. *Motion Picture News*, 12 July 1930.
11. *Photoplay*, June 1930.
12. *Photoplay*, June 1930.
13. *The Oakland Tribune*, 31 July 1930.
14. *The Bismarck Tribune*, 1 August 1930.
15. *The Morning News*, 1 August 1930.
16. *Talking Screen*, September 1930.
17. *Inside Facts of Stage and Screen*, 4 October 1930.
18. *Motion Picture News*, 23 August 1930.
19. *Pittsburgh Press*, 24 November 1930.
20. *Photoplay*, November 1930.
21. *Picture Play Magazine*, December 1930.

Eight

1. *Motion Picture*, January 1931.
2. *Dunkirk Evening Observer*, 19 February 1931.
3. *The Evening News*, 7 March 1931.
4. *Variety*, 11 March 1931.
5. *The Philadelphia Inquirer*, 14 March 1931.
6. *Chicago Tribune*, 26 March 1931.
7. *Brooklyn Daily Eagle*, 29 March 1931.
8. *St. Louis Post-Dispatch*, 11 August 1935.
9. *Philadelphia Inquirer*, 29 March 1931.
10. *L.A. Times*, 1 April 1930.
11. *Variety*, 1 April 1931.
12. *Pittsburgh Post-Gazette*, 6 June 1931.
13. *Chicago Tribune*, 18 June 1931.
14. *The Film Daily*, 12 July 1932.
15. *Motion Picture Daily*, 11 July 1931.
16. *The Palm Beach Post*, 20 August 1931.
17. *Chicago Tribune*, 12 September 1931.
18. *Pittsburgh-Post Gazette*, 22 August 1931.
19. *Pittsburgh Post-Gazette*, 14 October 1931.
20. *Oakland Tribune*, 23 October 1931.
21. *The Pittsburgh Press*, 25 October 1931.
22. *Argus-Leader*, 13 November 1931.
23. *St. Cloud Times*, 14 November 1931.
24. *Variety*, 17 November 1931.
25. *Variety*, 24 November 1931.
26. *Oakland Tribune*, 8 December 1931.
27. *The Film Daily*, 9 December 1931.
28. *Motion Picture*, March 1932.

Nine

1. *Oakland Tribune*, 8 January 1932.
2. *Motion Picture Herald*, 30 January 1932.
3. *Variety*, 15 March 1932.
4. *Film Daily*, 21 February 1932.
5. *Oakland Tribune*, March 10, 1932.
6. *The Los Angeles Times*, 15 March 1932.
7. *Oakland Tribune*, 1 April 1932.
8. *Variety*, 10 May 1932.
9. *Motion Picture Herald*, 9 April 1932.
10. *Variety*, 10 May 1933.
11. *Variety*, 2 August 1932.
12. *Variety*, 4 October 1932.
13. *Variety*, 8 November 1932.
14. *The Minneapolis Star Tribune*, 31 October 1932.
15. *Poughkeepsie Eagles-News*, 9 January 1933.
16. *The Brooklyn Daily Eagle*, 23 January 1933.
17. *Middletown Times Herald*, 3 May 1933.
18. *Variety*, 4 July 1933.
19. *Pittsburgh Post-Gazette*, 25 August 1933.
20. *The Film Daily*, 30 August 1933.
21. *Bradford Evening Star*, 18 November 1933.
22. *Variety*, 19 December 1933.
23. *The Film Daily*, 1 February 1934.
24. *The Film Daily*, 25 August 1934.

25. *The Wilkes-Barre Record*, 5 November 1934.
26. Mary would have been 32 years old, not 23 years as noted on the charge.

Ten

1. She was actually 33 years old.
2. Mary never appeared in this play nor was it ever staged. Linder wrote more than one hundred plays and wrote and appeared in vaudeville. In 1940 he was sued by Mae West over the production of *Diamond Lil*, which he claimed he had written under the title of *Chatham Square*. He lost the suit and Mae West was awarded one million dollars in damages. Linder died at age 79 of a heart attack in 1950.
3. *The Pittsburgh Press*, 6 January 1935.
4. *Miami Daily News*, 9 July 1935.
5. *The Salt Lake Tribune*, 10 July 1935.
6. *The Pittsburgh Press*, July 10, 1935.
7. *The Philadelphia Inquirer*, 17 July 1935.
8. *The Morning News*, 22 August 1935.
9. *Variety*, 28 August 1935.
10. *The Los Angeles Times*, 10 October 1935.
11. *Variety*, 18 December 1935.
12. *Variety*, 25 December 1935.
13. *The Ottawa Journal*, 11 January 1936.
14. *Variety*, 29 January 1936.
15. *The Brooklyn Daily Eagle*, 30 January 1936. Although a picture of Mary appeared in the paper in this article, other sources, including a copy of the original playbill, say the actress was Doris Nolan, so it could well be that Mary was just a guest star for the one matinee performance.
16. *Variety*, 1 April 1936.
17. *Detroit Free Press*, 25 May 1936.
18. *The Pittsburgh Press*, 31 July 1936.
19. *Chicago Tribune*, 18 October 1936.
20. *The Gettysburg Times*, 10 December 1936.
21. *Oakland Tribune*, 5 May 1937.
22. *The Pittsburgh Press*, 6 May 1937.
23. *Variety*, 12 May 1937.
24. *The Baltimore Sun*, 26 May 1937.
25. *The Plain Speaker*, 3 June 1937.
26. The Mr. X she referred to would be Eddie Mannix so one assumes she may have been under a court order never to mention him again by name
27. *The Fresno Bee*, 4 June 1937.
28. *Variety*, 4 August 1937.
29. *Brooklyn Daily Eagle*, 19 August 1937.
30. *The Plain Speaker*, 20 October 1937.
31. Marianne Ruuth, *Cruel City: The Dark Side of Hollywood's Rich and Famous*.
32. *The San Bernardino County Sun*, 22 April 1948.
33. *The Los Angeles Times*, 25 April 1948.
34. *The Town Talk*, 10 May 1948.
35. *The Gaffney Ledger*, 4 November 1948.
36. *Los Angeles Times*, 2 November 1948.

37. Los Angeles Times, 5 November 1948.
38. *Los Angeles Times*, 1 November 1948.
39. *Reading Eagle*, 2 July 1950.

Eleven

1. Hickory is actually around 250 miles from Louisville.
2. In her story, Mary had conveniently left out appearing in two stage productions before she appeared in the Follies. Why she did this is unknown.
3. Vivienne Segal was in the 1924 *Follies*, not the 1923 *Follies* with Mary.
4. Will Rogers was never in the *Follies* with Mary. Will was in the *Follies* in 1922, 1924 and 1925. Mary was only in the *Follies* in 1923. Will left the *Follies* in the summer of 1923 to do silent film comedies for Hal Roach.
5. Bert and Betty Wheeler were in the 1923 *Follies* with Mary.
6. Lina Basquette was in the *Follies* in 1925 and 1925, not in the 1923 version.
7. Paulette Duval was in the 1923 *Follies*
8. Hilda Ferguson was in the 1923 *Follies*. As Mary noted in her story, Hilda became an alcoholic and died at 29 in a New York Hospital from peritonitis after collapsing on the stairway of a rundown speakeasy.
9. Brooke Jones was in the 1923 *Follies*
10. Both Edna Leedon and Dave Stamper were in the 1923 *Follies*, as well as the *Follies* in 1924 and 1925.
11. Ann Pennington was in the summer edition of the *Follies* in 1923, but not the one Mary was in. She also appeared in the 1924 edition of the *Follies*.
12. Bert Wheeler was a popular stage and movie comedian who was teamed with Robert Woolsey for many years. He got his first break with Gus Edwards, working later as actor in several shows, among them "The Gingerbread Man" and "When Dreams Come True". During this show he met his first wife, Margaret Grae, with whom he formed up a successful vaudeville team. Although being asked several times to make movies (among them a request by Harold Lloyd), he stayed with vaudeville. In 1926 they divorced, and his wife soon married another actor. In 1927 he was signed by Florenz Ziegfeld for his show "Rio Rita", where he was teamed with Robert Woolsey. They clicked and formed a comedy team that lasted until 1938 when Woolsey died. When Ziegfeld sold the screen rights of Rio Rita to the newly formed RKO studio as their official debut, they were the only actors in the cast who repeated their stage roles. During the 30s, while they made many comedies in Hollywood, Wheeler married and was divorced twice. After Woolsey's death, he continued as single, mostly on the stage, but sometimes also on

the screen. His last years were darkened with financial difficulties and failing health. Furthermore, two weeks before his own death on January 18, 1968 his daughter died of cancer. Betty Wheeler was born Margaret Grae and performed with Bert in the 1920's as "Bert and Betty Wheeler".

13. Jessie first appeared on stage in 1918 when she was discovered by Jake Schubert. She was quickly stolen away by Florenz Ziegfeld who put her in his 1919 edition of the Midnight Frolic...the more "risqué" version of the Follies. She continued to work on the rooftop, but also appeared in the Ziegfeld Follies from 1921 until 1924. Jessie soon became more famous (or infamous) for her life off the stage. Jessie had her fair share of suitors and husbands for that matter. Her first marriage was to a black face comedian named Oliver de Brow. The two had a daughter named Ann. Apparently the two divorced after Oliver killed a man in a duel. Her second "supposed" marriage was to another performer named Lew Reed. After that, she married advertisement executive, Bill Young, then millionaire Dan Caswell. Her last husband was Leonard Reno, who visited her in the hospital before she died. He and even his new wife at the time donated blood to try and save Jessie's life. Obviously, none of the marriages lasted. Her ex-husbands found her to be greedy, manic, and too high maintenance. By 1935, Jessie was alone and broke. She got a few dollars from various theater charities occasionally, that kept her fed and clothed. Jessie Reed passed away at age 42.

14. $2,000 would be the equate to around $28,000 in 2018.

15. Arnold Rothstein was a racketeer, businessman and gambler who became a kingpin of the Jewish mob in New York City. He was widely reputed to have organized corruption in professional sport, including conspiring to fix the 1919 World Series. Rothstein refused to pay a large debt resulting from a fixed poker game and was murdered in 1928.

16. Frank did go back on the stage, and was appearing in Detroit in October 1926, and was hospitalized in November that year with pneumonia.

17. Frank was officially divorced from Edna on November 28, 1925; however, he was in the United States at the time and spent Thanksgiving with Edna and their son that year.

18. There is no record of a Dr. Robert Reinhart on the *Columbus* with Mary. There were three German men on board with Mary, with two of them having similar names being a Robert Stern, 60 and Reinhold Thiel, 42. There are passenger records of a Robert Reinhart who was from Germany, lived in Eureka, California but he was not a Doctor.

19. The film was actually released in 1927 as *Memoirs of a Nun* or *Erinnerungen Einer Nonne.*

20. Helen Lee Worthing was the "it" girl of the silent screen era, a stunning ex-Ziegfeld beauty, who would go on to star with John Barrymore in movies. Helen fell in love with a prominent African American doctor at a time when interracial relationships were a total anathema to a Hollywood career. Helen died in Los Angeles, on 27 August 1948 from an overdose of sleeping tablets. Scrawled on the cover of a pulp magazine found in her littered room was written: "I Can't Stand Another Straw, It Would Be Too Much."

21. In February 1952, *Ebony Magazine* published Helen's story which she had written just before she died. In the series of articles, she mentions running into Mary, and mentions that when Mary drives her home, Mary confided in Helen about her own battle with narcotics. Helen makes no mention of going to Mary's house after slashing her wrists.

22. "Casalda" was Alma Rubens, who was a film actress and stage performer. She had begun her career in the mid-1910s, and she quickly rose to stardom in 1916 after appearing opposite Douglas Fairbanks in *The Half Breed.* For the remainder of the decade, she appeared in supporting roles in comedies and drama. In the 1920s, Rubens developed a drug addiction which eventually ended her career. She died in January 1931, at age 33, shortly after being arrested for cocaine possession.

23. In Alma Ruben's 1930 memoir, she mentions this incident with the ghostly apparition being Julia Bruns, who was a silent film actress and model who had died of alcoholic poisoning in 1927, aged 32. Alma completed her memoir the day before she left New York on 15 December 1930. She was subsequently arrested in San Diego on 5 January 5 1931, for cocaine possession and trying to smuggle morphine into the United States from Mexico. She was jailed but was released on a $5,000 bond to await trial. She had caught a cold however, which turned into pneumonia, and because of the abuse she had put her body through, she did not survive this, and died on January 22, 1931.

24. The man Mary is referring to is Eddie Mannix.

25. *Carnival Girl* was eventually released as *Young Desire.*

26. Dutch Schultz was a New York City-area Jewish-American mobster of the 1920s and 1930s who made his fortune in organized crime-related activities, including bootlegging and the numbers racket. Weakened by two tax evasion trials led by prosecutor Thomas Dewey, Schultz's rackets were also threatened by fellow mobster Lucky Luciano. To avert his conviction, Schultz asked the governing body of the Mafia, the Commission, for permission to kill Dewey, which they refused. When Schultz disobeyed them, and tried to kill Dewey, the Commission ordered his murder in 1935.

27. This would have been in December 1935.

Bibliography

Anderson, Mark Lynn. *Twilight of the Idols: Hollywood and the Human Sciences in 1920s America.* Berkeley: University of California Press, 2011.

Ankerich, Michael G. *Dangerous Curves Atop Hollywood Heels.* Albany, Georgia: BearManor Media, 2015.

Cooper, Miriam. *Dark Lady of the Silent: My Life in Early Hollywood.* New York: Bobbs-Merrill Company, 1973.

Dempsey, David. *The Triumphs and Trials of Lotta Crabtree.* New York: William Morrow, 1968.

Eyman, Scott. *Lion of Hollywood: The Life and Legend of Louis B. Mayer.* New York: Simon & Schuster, 2012.

Farnsworth, Marjorie. *The Ziegfeld Follies.* New York: Putnam, 1956.

Fleming, E.J. *The Fixers: Eddie Mannix, Howard Strickling and the M-G-M. Publicity Machine.* Jefferson, N.C.: McFarland, 2005.

Golden, Eve. *Golden Images: 41 Essays on Silent Film Stars.* Jefferson, N.C.: McFarland, 2001.

Hudovernik, Robert. *Jazz Age Beauties: The Last Collection of Ziegfeld Photographer Alfred Cheney Johnston.* New York: Universe, 2006.

Keaton, Buster. *My Wonderful World of Slapstick.* London: Allen and Unwin, 1967.

Mordden, Ethan. *Ziegfeld: The Man Who Invented Show Business.* New York: St. Martin's Press, 2008.

Musto, David F. *The American Disease: Origins of Narcotic Control.* New York: Oxford University Press, 1999.

Oshinsky, David. *Bellevue: Three Centuries of Medicine and Mayhem at America's Most Storied Hospital.* New York: Doubleday, 2016.

Page, Will A. *Behind the Curtains of the Broadway Beauty Trust.* New York: Edward A. Miller Publishing, 1926.

Ruuth, Marianne. *Cruel City: The Dark Side of Hollywood's Rich and Famous.* Malibu, CA.: Roundtable Pub, 1991.

Sann, Paul. *The Lawless Decade: A Pictorial History of a Great American Transition: From the World War I Armistice and Prohibition to Repeal and the New Deal.* New York: Crown, 1957.

Shields, David S. *Still: American Silent Motion Picture Photography.* Chicago: University of Chicago Press, 2013.

Slide, Anthony. *New York City Vaudeville.* Charleston, SC: Arcadia, 2006.

Slide, Anthony. *A Special Relationship: Britain Comes to Hollywood and Hollywood Comes to Britain.* Jackson, Miss.: University of Mississippi Press, 2015.

Slide, Anthony. *The Vaudevillians: A Dictionary of Vaudeville Performers.* Westport, Conn.: Arlington House, 1981.

Smith, Ronald L. *Comedy Stars at 78Rpm: Biographies and Discographies of 89 American and British Recording Artists, 1896–1946.* Jefferson, N.C.: McFarland, 1998.

Trav, S.D. *No Applause—Just Throw Money: Or the Book That Made Vaudeville Famous.* New York: Faber & Faber, 2005.

Wollstein, Hans J. *Strangers in Hollywood.* Metuchen, N.J.: Scarecrow Press, 1994.

Newspapers

Argus-Leader
The Baltimore Sun
The Bismarck Tribune
Bradford Evening Star
Bridgeport Telegram
The Brooklyn Daily Eagle
Chicago Tribune
The Cincinnati Enquirer
The Decatur Daily Review
Delaware County Daily Times
The Detroit Free Press
Dunkirk Evening Observer
The Evening News
Fitchburg Sentinel
The Fresno Bee
The Gaffney Ledger
The Gettysburg Times
The Jacksonville Daily Journal
The Kentucky Explorer
Lincoln Evening Journal
The Los Angeles Times

Bibliography

Medford Mail Tribune
The Miami News
Middletown Times Herald
Minneapolis Star Tribune
The Morning Call
The Morning News
New York Times
The News-Herald
Oakland Tribune

The Ottawa Journal
The Palm Beach Post
The Philadelphia Inquirer
Pittsburgh Daily Post
Pittsburgh Post-Gazette
Pittsburgh Press
The Plain Speaker
Poughkeepsie Eagles-News
Reading Eagles

Index

Index